The Patterns of Social Behavior series
Zick Rubin, *Harvard University, General Editor*

This series brings both psychological and sociological perspectives to bear on the ways in which people affect one another. Each volume explores research and experience on a particular aspect of social behavior and considers its personal and social implications.

JOSEPH PLECK received a degree in Social Relations and his doctorate in Clinical Psychology from Harvard University. He is now teaching and doing research at the Residential College and the Institute of Social Research, both at the University of Michigan. He has lectured and written widely on male sex roles and men's liberation.

JACK SAWYER received degrees in mathematics from Iowa State University, psychology from Ohio State University, and industrial psychology from Purdue University, then worked as a personnel research psychologist with the Department of the Army. He later taught social psychology and did research at the University of Chicago, Northwestern University, and Harvard University. He has been active in the civil rights movement, the anti-war movement, Psychologists for Social Action, and male liberation. He is now affiliated with the Wright Institute and the University of California at Berkeley.

To the men and women with whom we have shared
or have yet to share
in the joy and struggle of liberation

MEN AND MASCULINITY

Edited by

JOSEPH H. PLECK
and
JACK SAWYER

PRENTICE-HALL, INC., Englewood Cliffs, New Jersey

Library of Congress Cataloging in Publication Data

PLECK, JOSEPH H COMP.
Men and masculinity.

(The Patterns of social behavior series) (A Spectrum book)
Bibliography: p.
1. Men. 2. Sex role. 3. Men—Psychology.
I. Sawyer, Jack, joint comp. II. Title.
HQ1067.P6 301.41'1 74-13395
ISBN 0-13-574319-2
ISBN 0-13-574301-X (pbk.)

ABOUT THE COVER—SIGNS AND SYMBOLS TRADITIONALLY ASSOCIATED WITH MEN AND MASCULINITY:

A SPECTRUM BOOK

5 6 7 8 9 10

Printed in the United States of America

PRENTICE-HALL INTERNATIONAL, INC. (LONDON)
PRENTICE-HALL OF AUSTRALIA PTY., LTD. (SYDNEY)
PRENTICE-HALL OF CANADA, LTD. (TORONTO)
PRENTICE-HALL OF INDIA PRIVATE LIMITED (NEW DELHI)
PRENTICE-HALL OF JAPAN, INC. (TOKYO)

CONTENTS

Introduction

About three or four years ago, we both started asking ourselves what it means to be "a man." Is it true that to be a man, we have to achieve something considered worthwhile? Neither of us accepted this intellectually, but we knew that we personally were highly anxious about doing well. We began to see our anxiety about performance as something we had started learning as small boys. We remembered praise for being "a little man," which meant doing a good job. We saw how we had come to believe that we were worthwhile *because* we performed well.

We also remembered learning that "big boys don't cry." As adults, we have found it hard to recognize and express our feelings, especially feelings of tenderness or vulnerability. We both considered it acceptable for men to be sympathetic to others, to be silly, to feel hurt, and to cry. Yet we ourselves kept these emotions, when we felt them, mostly inside us.

These were old problems. But it was new to think of them not as individual shortcomings but as ideas we had learned in growing up male. Maybe now, with effort, we could learn to express feelings more easily and reduce our anxiety about performance.

If we learned these ideas as males, it made sense to talk about them with other men. We each joined with a group of men discussing their masculine role. In these groups, we learned that *we were not the only ones* with doubts. The world still seemed to say that the best man is the one who wins and real men keep their cool, but we found that other men were also questioning such values. This was a relief and a step toward understanding and change.

Recently, more men have begun to question whether the masculine role we learned so unconsciously is either necessary or desirable. Men's consciousness-raising groups devoted to such questions have developed in all parts of the country. Conferences and workshops have explored the masculine role. Some groups of men have organized "men's centers" where men can meet others interested in issues of masculinity. Since 1971, a periodical called *Brother: A Forum for Men Against Sexism* has been published by men in the San Francisco Bay Area. Men have written personal accounts of their own change, and others have analyzed and reported changes occurring generally in the masculine role. This book brings together some of these writings, both personal and general, from a wide variety of publications. We ourselves have learned from these accounts, and we hope they prove helpful to others.

Many men, including both of us, have been stimulated to question the masculine role through our relationship with a woman who was questioning her role. Women seek equality because it is their desire and their right; but, in our experience, women's liberation also holds incidental benefits for men. For us, it provoked initial questioning and suggested some first steps. Basically, however, it is up to us men to free ourselves of the restrictions the masculine role places upon us.

This book deals mainly with the experience of males who are white, middle-class, heterosexual, and live in the United States. This is a distinctly advantaged group, with disproportionate access to society's wealth and respect. Advantage, according to the masculine role, should be made the most of. Yet some of these advantaged men are finding, as accounts in this book relate, that the traditional masculine pursuit of power, prestige, and profit will not fulfill their lives.

We feel on uncertain ground about the relation of homosexuality to the liberation of men, partly because we have not come fully to terms with it in our own lives. We know that gay males were the first to articulate the psychic costs exacted from males whose behavior does not match the traditional masculine requirements. Gay males were the first to challenge the legitimacy of these prescriptions for masculinity, and were also the first to explore how collective action and mutual support could loosen their hold on men.

The openness experienced in men's groups frequently leads to questions of physical and sexual relations among men. We consider it highly desirable that these questions be dealt with. But we are not sure of the answers—whether, for example, liberation from the strictures of the masculine role requires that we be open to sexual relations with other men. We believe that gay liberation is helping both homosexual and heterosexual men to reclaim parts of our humanity that were invalidated and abandoned during our masculine role training. As it stands, though, "male liberation" is distinct from gay male liberation.

The 31 articles in this book are organized into seven sections, each preceded by an introduction. The first section, "Growing Up Male," tells how we learn the masculine role in the first place and how this role disposes us to seek achievement and to suppress emotion. In the next five sections, personal accounts and general reports show how the masculine role influences our adult lives in our relations with women, with children, with other men, with work, and with the larger society. The last section of articles, "Men's Liberation," describes how men are getting together to explore and change themselves. A final section contains an extensive classified bibliography on men and masculinity.

1

GROWING UP MALE

"Is it a boy or a girl?" That's the first question society asks about us, and it marks the beginning of a continuing process of social influence. Boys are treated, and are expected to behave, in certain ways defined as masculine. Brian Allen's fable, "A Visit from Uncle Macho," suggests the force of the demands to grow up masculine, and the anxiety these demands create. Ruth Hartley's analysis of male socialization describes more specifically what is expected. Basically, the masculine role says that we males are supposed to seek achievement and suppress emotion. We are to work at "getting ahead" and "staying cool."

As boys we learn that getting ahead is important in both work and play. Grades are handed out in school, teams are chosen on the playground, and both of these events tell us how well we are doing and how much better we could be doing. Sports is a major route for conveying the masculine role to boys. Here our masculinity is tested in immediate physical competition with others. Moment by moment, our performance is measured in relation to others. Both in winning and in losing, the masculine role exerts strong influence, as two articles in this section, one from each perspective, illustrate.

The author of "Out in Right Field" was poor at sports and dreaded them. The author of "When I Was About Fourteen" was good at sports and loved them. But sports were important to both: each accepted as legitimate a status system based upon athletic ability, and a common anxiety ran through their experience. The main difference was that one boy was *sure* he wouldn't do well, and the other was *afraid* he wouldn't.

That even this successful male showed anxiety shows how the masculine drive for success can never be fulfilled, even by those at the top. It is not enough to win once, we have to keep winning. The continuing evaluation in relation to others encourages us to keep trying, but also insures that we can't ever really make it, once and for all. Our learned need to keep proving ourselves helps explain why many of us—no matter how hard we work or how much we achieve—remain vaguely dissatisfied with our lives.

As males grow older, the bases for evaluation change, but the importance of establishing a ranking of worth among individuals remains. As adults, the physical skills that were reflected in sports become less important than the mental and social skills that are reflected in prestige and income. What we learn growing up prepares us for these adult skills and rewards. As adolescents, one important area we were rated on was our social facility with females. Trying to get on well with females created anxiety for many of us, but mainly we accepted the situation as just another place where we should try to ignore our fears and go ahead.

Staying cool, no matter what, was part of what we learned growing up male. We knew that big boys didn't cry, and that real men didn't get too excited except in places like football games. Spontaneous emotion—positive or negative—was suppressed or restricted to certain settings. We learned to mute our joy, repress our tenderness, control our anger, hide our fear. The eventual result of our not expressing emotion is not to experience it. Finally, as Marc Fasteau writes in "Why Aren't We Talking?" we men simply lose the ability to be open with others.

Our restriction of emotionality compounds the stress put upon us by our striving to get ahead; we are often unable to acknowledge fully how the striving makes us feel. We suffer in many ways that may relate to the strain our emotional denial places upon our physical body. Compared with women, we die younger, have more heart attacks, and contract more stress diseases. Sidney Jourard, in "Some Lethal Aspects of the Male Sex Role," notes how we men are less aware of our own emotional life, disclose ourselves less to others, and find difficulty in loving and being loved.

The drive toward getting ahead and staying cool has functioned, more or less well, for men as individuals and for society as a whole, for a long time. Much work has been accomplished, and many troubling feelings have been avoided. The masculine role has provided answers about who we are and what to do. But, as the articles in this section show, some men are now finding what the masculine role offers to be insufficient. Some of us no longer find our fulfillment in external rewards that come from meeting masculine standards; instead we seek internal satisfaction that comes from fuller emotional involvement in our activities and relationships.

A Visit from Uncle Macho

Brian Allen

BRIAN ALLEN *is a counselor who received his training at the Radical Psychiatry Center in Berkeley, California. He is currently the Youth Advisor for the Contra Costa County Drug Education Center. Mr. Allen lives with his wife and two daughters in Berkeley.*

"Wake up, boy, the early bird gets the worm, you know!"

Mark rolled over and rubbed the sleep from his eyes, then he squinted up through the semi-darkness of the early morning at the figure standing beside the bed. Towering over Mark was a large man with a red face, a crew cut, and a thick neck that bulged over his shirt collar.

"Strong silent type, eh?" the man observed, "A real chip off the old block!"

Suddenly, Mark became frightened by this strange man in his bedroom and he began to cry.

"Hey, cut that out, young fellow!" the man said, leaning over and snapping his fingers in front of Mark's face, "Big boys don't cry."

Mark noticed for the first time that the man had a brown leather briefcase in his hand, one just like his father carried to work in the morning and brought home at night. The man spoke again, this time in a very business-like tone of voice.

"I'm your fairy godfather, but you can call me Uncle Macho. We have some very important business to discuss, you and I, man to man." Mark swallowed hard and blinked.

"But I'm not a man yet. I'm just a little boy."

"But you will be a man before long," Uncle Macho replied, "and you must begin preparing as soon as possible. You are five years old today and it's high time you began thinking about how to get a jump on the other guy and get ahead in this dog-eat-dog world."

Mark became confused and a bit frightened once again. A tear crept

---

From Brian Allen, "Liberating the Manchild," *Transactional Analysis Journal,* April 1972, 2(2), 68–71. Reprinted by permission of the International Transactional Analysis Association, Inc.

to the corner of his eye, climbed over a long, dark lash, and spilled onto his cheek, but the big man continued, seeming not to notice.

"Mark, I have a present for you here, the most important birthday present you will ever receive. What I have here will tell you what you need to know to become a man."

What Uncle Macho withdrew from the briefcase didn't look like any birthday present Mark had ever seen. It was nothing but a plain cardboard folder with some sheets of paper inside. Uncle Macho continued, speaking rapidly, like the used-car salesman on T.V.

"This is your script, Mark, and each of the great men in history has followed one like it, just as you will follow this one."

"Is it O.K. if my parents help me," Mark asked, still puzzled, "I'm only in kindergarten and I don't read too well yet."

"Of course they will help you, "Uncle Macho replied, but added quickly, "however, you must never *ask* them for help. In fact, you must never ask *anyone* for help, or even let anyone know that you are confused or frightened. That's part of learning to be a man. But all that is in the script. And don't worry about the words too much: there are plenty of pictures."

Mark opened the script in the middle and sure enough, there was a picture of a muscular-looking man in swim trunks carrying a pretty girl along a beach. Below the picture it said, "Dominate women." Mark wasn't sure what "dominate" meant, but he decided it had something to do with swimming. He looked up at Uncle Macho and smiled knowingly.

"Getting the idea already I see," said Macho with a wink, as he fastened the clasp on the briefcase. "Bright boy. You'll go far . . . in more ways than one." Then he buckled the straps and rose to his feet. Mark saw through the window behind his rocking horse that the sun was just beginning to come up.

"I've got to be going now," the fairy godfather said, "but I'll be seeing you again when you're about thirteen. That's when young men begin to have a lot of trouble with their scripts."

Mark looked up from the page with a puzzled expression on his face. "What will you do then?" he asked.

"I'll ride your ass," said Uncle Macho, as he strode out the door, "that's what I'll do!"

Sex-Role Pressures and the Socialization of the Male Child

Ruth E. Hartley

DR. RUTH HARTLEY *has been chairman of the growth and development concentration at the University of Wisconsin–Green Bay since 1968. She previously taught at Brooklyn College, City College of New York, Long Island University, and the University of Hawaii.*

Dr. Hartley is the author and co-author of numerous articles and papers on sex-role concepts and wrote the chapter "American Core Culture: Changes in Continuities," in Sex Roles in Changing Society. *Much of her recent work has focused on sex-role concepts of children and the implications of current changes in sex-role patterns.*

Demands that boys conform to social notions of what is manly come much earlier and are enforced with much more vigor than similar attitudes with respect to girls. Several research studies, using preschool children as their subjects, indicate that boys are aware of what is expected of them because they are boys and restrict their interests and activities to what is suitably "masculine" in the kindergarten (2, 3, 8, 10, 23) while girls amble gradually in the direction of "feminine" patterns for five more years (2, 3). In other words, more stringent demands are made on boys than on girls and at an early age, when they are least able to understand either the reasons for or the nature of the demands. Moreover, these demands are frequently enforced harshly, impressing the small boy with the danger of deviating from them, while he does not quite understand what they are. To make matters more difficult, the desired behavior is rarely defined positively as something the child *should* do, but rather, undesirable behavior is indicated negatively as something he should *not* do or be—anything, that is, that the parent or other people regard as "sissy." Thus, very early in life the boy must either stumble on the right path or bear repeated punishment without warning when he accidentally enters into the wrong ones. This situation gives us practically a perfect combination

From Ruth E. Hartley, "Sex-role Pressures in the Socialization of the Male Child," *Psychological Reports,* 1959, 5, 457–68. Reprinted with permission of author and publisher.

for inducing anxiety—the demand that the child do something which is not clearly defined to him, based on reasons he cannot possibly appreciate, and enforced with threats, punishments, and anger by those who are close to him. Indeed, a great many boys do give evidence of anxiety centered in the whole area of sex-connected role behaviors, an anxiety which frequently expresses itself in overstraining to be masculine, in virtual panic at being caught doing anything traditionally defined as feminine, and in hostility toward anything even hinting at "femininity," including females themselves. This kind of overreaction is reminiscent of the quality of all strong emotion precipitated early in life before judgment and control have had a chance to develop.

This, however, is only one source of difficulty. Another related one comes from the simple fact that fathers are not at home nearly as much as mothers are. This means that the major psychodynamic process by which sex-roles are learned—the process of identification—is available only minimally to boys since their natural identification objects, their fathers, are simply not around much of the time to serve as models (5, 21). Illustrative of the children's awareness of this state of affairs, many subjects expressed themselves in the following vein: "My father . . . . I don't see him very often." "It's harder to know about boys (than about girls) . . . . Father hardly has time to talk to me." "Men are harder to tell about . . . . to tell the truth, my father isn't around much."

The absence of fathers means, again, that much of male behavior has to be learned by trial and error and indirection. One outcome of this state of affairs is the fact that boys, as a group, tend to resemble their fathers in personality and attitudes much less than girls resemble their mothers. This has been impressively documented by the results of a number of research studies conducted by different workers using different subjects and collecting data by different methods (1, 13, 14, 24, 26).

In addition to the effect of the relative absence of fathers from boys' experience, we also have evidence that the relations between boys and their fathers tend to be less good than those between girls and their mothers or fathers (16, 17, 20). Since identification is affected by the quality of relationships existing between the child and the identification model (18, 27), this diminishes still further the boy's chance to define his sex-roles easily and naturally by using his male parent as a model (4, 19). Boys having trouble in sex-roles, for example, often report their fathers as the punishing agents, their mothers as protectors. Fathers in general seem to be perceived as punishing or controlling agents (6, 7).

Where, then, we might ask, *do* boys find meaningful, positive guides for the specifics of their behavior as males? The answer seems to point largely to their peer groups and somewhat older youths. For a boy, then, contact with, and acceptance by, his peers is tremendously important, because he has to look to them to fill in the gaps in his information about his role as a male, and he has to depend on them to give him practice in it. Unfortunately, both the information and the practice he gets are distorted. Since his peers have no better sources of information than he has, all they can do is to pool the impressions and anxieties they derived from their early training. Thus, the picture they draw is at once oversimplified and overemphasized. It is a picture drawn in black and white, with little or no modulation, and it is incomplete, including only a few of the many elements that go to make up the role of the mature male. Thus, we find overemphasis on physical strength and athletic skills (9, 22, 28), with almost a complete omission of tender feelings or acceptance of responsibility toward those who are weaker. It is, after all, a picture drawn by children and it is not enough. Unfortunately, it is almost all that many boys have to go by, and its power to induce anxiety is amply attested (11, 12, 15, 25, 28).

And now we come to what is perhaps the source of greatest difficulty for the growing boy—the conflict in role demands that our social structure imposes on him. On the one hand, we have insisted that he eschew all "womanly" things almost from the cradle, and enforced these demands in a way that makes whatever is female a threat to him—for that is what he must not be. Ordinarily, one responds to a threat by trying to escape from it or by trying to destroy the threatening object. But this the boy cannot do, for society puts him directly under the jurisdiction of women, without relief, for most of his waking day. On the one hand, he is told that he is supposed to be rugged, independent, able to take care of himself, and to disdain "sissies." On the other, he is forced into close contact with the epitome of all sissy-things—women—for most of his day and he is commanded to obey and learn from them. In other words, he is compelled to knuckle under to that which he has been taught to despise. Need we wonder that he tends to rebel at times or has trouble making a smooth adjustment?

Moreover, the demeanor of the women with whom he is forced to associate is often such that the boy feels that women just don't like boys. We found many indications of this belief in our subjects' responses to a hypothetical adoption story that they were asked to complete. Almost invariably mothers were assumed to prefer girls to boys. The reasons given for this were drawn from the boys' own experience with their mothers: "She says boys are rough." "A girl wouldn't be so wild—she would not run so much and play rough . . . . a girl is more kind." If a mother is assumed to want a boy, it is for a nefarious purpose, as in the following: "She'd want a boy so she can give him to the Indians . . . . girls are always good."

Admittedly, the pressures of male-oriented socialization are not exerted on all equally. Some suffer more than others, notably those with physical endowments or special abilities which are not congruent with the common cultural definition of the male role, and those who have even poorer opportunities than usual for forming sex-appropriate identifications. Thus, the small boy, the weak boy, the boy whose physical coordination is poor—these are especially penalized. But the lad with better-than-average endowments also suffers if those endowments happen to be in areas not included in the culture's definition of what is "masculine"—music, for example, or art. It takes an unusually rugged physique to offset the disadvantage of a creative talent.

To illustrate what we mean by the "demands" of the male role, let me quote from the boys themselves. This is what they tell us boys have to know and be able to do—their view of the masculine role at their own age level (8 and 11 years): they have to be able to fight in case a bully comes along; they have to be athletic; they have to be able to run fast; they must be able to play rough games; they need to know how to play many games—curb-ball, baseball, basketball, football; they need to be smart; they need to be able to take care of themselves; they should know what girls don't know—how to climb, how to make a fire, how to carry things; they should have more ability than girls; they need to know how to stay out of trouble; they need to know arithmetic and spelling more than girls do. (The last point is probably the greatest blow of all for an 8-year-old.)

We learn a little more when we ask, "What is expected of boys?" We find that they believe grown-ups expect them to be noisy; to get dirty; to mess up the house; to be naughty; to be "outside" more than girls are; not to be crybabies; not to be "softies"; not to be "behind" like girls are; and to get into trouble more than girls do. Moreover, boys are not allowed to do the kind of things that girls usually do, but girls may do the kind of things that boys do.

Going beyond the immediate present, this is what the boy sees as his future, described in terms of the things men need to know and be able to do: they need to be strong; they have to be ready to make decisions; they must be able to protect women and children in emergencies; they have to have more manual strength than women; they should know how to carry heavy things; they are the ones to do the hard labor, the rough work, the dirty work, and the unpleasant work; they must be able to fix things; they must get money to support their families; they need "a good business head." In addition to their being the adventurers and protectors, the burden bearers, and the laborers, they also need to know how to take good care of children, how to get along with their wives, and how to teach their children right from wrong.

We are also told that, in contrast to women, men are usually in charge of things; they work very hard and they get tired a lot; they mostly do things for other people; they are supposed to be bolder and more restless, and have more courage than women. Like boys, they, too, mess up the house.

On the positive side, men mostly do what they want to do and are very important. In the family, they are the boss; they have authority in relation to the disposal of monies and they get first choice in the use of the most comfortable chair in the house and the daily paper. They seem to get mad a lot, but are able to make children feel good; they laugh and make jokes more than women do. Compared with mothers, fathers are more fun to be with; they are exciting to have around; they have the best ideas.

One wonders, looking over these items, whether the compensations are enough to balance the weight of the burdens that boys see themselves as assuming in order to fulfill the male role adequately. Looked at from this point of view, the question is not why boys have difficulty with this role, but why they try as hard as they do to fulfill it. Perhaps a glance at the characteristics of the female role from the boys' eye view can give us the answer.

Concerning girls, boys tell us: they have to stay close to the house; they are expected to play quietly and be gentler than boys; they are often afraid; they must not be rough; they have to keep clean; they cry when they are scared or hurt; they are afraid to go to rough places like rooftops and empty lots; their activities consist of "fopperies" like playing with dolls, fussing over babies, and sitting and talking about dresses; they need to know how to cook, sew, and take care of children, but spelling and arithmetic are not as important for them as for boys. Though reeking of limitation and restraint, this picture is not very full. Not until we ask about adult women do we get any sort of depth or reflection of the affective aspects of the female role.

Concerning adult women we are told: they are indecisive; they are afraid of many things; they make a fuss over things; they get tired a lot; they very often need someone to help them; they stay home most of the time; they are not as strong as men; they don't like adventure; they are squeamish about seeing blood; they don't know what to do in an emergency; they cannot do dangerous things; they are more easily damaged than men; and they die more easily than men. Moreover, they are "lofty" about dirty jobs; they feel themselves above manual work; they are scared of getting wet or getting an electric shock; they cannot do things men do because they have a way of doing things the wrong way; they are not very intelligent; they can only scream in an emergency where a man would take charge. Women are the ones who have to keep things neat and tidy and clean up household messes; they feel sad more often than men. Although they make children feel good, they also make boys carry heavy loads; haul heavy shopping carts uphill; keep them from going out when they want to go, or demand that they stay out when they want to come in. They take the pep out of things and are fussy about children's grades. They very easily become jealous and envy their husbands.

Concerning women's traditional household activities, we get the following reflections: "They are always at those crazy household duties and don't have time for anything else." "Their work is just regular drudging." "Women do things like cooking and washing and sewing because that's all they can do." "If women were to try to do men's jobs the whole thing would fall apart with the women doing it." "Women haven't enough strength in the head or in the body to do most jobs." "In going to adventurous places women are pests—just a lot of bother. They die easily and they are always worried about their petticoats." "I don't know how women would get along without men doing the work." Natural exploiters, women are good people to stay away from because, as one boy told us, "If I play with my mother, I'll end up doing the dishes and she'll be playing with my father."

When he sees women as weak, easily damaged, lacking strength in mind and in body, able to perform only the tasks which take the least strength and are of least importance, what boy in his right senses would not give his all to escape this alternative to the male role? For many, unfortunately, the scramble to escape takes on all the aspects of panic, and the outward semblance of non-femininity is achieved at a tremendous cost of anxiety and self-alienation. From our data, we would infer that the degree of anxiety experienced has a direct relationship to the degree of pressure to be "manly" exerted on the boy, the rigidity of the pattern to which he is pressed to conform, the availability of a good model, and the apparent degree of success which his efforts achieve.

REFERENCES

1. Beier, E. G., & Ratzeburg, F. The parental identification of male and female college students. *J. abnorm. soc. Psychol.*, 1953, 48, 569–572.

2. Brown, D. G. Sex-role preference in young children. *Psychol. Monogr.*, 1956, 70, No. 14 (Whole No. 421).

3. Brown, D. G. Sex-role development in a changing culture. *Psychol. Bull.*, 1958, 54, 232–242.

4. Cava, E. L., & Raush, H. L. Identification and the adolescent boy's perception of his father. *J. abnorm. soc. Psychol.*, 1952, 47, 855–856.

5. Cottrell, L. The adjustment of the individual to his age and sex roles. *Amer. sociol. Rev.*, 1942, 7, 617–620.

6. Emmerich, W. Young children's discriminations of family roles. Paper read at the Society for Research in Child Development, Bethesda, Md., March, 1959.

7. Emmerich, W. Parental identification in young children. *Genet. Psychol. Monogr.*, 1959, 60, 257–308.

8. Fauls, L. B., & Smith, W. D. Sex-role learning of five-year-olds. *J. genet. Psychol.*, 1956, 89, 105–117.

9. Feinberg, M. R., Smith, M., & Schmidt, R. An analysis of expressions used by adolescents at varying economic levels to describe accepted and rejected peers. *J. genet. Psychol.*, 1958, 93, 133–148.

10. Gilbert, G. M. A survey of "referral problems" in metropolitan child guidance centers. *J. clin. Psychol.*, 1957, 13, 37–40.

11. Goodenough, E. W. Interest in persons as an aspect of sex difference in the early years. *Genet. Psychol. Monogr.*, 1957, 55, 287–323.

12. Gray, S. W. Masculinity-femininity in relation to anxiety and social acceptance. *Child Developm.*, 1957, 28, 204–214.

13. Gray, S. W., & Klaus, R. The assessment of parental identification. *Genet. Psychol. Monogr.*, 1956, 54, 87–109.

14. Lazowick, L. M. On the nature of identification. *J. abnorm. soc. Psychol.*, 1955, 51, 175–183.

15. MacDonald, M. W. Criminally aggressive behavior in passive effeminate boys. *Amer. J. Orthopsychiat.*, 1938, 8, 70–78.

16. Meltzer, H. Sex differences in parental preference patterns. *Char. & Pers.*, 1941, 10, 114–128.

17. Meltzer, H. Sex differences in children's attitudes to parents. *J. genet. Psychol.*, 1943, 62, 311–326.

18. Mowrer, O. H. *Learning theory and personality dynamics.* New York: Ronald, 1950.

19. Mussen, P. H., & Payne, D. E. Parent-child relations and father identification among adolescent boys. *J. abnorm. soc. Psychol.*, 1956, 52, 358–362.

20. Nimkoff, M. F. The child's preference for father or mother. *Amer. sociol. Rev.*, 1942, 7, 517–524.

21. Parsons, T. Age and sex in the social structure of the United States. *Amer. sociol. Rev.*, 1942, 7, 604–616.

22. Pope, B. Socio-economic contrasts in children's peer culture prestige values. *Genet. Psychol. Monogr.*, 1953, 48, 157–220.

23. Rabban, M. Sex-role identification in young children in two diverse social groups. *Genet. Psychol. Monogr.*, 1950, 42, 81–158.

24. Roff, M. Intra-family resemblances in personality characteristics. *J. Psychol.*, 1950, 30, 199–227.

25. Ronge, P. H. The feminine protest. *Amer. J. indiv. Psychol.*, 1956, 2, 112–115.

26. Schoeppe, A. Sex differences in adolescent socialization. *J. soc. Psychol.*, 1953, 38, 175–185.

27. Symonds, P. M. *The dynamics of human adjustment.* New York: Appleton-Century-Crofts, 1946.

28. Tuddenham, R. D. Studies in reputation: I. Sex and grade differences in school children's evaluation of their peers. II. The diagnosis of social adjustment. *Psychol. Monogr.*, 1952, 66, No. 1 (Whole No. 333).

When I Was about Fourteen . . .

Peter Candell

PETER CANDELL *describes himself this way: "For the past two years I have been with The Moving Men Theater Co. of Berkeley. We create our plays collectively, and they are based on our lives: our fantasies and addictions, pasts and futures, our personalities and politics as American men in the 1970's."*

When I was about fourteen I slapped this kid Jeff Cook across the face right in the middle of a football huddle. I was boiling inside because he wasn't playing seriously. (I think it was the summer after I bit Barry Paley in the stomach after I tackled him, also during a football game. I remember being really embarrassed when his father came up to me later and bawled the hell out of me in front of other people. He couldn't understand why I wanted to bite his son and leave those ugly teeth marks. I didn't like Barry Paley.) Jeff Cook was a nice kid.

He was just goofing at a time when I was most serious and I slapped him out of pure rage. In fact I used to get pissed off a lot when we played ball whenever someone showed any signs of having fun, if that seemed more important to the kid than winning.

A softball or football game to me was deadly serious: if we won, the day was fine; if we lost, everything would be a little bitter for a while. If we won, I'd try to figure out how much I contributed to the victory. If we lost, I mulled over my mistakes, real and imagined, for hours. If I made a good play, I was a hero. An error, and I was a total failure. I still don't take my mistakes very lightly, even when they're trivial. And I remember my own greatest moments in sports vividly.

Jeff Cook probably felt that day, before I slapped him, anyway, the way that I wanted to feel today when I played football, only I couldn't. He must've been really bored during that game, because he wasn't getting much of a chance to do anything except stand on the line and "block" every play. Anybody who plays touch football knows that the

---

Peter Candell, "When I was about fourteen . . . ," *Brother: A Forum for Men Against Sexism* (P. O. Box 4387, Berkeley, Calif. 94704), April 1972, #4, p. 6. Reprinted by permission. This article by itself should not be considered representative of the politics of the staff of *Brother*. Each issue was meant to be seen as a whole.

most boring position is on the line blocking somebody play after play. And in most games, the guys who are the worst players get the job as linemen, while two or three "stars" do all of the running, passing and catching.

Anyway Jeff Cook was one of these linemen and was undoubtedly bored stiff, for good reason, so he was goofing off, which seems to me now to be the best way to deal with the situation. Because he was entertaining himself and the other linemen, and also, although he may not have known it, he was goofing on us "stars" who were so serious. And I must have known somehow that he was goofing on me especially and I couldn't take it so I gave it to him.

Today I was treated like Jeff Cook on the football field. I was chosen last in two different games and I was pretty much ignored the whole day when plays were called in the huddle.

I guess it happened because I'm small and I didn't know anyone else playing. It was obvious early in the day there was a pecking order of "stars" based on who knew who and also on how tough a guy talked and acted. Since I didn't know anyone, the only way for me to break through that pecking order and get into the game was to start acting really tough. But I can't do that, it's just not my style. So I just kept my mouth shut and went through the motions sulking to myself, dragging my ass and my sense of pride through the mud on that wet field. It would have done me good to goof on the whole thing the way Jeff Cook did, but I couldn't do that either. I was too hurt.

But the thing is I really understood male chauvinism during those games today, and I felt it. I felt pushed around, ignored, used, and worst of all, powerless to do anything about it, except to leave. I felt like a little girl surrounded by all the older boys on the block.

My brother Steve used to lose his temper with me, just the way I did with Jeff Cook, except with Steve it was usually a punch in the arm. I loved my brother and his punches and noogies told me he loved me too. And I feel sad now to think how far away I am from my brother, because I have been searching for new brothers ever since he went away to summer camp when he was about thirteen and I was about nine, but it's never been the same.

I think I learned a lot of the jock mentality from my brother. He was always serious during a game, too. I guess he learned from my father, who probably learned it from his father. I knew I was admired for having such good "spirit." Incredible.

The summer I was 15 I got to play softball with the men's teams which is like being called up to the majors after years of playing Class C ball. It was a rite of passage. My manhood was on the line. They put me in right field which is usually where the worst player on the team was put and I knew that I had to prove myself and it wouldn't be easy in right field because you were lucky to get one chance a game out there.

There I was in right field spiritually urging the pitcher on with such gems as "no batta, baby, no batta," "right pastim," "lettim hitit, letim hitit," and the like, the visor of my baseball cap pulled down tight on my crew cut and over my eyes and there it was: A high foul ball behind first base, normally an easy play for the first or second baseman, but way out of reach of the old men with no legs playing these positions on OUR TEAM.

I take off at full speed not knowing whether I would reach it but knowing very clearly that this is *my chance*. My cap flies off my head, which must have been pre-ordained, and a second later I one-hand it as cool as can be, still moving at top speed. I glance to the left as I hear the applause from the thirty or so fans and there's MOM kvelling, beaming, in a lounge chair she brought from the bungalow. My catch is the third out so I continue on to the sidelines and I hear voices congratulating my mother for having such a good athlete for a son: "Quite a kid you've got there, Netti." Everybody on the team pounds my back as they come in from the field, letting me know that I've MADE IT.

But I know enough not to blow my cool so all I do is mumble thanks under a slightly trembling upper lip which is fighting the rest of my face, the rest of my being, from exploding with laughter and tears of joy. I don't even allow myself to smile because I know that it won't be just a smile, that if I let go even a quarter of an inch it will get beyond control and at the very least I'll giggle, which is unheard of on the ballfield.

I learned to be so cool partly from watching baseball stars on TV. The stars were always super-modest: they were responsible only for their failure, successes being due to Divine Intervention or Luck. My star, super-modest super-hero, was Mickey Mantle. What a name—Mickey Mantle—a born hero to millions of war babies who were freaking out on Bill Haley and the Comets the same year Mickey was on the way to the Triple Crown.

Mickey Mantle was far and away my most important person during those years. I lived through him, through his performance on the baseball field. Blond, crew-cut, strong, very strong, handsome and innocent—downright dumb in fact. He had a certain way of running after he hit a homerun, hunching his shoulders and clinking his arms, bent sharply at the elbow, up and down, but not backwards and forwards the way most other people do, which made him look even stronger; and so I started to run like him going to position or coming back in and very soon I was doing it without realizing I was doing it. In fact, I'm not even sure I ever was actually *aware* I was doing it but I was sure as hell doing it.

The whole vicarious masculinity thing went on for a long time, and when Mickey started fading out in the early sixties, I was still hooked on New York teams, which amounted to almost the same thing.

I rooted passionately for all the New York teams, getting most involved with the ones that were winning, and to *this day,* fans, to this day, I occasionally follow Giants football and Knicks basketball in the *Chronicle* sports pages, and *it still matters* whether they win or lose.

Out in Right Field

Throughout my entire school career, the time of day I dreaded most was Gym class. Whereas other kids seemed to look forward to Gym as some sort of relief from sitting at a desk and listening to a teacher, I dreaded the thought of sports.

The curse followed me throughout my entire life. In elementary school, part of the year we played baseball outdoors. The two best players (never me) were captains and they chose—one by one—players for their teams. The choosing went on and on, the better players getting picked first and me and my type last.

During the game I always played the outfield. Right field. Far right field. And there I would stand in the hot sun wishing I was anyplace else in the world. Every so often a ball looked like it was coming in my direction and I prayed to god that it wouldn't happen. If it did come, I promised god to be good for the next thirty-seven years if he let me catch it—especially if it was a flyball. The same thing occurred when it was my turn to bat. It was bad enough, but if there were any runners on base—or any outs—and it all depended on me—I knew we were lost.

The rest of the year in elementary school consisted of indoor Gym class, some of which were coed. The coed Gym classes consisted of things like dance lessons. The teachers would teach us essential dances like the fox trot, the mambo and the merengue. These were always a chore because it was you and your girl partner—usually matched by height—and I of course was the shortest—and matched up with the shortest girl—who towered over me anyway. Dances like the Virginia Reel and square dancing, which were a group thing, I usually enjoyed a lot. A lot, that is, until it became clear from the actions of the rest

---

From *Unbecoming Men: A Men's Consciousness-Raising Group Writes on Oppression and Themselves,* Times Change Press (c/o Monthly Review Press, 62 W. 14th St., New York, NY 10011, $1.75 plus 35¢ handling), 1971, pp. 36–38. Reprinted by permission.

of the guys in dance class that I was the only one having a good time. After that even that type of dancing was awful.

Junior high school was equally awful. For it was in junior high that real Gym classes started—Gym class with lockers and smelly locker rooms and gym uniforms and showers with eight million other guys.

I hated the sight of my gym uniform. The locker room stench almost knocked me out. And during Gym class I tried my best not to exert myself, so I wouldn't sweat too much, so I wouldn't have to take a shower with eight million other guys.

In junior high we still did things like play baseball. But things started to get rougher and rougher. We did things like wrestling. And gymnastics. To this day I can't climb a pole or a rope. Calisthenics were and are a bore.

High school was the same old stuff. However, in high school, sports started taking on new dimensions because the most highly prized girls looked to the best athletes. The football and basketball players. I was out of the competition from the beginning, but that didn't make it any the less awful.

There was absolutely no relief from sports in the early part of my life, for it happened not only in school, but also at home. My older brother was a good athlete. He went to ballgames and even tried out for and made some teams. He plastered our room with hateful pictures of the Dodgers at bat. Sports consumed his entire life, and he would get home from school, change his clothes and run out to play.

My father related to my brother completely in this way. They had a fine sports relationship, and would go off to ballgames together—or talk at the dinner table of the day's ballgames or the latest standings, which they both knew by heart. I was completely left out of this. After a while I grew resentful and wanted no part of it. Yet, every so often my father would try. He would take me out back for a while with a ball, bat and glove and try to make a man out of me. Patiently he would throw a ball in my direction and I swung and missed it. After he quickly grew tired of that he would once again explain to me how to use the fielding glove he stuck on my hand and I would try my hand at catching. I soon grew tired of this—mainly because I missed so often and had to go chasing down the block after the ball. These sessions never lasted very long. Even Sundays were no relief—the television was usually on and blasting a ballgame. I grew to hate the sound of Mel Allen's voice.

My father and brother seemed to have a great relationship. I didn't. Neither with my father, nor with my brother. I guess I was left to my mother. We seemed to get along fine.

Why Aren't We Talking?

Marc Fasteau

MARC FASTEAU *is a graduate of Harvard Law School who has litigated in the area of sex discrimination. A former assistant in foreign affairs to Senator Mike Mansfield, he has written a book about the personal and public costs of the masculine role. The book, entitled* The Male Machine, *was published in 1974 by McGraw-Hill.*

Can you imagine men talking to each other saying: "Are you sure you're not angry at me?" . . . "I'm not as assertive as I would like to be." . . . "I feel so competitive that I can't get close to anyone." . . . "I just learned something important about myself that I've got to tell you." . . . "I don't have the self-confidence to do what I really want to do." . . . "I feel nervous talking to you like this."

It just doesn't happen.

A lot of men sympathize with the Women's Movement, or at least with demands for equal treatment on the job and under the law. Some even accept and enjoy having women as equals in their personal lives. It takes only a little more imagination to see that the changes being brought about by feminism will directly benefit men as well as women. I have the theory down pat; I believe it and have even spent time proselytizing for this point of view on college campuses. But because men have not yet begun to talk to each other honestly, men's liberation is still just an idea. I feel like a navigator who has been to school, but has few shipmates and no ship.

As a man, my conditioning and problems are not only different, but virtually the inverse of those of most women. We've been taught that "real men" are never passive or dependent, always dominant in relationships with women or other men, and don't talk about or directly express feelings; especially feelings that don't contribute to dominance. A few of us have begun to free ourselves of these constraints. But so far we may have had unsettling personal insights, our fair share of the housework, slightly better understanding of the Masculine-Mystique reasons why this country is still fighting in Indochina—but very little

---

Marc Fasteau, "Why Aren't We Talking?," *Ms.*, July 1972, p. 16. Reprinted by permission.

else. Each of us is still pretty much going it alone. There is nothing among men that resembles the personal communication that women have developed among themselves. We don't know very much about ourselves, and we know even less about each other.

Now, in particular, we feel "left out," because we see how the women around us are making contact with each other, but our sense of isolation is also an independent and critical element of sex role conditioning itself. We are taught not to communicate our personal feelings and concerns. Most of our friendships simply don't run very deep. For example, looking back, I realize that my only points of contact with one of my closest friends of several years ago were playing poker and tennis together, eating dinners cooked by his wife, and rehashing the Vietnam war and other "large" problems. Never anything personal. I enjoyed tennis and poker and still do, but the conversations always left me with a feeling of strain and dissatisfaction that I wouldn't identify. In our case, we both had "credentials and prospects" within the "liberal establishment." We recognized this about each other, and this recognition was the basis of mutual respect and a precarious sense of equality. Competition, overt in games and covert in measuring our career progress, ran through the relationship. We didn't know what to do except compete, and the competition constantly threatened the balance upon which the friendship depended. Losing at poker three times running could be balanced by winning at tennis, by a step up in government.

We always needed an excuse to talk. Getting together for its own sake would have been frightening. Talking personally and spontaneously involves revealing doubts, plans which may fail, ideas which haven't been thought through, happiness over things the other person may think trivial—in short, making ourselves vulnerable. That was too risky.

The most painful thing, in retrospect, is that we thought we were the best of friends. Some men are better off than we were. Others are in worse shape, disguising and channeling their feelings in grotesque ways. Some months ago I saw two men, obviously friends out together, watching a football game in a bar. Their entire conversation consisted of grunts and exclamations and nudges after particularly exciting plays. It's a phenomenon not restricted to professional men or athletes or factory workers. It's simply part of our male culture.

Some men will admit that they can't talk to men, and are only really able to talk about their feelings to women. But even these intimacies are often structured into a safe framework. "Safe" because they think the woman is a subordinate, and therefore nonthreatening, nonjudging. Moreover, what men are really asking from women in these situations is the simple reassurance that, despite their problems and setbacks, they are still "real men," still needed and respected. Of course, comfort and reassurance are legitimate demands of every human being, but it is significant that there is rarely any real discussion of the problem or of the feelings involved. That kind of analysis requires more insight and willingness to probe than most men feel they can afford. It also can place the woman, at least temporarily, in the dreaded position of being the stronger one instead of the passive supporter.

As part of the women's process of gaining the freedom to be full human beings, they are talking to each other about subjects almost forbidden to men. And in so doing they have thrown a spotlight on the obstacles to communication among men. We ought to want to break through these barriers for the pleasure of getting to know ourselves and each other better. Until we do, men's liberation will remain an idea instead of a movement.

Some Lethal Aspects of the Male Role

Sidney M. Jourard

The author was born in Canada, and educated at the University of Toronto and the University of Buffalo, where he received his Ph.D. in Clinical Psychology in 1953. He has taught at various universities and presently is Professor at the University of Florida. He has published several books including The Transparent Self, Disclosing Man to Himself, *and* Healthy Personality: An Approach from the Viewpoint of Humanistic Psychology.

Men die sooner than women, and so health scientists and public health officials have become justly concerned about the sex difference in death age. Biology provides no convincing evidence to prove that female organisms are intrinsically more durable than males, or that tissues or cells taken from males are less viable than those taken from females. A promising place to look for an explanation of the perplexing sex-differential in mortality is in the transactions between men and their environments, especially their interpersonal environments. In principle, there must be ways of behaving among people which prolong a man's life and insure his fuller functioning, and ways of behaving which speed a man's progress toward death. The present paper is devoted to an overview of some aspects of being a man in American society which may be related to man's acknowledged faster rate of dying.

The male role, as personally and socially defined, requires man to appear tough, objective, striving, achieving, unsentimental, and emotionally unexpressive. But seeming is not being. If a man *is* tender (behind his *persona*), if he weeps, if he shows weakness, he will likely be viewed as unmanly by others, and he will probably regard himself as inferior to other men.

Now, from all that we can fathom about the *subjective* side of man, as this has been revealed in autobiography, novels, plays, and psychotherapists' case histories, it seems true that men are as capable as women at responding to the play of life's events with a broad range of feelings. Man's potential thoughts, feelings, wishes and fantasies know no bounds, save those set by his biological structure and his personal history. But the male role, and the male's self-structure will not allow man to acknowledge or to express the entire breadth and depth of his inner experience, to himself or to others. Man seems obliged, rather, to hide much of his real self—the ongoing flow of his spontaneous inner experience—from himself and from others.

MANLINESS AND LOW SELF-DISCLOSURE

Research in patterns of self-disclosure has shown that men typically reveal less personal information about themselves to others than women (Jourard 1961a; Jourard and Lasakow, 1958; Jourard and Landsman, 1960; Jourard and Richman, 1963). Since men, doubtless, have as much "self," i.e., inner experience, as women, it follows that men have more "secrets" from the interpersonal world than women. It follows further that men, seeming to dread being known by others, must be more continually tense (neuromuscular tension) than women. It is as if "being manly" implies the necessity to wear neuromuscular "armor," the character armor which Reich (1948) wrote about with such lucidity. Moreover, if a man has "secrets," "something to hide," it must follow that other people will be a threat to him; they might pry into his secrets, or he may, in an unguarded moment, reveal his true self in its nakedness, thereby exposing his areas of weakness and vulnerability. Naturally, when a person is in hostile territory, he must be continually alert, hypertonic, opaque, and restless. All this implies that trying to seem manly is a kind of "work," and work imposes stress and consumes energy. Manliness, then, seems to carry with it a chronic burden of stress and energy-expenditure which could be a factor related to man's relatively shorter life-span.

If self-disclosure is an empirical index of "openness," of "real-self being," and if openness and real-self being are factors in health and wellness, then the research in self-disclosure seems to point to one of the potentially lethal aspects of the male role. Men keep their selves to themselves, and impose thereby an added burden of stress beyond that imposed by the exigencies of everyday life. The experience of psychosomatic physicians who undertake psychotherapy with male patients suffering peptic ulcers, essential hypertension and kindred disorders seems to support this contention. Psychotherapy is the art of promoting self-disclosure and authentic being in patients who withhold their real selves from expression, and clinical experience shows that when psychotherapy has been effective with psychosomatic patients, the latter change their role-definitions, their self-structures, and their behavior in the direction of greater spontaneity and openness, with salutory consequences to their bodies. The time is not far off when it will be possible to demonstrate with adequately controlled experiments the nature and degree of correlation between levels and amounts of self-disclosure, and proneness to illness and/or early death age.

MANLINESS: THE LACK OF INSIGHT AND EMPATHY

There is another implication of the fact that men are lower self-disclosures than women, an implication that relates to self-insight. Men, trained by their upbringing to assume the "instrumental role," tend more to relate to other people on an *I—It* basis than women (Buber, 1937).[1] They are more adept than women at relating impersonally to others, seeing them as the embodiment of their roles rather than as persons enacting roles. Women (often to the despair of business-like men) seem to find it difficult to keep their interpersonal relationships *im*personal; they sense and respond to the feelings of the *other* person even in a supposedly official transaction, and they respond to their

[1] There is an interesting implication of these observations for the training of male psychotherapists. It seems true that effective psychotherapists of whatever theoretical school are adept at establishing a warm, bilaterally communicative relationship with their patients, one characterized by a refraining from manipulation on the part of the therapist. The effective therapists do not "take over" the patient's problems, or "solve them" for the patient. Rather, they seem to "be and to let be" (Rogers, 1958). This mode of being is quite alien to the modal male. Indeed, it can be discerned among beginning therapists that there is often considerable dread of such passivity, because it constitutes a threat to masculine identity. Beginning therapists seem to be most fascinated by "manly," active techniques such as hypnosis, reflection, interpretation, etc.—the kinds of things which will be difficult for them to master, but which will make them feel they are *doing something* to the patient which will get him well. These techniques, however, leave the self of the therapist hidden behind the mask of his professional role, and have limited effectiveness.

own feelings toward the other person, seeming to forget the original purpose of the impersonal transaction.

Now, one outcome that is known to follow from effective psychotherapy (which, it will be recalled, entails much self-disclosure from the patient to the therapist) is that the patient becomes increasingly sensitized to the nuances of his own feelings (and those of the therapist) as they ebb and flow in the relationship. The patient becomes more adept at labeling his feelings (Dollard and Miller, 1950, pp. 281–304), diagnosing his own needs, and understanding his own reactions. Co-incident with this increase in insight is an increase in empathy with others, an increase in his ability to "imagine the real" (Buber, 1957). Studies of leadership show that the leaders of the most effective groups maintain an optimum "distance" from their followers, avoiding the distraction thereby of overly intimate personal knowledge of the followers' immediate feelings and needs (Fiedler, 1957). But not all of a man's everyday life entails the instrumental leadership role. For example, a man may "lead" his family, but he is not a father twenty-four hours a day. Personal life calls both for insight and for empathy. If practice at spontaneous self-disclosure promotes insight and empathy, then perhaps we have here one of the mechanisms by which women become more adept at these aspects of their so-called "expressive" role. Women, trained toward motherhood and a comforting function, both engage in and receive more self-disclosure than men (Jourard and Richman, 1963).

Let us now focus upon insight, in the sense that we have used the term here. If men are trained, as it were, to ignore their own feelings, in order more adequately to pursue the instrumental aspects of manliness, it follows that they will be less sensitive to what one might call "all-is-not-well signals," as these arise in themselves. It is probably a fact that in every case of outright physical or mental illness, earlier signs occurred which, if noted and acted upon, would have averted the eventual breakdown. Vague discomfort, boredom, anxiety, depression probably arose as consequences of the afflicted person's way of life, but because these signals were "weak," or else deliberately or automatically ignored, the illness-conducive way of life persisted until breakdown finally forced a respite, a withdrawal from the illness-producing role. The hypothesis may be proposed that women, more sensitized to their inner experience, will notice their "all-is-not-well signals" sooner and more often than men, and change their mode of existence to one more conducive to wellness, e.g., consult a doctor sooner, or seek bed-rest more often than men. Men, by contrast, fail to notice these "all-is-not-well signals" of weaker intensity, and do not stop work, nor take to their beds until the destructive consequences of their manly way of life have progressed to the point of a "stroke," or a total collapse. It is as if women "amplify" such inner distress signals even when they are dim, while men, as it were, "tune them out" until they become so strong they can no longer be ignored.

Accordingly, manly men, unaccustomed to self-disclosure, and characterized by lesser insight and lesser empathy than women, do violence to their own unique needs, and persist in modes of behavior which to be sure, are effective at changing the world, but no less effective in modifying their "essence" from the healthy to the moribund range.

A curious exception to these patterns has been noted among college males Mechanic and Volkart (1961, p. 52) have proposed the term "illness behavior" to describe "the way in which symptoms are perceived, evaluated, and acted upon by a person who recognizes some pain, discomfort, or other sign of organic malfunction." Visiting a physician at a university infirmary following perception of some malaise thus qualifies as a type of "illness behavior." Some as yet unpublished research at the University of Florida Student Infirmary has shown that male students consulted the Infirmary one and one half times more frequently than comparable female students during the year under study. A breakdown according to religious denomination showed, moreover, that of the "high users" of the Infirmary, Jewish male students were represented with nearly double the frequency of males affiliated with Methodist, Baptist, Catholic, and other religious groups. A completely independent study (Jourard, 1961b) of self-disclosure patterns among members of different religious denominations on the University of Florida campus showed that Jewish males were significantly higher disclosers than were comparable Methodist, Baptist, and Catholic males, none of the latter three groups differing significantly from one another. These findings imply that college males in general, and Jewish college males in particular, may depart from more stereotyped patterns of masculinity which prevail in the general population for the age range between 18 and 23.

MANLINESS AND INCOMPETENCE AT LOVING

Loving, including self-love, entails knowledge of the unique needs and characteristics of the loved person (Fromm, 1956). To know another person calls for empathy *in situ,* the capacity to "imagine the real," and the ability to "let be," that is, to permit and promote the disclosure of being. The receipt of disclosure from another person obviously must enhance one's factual knowledge about him, and also it must improve one's degree of empathy with him. But data obtained in the systematic study of self-disclosure have shown, not only that men disclose less to others than women, but also that of all the disclosure that does go on among people, *women are the recipients of more disclosure than men* (Jourard and Richman, 1963). This fact helps one better to understand why men's concepts of the subjective side of other people—of other men as well as of women and children—are often naïve, crude, or downright inaccurate. Men are often alleged, in fiction, to be mystified by the motives for the behavior of others, motives which a woman observer can understand instantly, and apparently intuitively. If this conjecture is true, it should follow that men, in spite of good intentions to promote the happiness and growth of others by loving actions, will often "miss the target." That is, they will want to make the other person happy, but their guesses about the actions requisite to the promotion of this goal will be inappropriate, and their actions will appear awkward or crude.

The obverse of this situation is likewise true. If a man is reluctant to make himself known to another person, even to his spouse—because it is not manly thus to be psychologically naked—then it follows that *men will be difficult to love*. That is, it will be difficult for a woman or another man to know the immediate present state of the man's self, and his needs will thereby go unmet. Some men are so skilled at dissembling, at "seeming," that even their wives will not know when they are lonely, bored, anxious, in pain, thwarted, hungering for affection, etc. And the men, blocked by pride, dare not disclose their despair or need.

The situation extends to the realm of self-love. If true love of self implies behavior which will truly meet one's own needs and promote one's own growth, then men who lack profound insight or clear contact with their real selves will be failures at self-loving. Since they do not know what they feel, want and need (through long practice at repression) men's "essences" will show the results of self-neglect, or harsh treatment of the self by the self.

It is a fact that suicide, mental illness, and death occur sooner and more often among "men whom nobody knows" (that is, among unmarried men, among "lone wolves") than among men who are loved as individual, known persons, by other individual, known persons. Perhaps loving and being loved enables a man to take his life seriously; it makes his life take on value, not only to himself, but also to his loved ones, thereby adding to its value for him. Moreover, if a man is open to his loved one, it permits two people—he and his loved one—to examine, react to, diagnose, evaluate, and do something constructive about *his* inner experience and his present condition when these fall into the undesirable range. When a man's self is hidden from everybody else, even from a physician, it seems also to become much hidden even from himself, and it permits entropy—disease and death—to gnaw into his substance without his clear knowledge. Men who are unknown and/or inadequately loved often fall ill, or even die as if suddenly and without warning, and it is a shock and a surprise to everyone who hears about it. One wonders why people express surprise when they themselves fall ill, or when someone else falls ill or dies, apparently suddenly. If one had direct access to the person's real self, one would have had many earlier signals that the present way of life was generating illness. Perhaps, then, the above-noted "inaccessibility" (Rickers-Ovsiankina, 1956) of man, in addition to hampering his insight and empathy, also handicaps him at self-loving, at loving others and at being loved. If love is a factor that promotes life, then handicap at love, a male characteristic, seems to be another lethal aspect of the male role.

THE MALE ROLE AND DISPIRITATION

Frankl (1955) has argued that unless a man can see meaning and value in his continuing existence, his morale will deteriorate, his immunity will decrease, and he will sicken more readily, or even commit suicide. Schmale (1958) noted that the majority of a sample of patients admitted to a general hospital suffered some depressing disruption in object relations prior to the onset of their symptoms. Extrapolating from many observations and opinions of this sort, the present writer proposed a theory of inspiritation-dispiritation. Broadly paraphrased, this theory holds that, when a man finds hope, meaning, purpose, and value in his existence, he may be said to be "inspirited," and isomorphic brain events weld the organism into its optimal, anti-entropic mode of organization. "Dispiriting" events, perceptions, beliefs, or modes of life tend to weaken this optimum mode of organization (which at once sustains wellness and mediates the fullest, most effective functioning and behavior), and illness is most likely to flourish then. It is as if the body, when a man is dispirited, suddenly becomes an immensely fertile "garden" in which viruses and germs proliferate like jungle vegetation. In inspirited states, viruses and germs find a man's body a very uncongenial milieu for unbridled growth and multiplication.

Now, from what has been said in previous sections, it seems clear that the male role provides many opportunities for dispiritation to arise. The best example is provided by the data on aging. It is a well-documented observation that men in our society, following retirement, will frequently disintegrate and die not long after they assume their new life of leisure. It would appear that masculine identity and self-esteem—factors in inspiritation for men—are predicated on a narrow base. If men can see themselves as manly, and life as worth-while, only so long as they are engaged in gainful employ, or are sexually potent, or have enviable social status, then clearly these are tenuous bases upon which to ground one's existence. It would seem that women can continue to find meaning, and *raisons d'être* long after men feel useless and unneeded.

Thus, if man's sense of masculine identity, as presently culturally defined, is a condition for continued existence, and if this is easily undermined by the vicissitudes of aging or the vicissitudes of a changing social system, then, indeed, the male role has an added lethal component. The present writer has known men who became dispirited following some financial or career upset, and who fell victims to some infectious disease, or "heart failure" shortly thereafter. Their wives, though affected by the husbands' reverses or death, managed to find new grounds and meaning for continued existence, and got on with living.

DISCUSSION AND SUMMARY

It has been pointed out that men, lower disclosers of self than women, are less insightful and empathic, less competent at loving, and more subject to dispiritation than women. The implication of these aspects of manliness for health and longevity was explored. As a concluding note, it seems warranted to step back, and look briefly at the problem of roles from a broader perspective.

Social systems need to delimit people's behavior in order to keep the systems functioning. No social system can use all of every man's self and yet keep the social system functioning well. This is what roles are for—sex roles as well as occupational, age, and familial roles. The role-definitions help men and women to learn just which actions they must perform, and which they must suppress in order to keep the social system functioning properly. But it should not then be thought that just because society cannot use all that a man is, that the man should then strive to root out all self that is neither useful, moral, nor in vogue.

If health, full-functioning, happiness and creativity are valued goals for mankind, then laymen and behavioral scientists alike must seek ways of redefining the male role, to help it become less restrictive and repressive, more expressive of the "compleat" man, and more conducive to life.

REFERENCES

BUBER, M. *I and Thou,* New York, Scribners, 1937.

BUBER, M. Elements of the interhuman. William Alanson White Memorial Lectures. *Psychiatry,* 1957, *20,* 95–129.

DOLLARD, J., AND MILLER, N. E. *Personality and Psychotherapy.* New York, McGraw-Hill, 1950.

FIEDLER, F. E. A note on leadership theory: The effect of social barriers between leaders and followers. *Sociometry,* 1957, *20,* 87–94.

FRANKL, V. E. *The Doctor and the Soul, An Introduction to Logotherapy.* New York, Knopf, 1955.

FROMM, E. *The Art of Loving.* New York, Harper, 1956.

JOURARD, S. M. Age and self-disclosure. *Merrill-Palmer Quart. Beh. Dev.,* 1961 (a), *7,* 191–197.

JOURARD, S. M. Religious denomination and self-disclosure. *Psychol. Rep.,* 1961 (b), *8,* 446.

JOURARD, S. M., AND LANDSMAN, M. J. Cognition, cathexis, and the "dyadic effect" in men's self-disclosing behavior. *Merrill-Palmer Quart. Behav. Dev.,* 1960, *6,* 178–186.

JOURARD, S. M., AND LASAKOW, P. Some factors in self-disclosure. *J. abn. soc. Pyschol.,* 1958, *56,* 91–98.

JOURARD, S. M., AND RICHMAN, P. Disclosure output and input in college students. *Merrill-Palmer Quart. Beh. Dev.,* 1963, *9,* 141–148.

MECHANIC, D., AND VOLKART, E. H. Stress, illness behavior and the sick role. *Amer. Sociol. Rev.,* 1961, *26,* 51–58.

REICH, W. *Character Analysis.* New York, Orgone Press, 1948.

RICKERS-OVSIANKINA, MARIA. Social accessibility in three age groups. *Psychol. Reports,* 1956, *2,* 283–294.

ROGERS, C. R. The characteristics of a helping relationship. *Pers. Guid. J.,* 1958, *37,* 6–16.

SCHMALE, A. H. Relation of separation and depression to disease. *Psychosom. Med.,* 1958, *20,* 259–277.

2

MEN AND WOMEN

The masculine role leads us to expect to find a woman to relate to, to relate to her in particular ways, and to experience certain satisfactions from the relationship. The first expectation is that we do relate: having a date, a lover, or a wife is a good thing. Once we are with a woman, then there are further expectations. As a man, we should provide strength in the relationship and take ultimate responsibility for it. At the same time, we should maintain our independence and our other activities. In return for fulfilling our role, a relationship with a woman promises one place in our life where we can relax, be open, and experience emotional closeness.

On the surface, this masculine prescription for having and relating to a woman may sound all right. But problems develop, when we fulfill the role as well as when we do not. When we do not have a date, a lover, or a wife, we feel lacking. When we do, we may question whether we are providing the expected strength in the relationship, and still maintaining our independence in the rest of our life. Failing these expectations may dishearten us. But meeting them may fail to bring the promised satisfactions.

A man who feels he should take ultimate responsibility in his relation with a woman, and does so, may find himself lonely and the woman ungrateful. A man who is successful in not letting his relationship disturb the rest of his life may find that his relationship suffers and does not provide the expected emotional warmth. The problem is that these more or less reasonable-sounding expectations for how we relate to women often have side-effects that destroy what we are seeking.

The result is that relating to women as the masculine role calls for often turns out to be both more difficult and less rewarding than it appears. One consequence is considerable anxiety, experienced if not acknowledged by many males. Julius Lester, in "Being a Boy," describes vividly his own anxiety in trying to act with females the way he thought he was supposed to.

Sexuality is the one area where male anxiety about performance operates strongly. Our training inhibits our sexual activity from following our feeling; instead the masculine role prescribes our sexual behavior. When the feeling and the role differ, we're in trouble. Julius Lester tells of suffering embarrassment from having an erection when he "shouldn't"; Sam Julty tells of suffering from not having one when he "should." In "A Case of 'Sexual Dysfunction' " Julty notes that when we get into bed seeking to fulfill a role of masculine power we are likely to end up disappointed in ourselves. When our relation with women, sexual and otherwise, is taken as another area in which we men must prove ourselves, it becomes one more area of anxiety.

Our relations with women suffer from both sides of the masculine role—the getting ahead that shows in proving oneself, and also the staying cool that shows in inexpressiveness. The need we feel to keep our emotions under control impedes our experiencing closeness with others. Many of us are emotional strangers in our own homes, and depend upon a woman to tell us what is happening. We are not always open to experiencing the emotional warmth we desire. We may find emotional coolness interfering with sexuality. Irving London, in "Frigidity, Sensitivity, and Sexual Roles," tells how emotional constriction limits the pleasure, nourishment, and energy men derive from sex.

We are only now learning in how many ways the masculine role has impoverished men's relations with women. The limitations of the feminine role have been more obvious, and today many women are freeing themselves of its restrictions. More women are now seeking competence in their own right rather than seeking fulfillment in their lives through looking after ours.

All men are being touched, to some degree, by the movement of women toward equality. As a principle, equality between men and women seems right to many of us. But our old needs stand in the way of achieving it. S. M. Miller, in "The Making of a Confused, Middle-Aged Husband," tells candidly how even though he valued his wife's career, he let her do most of the housework. Having time for his own work was more important than freeing some of that time for her.

For many of us women's questioning of their sex role has been a stimulus for us to question our own. Some of us have found that getting ahead and staying cool are less important to us than we thought, and experience more pleasure and less compulsion in both our work and our relationships than we used to. Perhaps, finally, we men will change the way we relate to women, not only because we consider it right, not only because they insist upon it, but also because we find it enhances our own lives.

Being a Boy

Julius Lester

JULIUS LESTER *is a writer and teaches Afro-American studies at the University of Massachusetts. His most recent books are* Long Journey Home *and* Two Love Stories. *Both have been published by Dial Press.*

As boys go, I wasn't much. I mean, I tried to be a boy and spent many childhood hours pummeling my hardly formed ego with failure at cowboys and Indians, baseball, football, lying, and sneaking out of the house. When our neighborhood gang raided a neighbor's pear tree, I was the only one who got sick from the purloined fruit. I also failed at setting fire to our garage, an art at which any five-year-old boy should be adept. I was, however, the neighborhood champion at getting beat up. "That Julius can take it, man," the boys used to say, almost in admiration, after I emerged from another battle, tears brimming in my eyes but refusing to fall.

My efforts at being a boy earned me a pair of scarred knees that are a record of a childhood spent falling from bicycles, trees, the tops of fences, and porch steps; of tripping as I ran (generally from a fight), walked, or simply tried to remain upright on windy days.

I tried to believe my parents when they told me I was a boy, but I could find no objective proof for such an assertion. Each morning during the summer, as I cuddled up in the quiet of a corner with a book, my mother would push me out the back door and into the yard. And throughout the day as my blood was let as if I were a patient of 17th-century medicine, I thought of the girls sitting in the shade of porches, playing with their dolls, toy refrigerators and stoves.

There was the life, I thought! No constant pressure to prove oneself. No necessity always to be competing. While I humiliated myself on football and baseball fields, the girls stood on the sidelines laughing at me, because they didn't have to do anything except be girls. The rising of each sun brought me to the starting line of yet another day's Olympic decathlon, with no hope of ever winning even a bronze medal.

Through no fault of my own I reached adolescence. While the pressure to prove myself on the athletic field lessened, the overall situation

---

Julius Lester, "Being a Boy," *Ms.*, June 1973, pp. 112–13. Reprinted by permission.

got worse—because now I had to prove myself with girls. Just how I was supposed to go about doing this was beyond me, especially because, at the age of 14, I was four foot nine and weighed 78 pounds. (I think there may have been one 10-year-old girl in the neighborhood smaller than I.) Nonetheless, duty called, and with my ninth-grade gym-class jockstrap flapping between my legs, off I went.

To get a girlfriend, though, a boy had to have some asset beyond the fact that he was alive. I wasn't handsome like Bill McCord, who had girls after him like a cop-killer has policemen. I wasn't ugly like Romeo Jones, but at least the girls noticed him: "That ol' ugly boy better stay 'way from me!" I was just there, like a vase your grandmother gives you at Christmas that you don't like or dislike, can't get rid of, and don't know what to do with. More than ever I wished I were a girl. Boys were the ones who had to take the initiative and all the responsibility. (I hate responsibility so much that if my heart didn't beat of itself, I would now be a dim memory.)

It was the boy who had to ask the girl for a date, a frightening enough prospect until it occurred to me that she might say no! That meant risking my ego, which was about as substantial as a toilet-paper raincoat in the African rainy season. But I had to thrust that ego forward to be judged, accepted, or rejected by some girl. It wasn't fair! Who was she to sit back like a queen with the power to create joy by her consent or destruction by her denial? It wasn't fair—but that's the way it was.

But if (God forbid!) she should say Yes, then my problem would begin in earnest, because I was the one who said where we would go (and waited in terror for her approval of my choice). I was the one who picked her up at her house where I was inspected by her parents as if I were a possible carrier of syphilis (which I didn't think one could get from masturbating, but then again, Jesus was born of a virgin, so what did I know?). Once we were on our way, it was I who had to pay the bus fare, the price of the movie tickets, and whatever she decided to stuff her stomach with afterward. (And the smallest girls are all stomach.) Finally, the girl was taken home where once again I was inspected (the father looking covertly at my fly and the mother examining the girl's hair). The evening was over and the girl had done nothing except honor me with her presence. All the work had been mine.

Imagining this procedure over and over was more than enough: I was a sophomore in college before I had my first date.

I wasn't a total failure in high school, though, for occasionally I would go to a party, determined to salvage my self-esteem. The parties usually took place in somebody's darkened basement. There was generally a surreptitious wine bottle or two being passed furtively among the boys, and a record player with an insatiable appetite for Johnny

Mathis records. Boys gathered on one side of the room and girls on the other. There were always a few boys and girls who'd come to the party for the sole purpose of grinding away their sexual frustrations to Johnny Mathis's falsetto, and they would begin dancing to their own music before the record player was plugged in. It took a little longer for others to get started, but no one matched my talent for standing by the punch bowl. For hours, I would try to make my legs do what they had been doing without effort since I was nine months old, but for some reason they would show all the symptoms of paralysis on those evenings.

After several hours of wondering whether I was going to die ("Julius Lester, a sixteen-year-old, died at a party last night, a half-eaten Ritz cracker in one hand and a potato chip dipped in pimiento-cheese spread in the other. Cause of death: failure to be a boy"), I would push my way to the other side of the room where the girls sat like a hanging jury. I would pass by the girl I wanted to dance with. If I was going to be refused, let it be by someone I didn't particularly like. Unfortunately, there weren't many in that category. I had more crushes than I had pimples.

Finally, through what surely could only have been the direct intervention of the Almighty, I would find myself on the dance floor with a girl. And none of my prior agony could compare to the thought of actually dancing. But there I was and I had to dance with her. Social custom decreed that I was supposed to lead, because I was the boy. Why? I'd wonder. Let her lead. Girls were better dancers anyway. It didn't matter. She stood there waiting for me to take charge. She wouldn't have been worse off if she'd waited for me to turn white.

But, reciting "Invictus" to myself, I placed my arms around her, being careful to keep my armpits closed because, somehow, I had managed to overwhelm a half jar of deodorant and a good-size bottle of cologne. With sweaty armpits, "Invictus," and legs afflicted again with polio, I took her in my arms, careful not to hold her so far away that she would think I didn't like her, but equally careful not to hold her so close that she could feel the catastrophe which had befallen me the instant I touched her hand. My penis, totally disobeying the lecture I'd given it before we left home, was as rigid as Governor Wallace's jaw would be if I asked for his daughter's hand in marriage.

God, how I envied girls at that moment. Wherever *it* was on them, it didn't dangle between their legs like an elephant's trunk. No wonder boys talked about nothing but sex. That thing was always there. Every time we went to the john, there *it* was, twitching around like a fat little worm on a fishing hook. When we took baths, it floated in the water like a lazy fish and God forbid we should touch it! It sprang to life like lightning leaping from a cloud. I wished I could cut it off, or at least keep it tucked between my legs, as if it were a tail that had been mistakenly attached to the wrong end. But I was helpless. It was there, with a life and mind of its own, having no other function than to embarrass me.

Fortunately, the girls I danced with were discreet and pretended that they felt nothing unusual rubbing against them as we danced. But I was always convinced that the next day they were all calling up their friends to exclaim: "Guess what, girl? Julius Lester got one! I ain't lyin'!"

Now, of course, I know that it was as difficult being a girl as it was a boy, if not more so. While I stood paralyzed at one end of a dance floor trying to find the courage to ask a girl for a dance, most of the girls waited in terror at the other, afraid that no one, not even I, would ask them. And while I resented having to ask a girl for a date, wasn't it also horrible to be the one who waited for the phone to ring? And how many of those girls who laughed at me making a fool of myself on the baseball diamond would have gladly given up their places on the sidelines for mine on the field?

No, it wasn't easy for any of us, girls and boys, as we forced our beautiful, free-flowing child-selves into those narrow, constricting cubicles labeled *female* and *male*. I tried, but I wasn't good at being a boy. Now, I'm glad, knowing that a man is nothing but the figment of a penis's imagination, and any man should want to be something more than that.

A Case of "Sexual Dysfunction"

Solomon "Sam" Julty

SOLOMON "SAM" JULTY, *author of* Auto Repairs You Can Do Yourself (*New York: Dafran House, 1972*) *and* How Your Car Works (*to be published by Harper and Row*) *is an automotive editor and freelance writer. His forthcoming book* The Man Trap (*Grosset and Dunlap*) *is an exposition of the problems—social, sexual, and medical—faced by sexually dysfunctioning men.*

My desk is in an office facing the main entrance to the Veterans Administration Building. I often sit and stare out the window at the very

Solomon "Sam" Julty, "A Case of 'Sexual Dysfunction,'" *Ms.*, November 1972, pp. 18, 20–21. Reprinted by permission.

mixed crowd going into the building. Among the multitude I see dozens of men who are amputees, paraplegics, and blind. Presumably they are ex-GIs.

I look at them, and I look at myself. I am a sexually dysfunctioning man (hell—why don't I come out and say I'm impotent), and I find that although we both suffer physical disabilities, theirs elicit concern and respect while mine elicits embarrassment and shame. The civilian population has a special regard for returning vets—people who made the sacrifice. War, battle wounds, disabilities are acceptable and "manly." Contrast this with the feeling of loss of manhood of the sexually dysfunctioning man. He doesn't accept this problem and no one else will, either. Wives and lovers are confused by his crushed feelings. Physicians, who don't know what else to say, pooh-pooh the man out of the examining room. Psychiatrists, who don't know much more, tell the man to concentrate on *not* thinking about it. Many men cannot discuss it with other men, nor with women, for fear they will lose a respect they cannot regain.

The result is a silence which blurs sexual perspectives and discards alternatives—all weighing down his organ yet further with guilt and shame.

My own erective dysfunction started at a time when, by all logic and reasoning, it shouldn't have. I was shifting gears in my attitudes toward myself; an impossible marriage was coming to a welcome end; everything was looking up. But over this scene was the big shadow—my sexual spirit was willing, but the flesh was occasionally weak.

I didn't know why then, but my reflex action was that nobody must know. If the secret homosexual is in a closet, I was locked in a large, barren room. The women I went to bed with were given stories of fatigue, nervousness, crises on the job, or just too much gin.

Then came the guilt. My sex role was supposed to be that of initiator, enticer, schemer, promise-maker—and I was failing to deliver. The penalty for nondelivery is guilt.

After striking out with two doctors, I finally whipped up the courage and dared to share my secret in my therapy group. All I saw through my own tears were the impassive faces of the women and the embarrassed faces of the men. Strike three—*Out!*

Dysfunction was bad enough, but rejection by those I thought could help was devastating. In the end, I became more determined than ever that the door to my room remain closed, bolted, and sealed.

But, prodded by the arrow of Eros and the hope that everything would be okay this time, I kept going to bed with women. And sooner or later I had to share my secret with them. What a down trip that was! Slowly I began to want to know not only why I had this problem but why I felt this way about the problem. I secretly looked for the answer in bookshops and libraries.

Well, if anyone is interested in the sexual dysfunction of women, female sex throughout history, sex techniques for the modern woman, sex and the movie queens, sex crimes against women, sex for the divorced woman, sex for old ladies in tennis shoes, drugstore remedies for frigidity, and home remedies for nymphomania—there is a lifetime of reading. But outside of books dealing with infamous dirty old men, there is pitifully little on the subject of men's difficulties with sex. And, significantly, most of the attention is focused on premature ejaculation rather than erective dysfunction. While the premature ejaculator does indeed have a serious problem, the mystique maintains that his manhood is not threatened as long as he can get it up.

To find out why there was so much literature about women and so little about men, I applied the axiom of Archimedes—"Everything has a common denominator." The common denominator here is that the overwhelming majority of the authors I read were men—who seemed to have conflicts in writing about themselves. I'm sure some of them suffer flaccid nights themselves, but to write about them requires some rough going against some pretty tough grain.

In scanning the books which dealt with men, I became irritated by the use of a certain word. The medical term which describes my problem is *impotency*. Why?

Potency means "powerful." Impotent means "without power." A man who cannot ejaculate is without power; a man who experiences physical pain during climax is without power; a man who ejaculates with pitifully little stimulation is without power; a man who cannot have or fails to maintain an erection is without power.

"Potency" and "impotency" are not only broad-sweep words, they are heavy words when applied to sexual relationships—which should have nothing to do with power. My rejection—and, I must admit, fear—of the potency concept in a sexual encounter with a woman is based on the awful and awesome responsibility that is packaged with that power. If it is my role to be *potent,* then I must become a potentate, a ruler. My license to rule then resides in my scepter. Thus, pleasure and satisfaction arrive by my command, not the woman's. Playing the power game is risky. I don't want to get into bed wearing a tottering crown. That's just too much responsibility and not enough fun.

While developing my thunder for the impotency concept, I couldn't help thinking how another broad-base, kill-'em-with-one-shot medical word is used against women—*frigidity*. Any woman who has any male-diagnosed hang-ups about sex is called frigid. A woman who is tired of balling seven times a night for two years is called frigid. A woman who fails to come once after 10 successive times at bat is frigid. The woman who cannot turn on to the guy who demands sex on the hood of a car during rush hour is frigid. We're going to have to do some turning around of the language which lays on concepts in place of diagnoses, and perpetuates myth instead of reality.

With that tucked in my head, I felt bold enough to talk to the men in my consciousness-raising group. Ours was a good group, and we all liked each other; our collective spirit made it a safe forum for me to spring my innermost secret. It did not fall on impassive ears, nor did it stun or bewilder my *compañeros*. They listened and asked questions. With the slowness and surety of a giant ocean wave, their involvement with the subject grew. Personal sexual experiences were piled high. My shame and guilt was being discussed by people who were reacting, encouraging, suggesting, debating. It felt good!

We spent many more meetings discussing our sexuality. For the first time in my life I began to hear men talk honestly about their sexual selves, without the bravado bullshit, without the conquest capers or the stud trips. The boldest truth I discovered was that I and a great number of other men had never before spent any time looking at our reflections in the pond of our true sexuality, but had been content to act like cherubs playing around on its role-playing banks.

I began to question the impact that erective dysfunctioning had on self-concepts of manhood. What made my *digestive* dysfunction, which is diabetes, acceptable to me and everyone else, and my *erective* dysfunction such a horror? I entered into heavy dialogue with myself.

I started sorting out my own behavior patterns into two laundry bags in my mind. They were labeled The Inner Me and Social Conditioning. When I finished sorting out I found that not all of my hang-ups belonged in the first laundry bag, but were carefully and properly distributed in both. The psychic and social worlds have a ying-and-yang relationship—one affecting the other, cause and effect flowing both ways.

I decided to investigate some of the "rules." The biggest myth is the belief "a stiff cock a man doth make." What bullshit! How readily men are willing to take a whole self, an entire life's experience, a bulk of accumulated learning, a set of potentials and attitudes and all the other intangible factors of life and invest them all in approximately 75 millimeters of spongy tissue, having an expansion capability of approximately 125 millimeters. *What a cruel joke it is to take a symbol and make it into the object it is supposed to symbolize.*

Men will have to stop believing all the things they read in pornographic books. Phrases like "his swelling manhood throbbed in her hands" and "he flaunted his manhood before her eyes" go nowhere in defining a man. Each man would do well to cop to the fact that, for better or for worse, *all* of him is a man. It took me a while, but I got there. I am still a man, even if a part of me is sometimes out to lunch.

Another myth I fell for is that any contact between two people must eventually result in an orgasm if it is not to be scored a failure. Now, I'm not knocking that nice exhausted, glowing tingle achieved with the full-flowered climax. But it's that damned goal-orientation which messes us up and takes its toll. The way it usually works is like this: if X is the point when physical vibes start bouncing between two people, there seems to be a compulsion to immediately set up point Y —the point of their respective orgasms. All the activities between X and Y—the dates, talks, exchange of feelings, the first kiss, holding, touching, the slow walk to the bedroom, the loosening of garments, etc., etc.—are not stations of enjoyment. They are only fueling stops toward the approaching nirvana of Y. As a result, that drive for "fulfillment" often turns into a siren song, luring both people to the rocks, and ruining any appreciation of the pleasures in just sailing along. Orgasm doth not a relationship make.

Many men (and possibly some women) still believe the con game we were taught by the older boys in high school. If we did some heavy petting and the girl would not provide that "release," we'd tell her that the testicles would swell, turn blue, and cause excruciating pain. While temporary discomfort can result from arousal without climax, it is far from fatal, far from excruciating, and far from blue-ing.

Another trap is the pressure to "make it." The man with the biggest box score is more of a man than anyone else. Tastes and preferences are shunted aside. Whether or not the particular woman is right for him is ignored; the moment, the place, the mood are disregarded; tune and tone of the physical self are never checked when it is time to be on the make. If there's a remote possibility that there will be any kind of play, men feel compelled to start pitching and hitting. And, if there are no viable possibilities, then start the fantasy trip. Keep that pot boiling, regardless of reality.

Too few men have ever really thought about what turns them on and how it relates to enjoyment or the lack of it. Everyone has his own quirks for what turns him on, but the guy who sticks to the goal of "screwing anything that walks" is headed for trouble.

It just may be that the tomcat syndrome is nothing but a cultural paper tiger. For a man without any dysfunction problems, this is still quite a burden to carry. But for the man with the problem, such an outlook is a disaster. When disaster strikes—at the moment the erection is lost—a single moment is turned into a state funeral. The first impulse is to head for a dark corner. But pure guilt keeps a man nailed to the scene. Then the silence. Whatever the cause of the silence, it is usually the woman who is forced to break it. "It there anything I can do? Is there anything I have done?" These are openers. Then escalation. "Has this ever happened before? Can you make it with anyone else?"

Whatever the cause of the man's dysfunction, be it psychological or physical, whatever reactions he may display, be it silence or rage, the problem is his. *He is the victim of his own reactions.*

Do relationships suffer because of a man's overreactions to his dysfunction? Of course. Do women suffer physical frustration at the fast lowering of the curtain before the act is over? Definitely. Are women affected by the problem? Yes. Are they responsible for it? No!

If the man is a real man, he'll try to stop this self-victimization. He can start by considering it a loss of a few moments before the end of an inning, but not the end of the ballgame. Relax! Get up and pour two glasses of wine and get back—close. Thoughts racing through the head? Spill them. No lies, no bullshit, just some straight words like, "Yeah, I have this problem, but don't worry about it because you have nothing to do with it. No, you don't have to do anything but relax and enjoy. If there is anything I need, I'll ask for it." Case closed. Proceed—onward and upward!

Another aspect of the problem has been bandied about lately, the proposition that more men are suffering erective dysfunction as a direct result of the Women's Movement, claiming that women have become so threatening to men that it scares the starch out of them.

The simple answer to that is that when we get to some healthy attitudes in man-woman relationships, when men begin to share power out of bed, they won't need so much of it in bed, either.

Men are expected to *do*—and do well. *Perform*—and perform well. There is roughhousing in the nursery, and Little League competition at school. Later on, Father is anxious to know if his son got laid the night before, and so is Mother, for that matter.

"Doing well" is where it's at. Doing his own thing and having weaknesses is *verboten*. Sent to college to learn a good profession so he can marry a good girl and become a good provider, he is made aware that each semester costs his parents 3,000 sacrifices. With some pride, Father gives him a gross of condoms so he doesn't get a girl "in trouble"—because that would spell the end of his success trip. Mother checks out his girl friends to make sure there is no one who will deter him from the goal. First you perform for parents. Later, you're playing a role for your wife.

Serious personal relationships start out with a certain set of holes punched into the card programmed into a man's head: the object is success.

As a lover, the expectations are the highest. Taught that he must be a hero in the world and a superstar in bed, God help him if he bombs out. He can fake his wealth, bullshit through his station in life, give a woman a snow job about his feelings for her, but he cannot conceal his dying dick or his non-climax. So what happens? He gets into bed and more pressure! Am I going to make it with her? Here it comes? No, there it goes. And let him fail once and the foundations tremble. The success is so tied to his cock that it makes no difference if he is tired, worried, drunk, stoned, unhappy, angry, dying of Hong Kong flu—no show of that magnificent symbol of manhood and he's had it. Whoever you were, you are no longer. The permit of your manhood is hereby revoked.

The way out of the maze is to tear up the sex roles. Feelings of defeat toward this problem are not individual but social. The solution is political. Roles which offer dubious rewards in exchange for heavy responsibilities should be put aside. The true measure of a man is neither the number of his war wounds nor the times he's bombed out in bed. His true measure is how he feels about himself and the human beings around him.

Frigidity, Sensitivity and Sexual Roles

Irving London, M.D.

DR. LONDON *attended Washington University School of Medicine. His postdoctoral work was done at the University of Minnestota Hospital and the University of California Hospital in San Francisco. He currently specializes in sleep research and is a sleep consultant to Innerspace, the California company that invented the flotation waterbed. He is a frequent guest on radio and television talk shows and does private counseling on how to get a good night's sleep without the use of drugs.*

For the past nine years I have been interested in the widespread problem of frigidity—its causes and effective solutions. This interest stemmed from a course I took as a medical student at Washington University with the now famous Dr. Masters. He gave a series of lectures on human sexual response. I was amazed at the reaction of my classmates. Masters presented a series of slides demonstrating the physical changes of sexual arousal and orgasm. This group of budding young doctors were crouched in their seats as though they were watching dirty movies. I observed their reaction. They blushed and squirmed

---

in their seats; in general the group seemed disquietingly uncomfortable yet fascinated with the content. Students would arrive early to get front row seats. As these lectures progressed I became aware of the general level of sexual ignorance which existed. Watching these reactions, I thought, "These are the authorities people will seek out to talk about their sexual problems!" I was struck by how hung up this "intellectually advanced" group was. I began to reflect on the causes and possible solutions to sexual problems.

American culture stimulates and promulgates sexual frustration. We are taught to regard the sexual act with deep guilt. Women are taught to withhold their genitals and to use the sexual act manipulatively rather than as a means of communication. Marriage programming with its inherent financial security is still extremely prevalent and sex is the prime level. This orientation promotes guilt, fear, and frustration while diminishing sensitivity, awareness, sensuality and communication.

Men are programmed to be "strong" and "aggressive." Practically from birth emotional sensitivity is squelched: "big boys don't cry; be strong; stand up straight; stomach in, chest out; take what you want; be a man." What "be a man" means in the American sense is to be emotionally sterile. What "be a man" means is don't feel anything. What "be a man" means is to be sexually inadequate.

Machismo and aggressiveness are in direct contradiction to sensitivity and intimacy. "Taking a woman" is supposed to fulfill this masculine urge. Perhaps this explains why 90% of all men ejaculate within the first two minutes of intercourse! It's not surprising that frigidity is extremely common. Sex as a means of communication is sorely lacking.

When doing frigidity counseling working for Masters and Johnson, I was struck by a recurring story. The man of the house would come home, have a couple of drinks, eat dinner, plop down in front of the television, drift off into a semi-stuperous state, and be helped to bed by his wife. Revived to a half-awake condition by this activity, he finds the stamina to roll over on top of his beloved and following a few furtive swipes, plunges home for a two minutes stint as he falls asleep. She, dejected, depressed, frustrated and guilt-ridden, lies in bed asking herself, "What's wrong with me? Why can't I climax?" Maybe they come for help.

In America sexual inhibitions and male-female roles interfere with full sexual response, enjoyment and orgastic release. Men in our society have been so completely programmed into not expressing feelings that intercourse often does not provide either transference of feeling, nourishment, or energy. Many men seem to ejaculate without having orgasm. If you have ever seen a pornographic movie you may have noticed that the male participants are stoically silent. I have experienced group sexual encounters and was amazed at the lack of sexual noises in the men. Sensitivity was also totally lacking. The men seemed like robots performing a programmed function with little or no emotional content.

I went through a period of my life with similar emotionless encounters. I was obsessed with sleeping with many women despite superficial feelings and empty experiences. My ego was salved by knowing I was sexually desirable. Gradually things changed. I began to tune in to my partner and empathize more with her. Sex became a deep tender form of communication. The more I opened myself and let my partner in, the more moving the experience became. My orgasms became fuller, more meaningful, and much more powerful. By tuning in more and more acutely, I was actually able to experience the emotional sensations of orgasm without ejaculating. Orgasms became a release for my entire self—body and mind. Much to my surprise I found this brought me closer to my lover. Instead of thinking I was a "sissy" she felt warm and close. She felt physically and emotionally full.

In my sexual counseling I often talked with couples about sensitivity and roles. It is risky for a man to open up and let another see him as he really is—a frail being with many fears, emotions and desires. The male role with its aggressive strong front is very thoroughly ingrained. In my counseling, I would try to soften this rigid armor. Many new techniques available today can help couples overcome society's structuring. Trust and risk-taking games can be useful. Reichian therapy, polarity therapy and massage produce extremely gratifying results. Sensitivity training, sensory awareness and role playing can also contribute to an emotional rebuilding. Sexual techniques must be taught and inhibitions worked through. Men must be offered the chance to be vulnerable, open, trusting and gentle, without feeling these to be negative "feminine" traits. I think the time is near when we will see widespread use of these techniques in sexual clinics and a gradual restructuring of male-female role relationships, with resulting diminution of sexual tension and a heightening of deep human sexual communication.

The Making of a Confused, Middle-Aged Husband

S. M. Miller

S. M. MILLER *is Chairperson, Department of Sociology, Boston University. He was formerly a professor of sociology and education at New York University and director of the Urban Center. He was president of the Eastern Sociological Society in 1970–71, a Guggenheim Fellow in 1972–73, and he is currently chairperson of the Research Committee on Poverty, Social Welfare, and Social Policy of the International Sociological Association. He is the coauthor of* The Future of Inequality *(1970) and* Social Class and Social Policy *(1968); editor of* Max Weber: A Reader *(1964); coeditor of* Applied Sociology *(1964); and author of* Comparative Social Mobility *(1960). His long-term interests are in inequality, and he has been working on the impact of economic and social policies upon social stratification.*

I have never had an intellectual problem with sexism. One reason may well have been the women who surrounded me as a child—my father's mother, my mother and two considerably older sisters—although I know it sometimes goes quite the other way. My father slept and my mother dominated—partly out of force of character and partly, one sister informed me fairly recently, because of the occupational and other failures of my father. He had tried to make it in America—and could not. His was the immigrant's rags-to-rags story, for he started as a factory worker, became a small businessman, only to be wiped out by the 1921 depression: he worked again as a machine operator and then started a dress store where he did the alterations and my mother was chief saleswoman. Again, his enterprise was rewarded by a depression—this time, that of the 1930s. He went back to working a machine in the lowest paid part of the garment industry, where he stayed until he retired in his early seventies. From the depression days on my mother worked as a saleslady. I was a "latchkey kid" from an early age, warming up the meals that were left for me by my mother.

From S. M. Miller, "The Making of a Confused, Middle-Aged Husband," *Social Policy*, July–Aug. 1971, 2(2), 33–39. Reprinted by permission of Social Policy Corporation, New York, New York 10010.

My mother was very smart and witty and so was my older sister. They were obviously intellectually well endowed, although not well educated. My mother had a few years of formal schooling; my sister just managed to graduate from high school. (I think I developed my repugnance to credentialism because I recognized that these were two very smart though not well-educated women.)

From this experience, I grew up regarding women as competent and capable of making family and economic decisions. (By contrast, my mother disliked cooking, and it was a shock to me when I began to eat away from home to discover what a bad cook she was.) Women worked and ran things well.

On the other hand, there was a notion that people frowned on women working, so we tried to hide the fact that my mother worked. I think I felt both shamed that my mother worked and irritated that "society" thought that it was wrong for women to work, especially when their incomes were needed.

Furthermore, sexism was, in principle, alien to the equalitarian and participatory circles in which my closest friends and I were passionately involved. We were out-of-sorts with the intellectual climate of the forties and fifties because of an egalitarian, populist, antielitist spirit. We criticized Stalinist democratic centralism and American "Celebration"-style pluralist democracy because of their inadequate attention to equality and participation for all. We could no more subscribe to intellectual rationalizations for female low status than we could condone the miseries of oppression and deprivation among other parts of the population.

A third reason I see myself as intellectually escaping sexism has more manifest emotional roots. Looking back, I don't believe that I could accept a woman who would center her life completely on me and devote herself to making me happy. (Children were not part of my purview.) At one level, the intellectual, how could one individual be worthy of such dedication by another? At the deeper and, I suspect now, more significant level, I rejected or stayed away from easily giving or male-centered women because I did not consider myself worthy of another person's total devotion or capable of evoking the sentiments which would sustain it beyond the initial impulse. Furthermore, it demanded an emotional response that I possibly could not make. In short, I did not think so well of myself that I could live with (overwhelming) devotion. As a consequence, I was usually involved with young women with strong career goals who were seeking their identity through work and not through family. They were my intellectual equals, if not superiors.

Thus, I had a good beginning, it seems to me, for having a marriage that did not embody sexist currents. But I don't see that my current life is very different from that of those who espoused or expounded more sexist values. Years ago a good friend told me that I had the reputation among the wives in our circle of being "an excellent husband," and he said, "You know, that's not a good thing." I now have the feeling that families that openly embrace both bourgeois and sexist values don't live very differently from us. I sense that we are engaged in a "lapsed egalitarianism," still believing in our earlier commitments and concerns about equality but having drifted from the faith in our daily life.

What happened? Probably the most important factor which accounts for the direction we took was our amazing naïveté about the impact of having children—a naïveté incidentally which I see today having a similarly devastating effect on many young parents. We just had no idea how much time and emotion children captured and how they simply changed your lives—even when we were able, as we were, to afford a housekeeper as a result of my wife's working.

The early years of child-rearing were very difficult. Our first son was superactive and did not sleep through the night. We were both exhausted. My wife insisted that I not leave everything to her; she fought with me to get me to participate in the care of our son and apartment. I took the 2 A.M. and 6 A.M. feedings and changings, for our ideology did not allow me to just occasionally help out; I had to "share" and really participate in the whole thing. I resented that degree of involvement; it seemed to interfere terribly with the work I desperately wanted to achieve.

Indeed, I have always felt put upon because of that episode of many months. To make matters worse, I did not know of other work-oriented husbands who were as involved as I with their children. True, I realized that my sons became much attached to each other and a lovely new element entered my life, but I resented the time and exhaustion, particularly since I was struggling to find my way in my work. I did not consider myself productive and was in the middle of struggling to clarify my perspective. I looked at the problem largely in terms of the pressure of my job, which required a lot of effort, and, more importantly, in terms of my personality and my inability to work effectively. While I wrote memoranda with great ease, I wasn't writing professional articles and books.

In retrospect, I think that it was the period of the McCarthy and Eisenhower years that was more significant in my lack of development. My outlook and interests were not what social science and society were responding to. That changed later, and I was able to savor in the sixties that infrequent exhilaration of one's professional work and citizen concerns merging and of gaining both a social science and popular audience and constituency. But I did not know in the 1950s that this would ensue and I felt resentment.

What I experienced was that I was working hard to make things easier for my wife, unlike my friends, and . . . I did not see rewards. Yes, she told me that she appreciated my effort, but my activities were never enough, my sharing was never full in the sense that I equally planned and involved myself with initiative in the care of child and house. She was tired too and irritated by child-care, and in turn, I was irritated by what seemed to be her absorption in taking care of children.

And there were always those male friends who did so little compared to me. I could and did tell myself that at some point along the line they would be paying heavy "dues" for their current neglect of their wives' plight, but it was small balm now. I wondered if I was not rationalizing my irritation by an intellectualizing metaphor about how you pay prices sooner or later and by a plaintively reassuring injunction never to envy anyone else, for who knew what lurked beyond the facade of family equanimity.

Things were further complicated by another factor—less typical of today's young marrieds—incomplete early socialization as a family member. For example, since I ate meals by myself as an adolescent and preadolescent, I developed the habit of reading while eating. Indeed, I am a compulsive reader, a "print nut." If there is nothing around to read, I will study the labels on ketchup bottles. The result is that marriage required a resocialization into talking to someone at mealtimes, not turning inward to my own thoughts or the *New York Times.*

Of course, the reading is only the personal iceberg tip of a larger problem of not closing myself to others and becoming inaccessible because of stress or intellectual absorption. I am now, again, in a conscious period of trying to make myself more accessible emotionally to my family, but it is a struggle. For example, when we vacation, I spend the first days devouring three to four mysteries a day, decompressing I call it, hardly talking to anyone. And, of course, when I am at a deadline or caught in my inability to work out an idea, or just unable to get to work—there are few other conditions for me than these three—I am rather inaccessible, to say the least. I work against this tendency but don't do notably well. While I do the mundane tasks of the household, psychologically I am often not much there. I think that I am winning the struggle against withdrawal, but what is a giant step to the battler may appear as a wiggle of progress to the beholder.

My wife has accommodated to my dislike of fixing things and "wasting time" on such things—not great matters in themselves, but symptomatic of the process of my disengagement from the burdens of home and family.

From a narrow perspective, I have useful incompetences, protecting me from diversions of my energy and focus. I don't like to fix things and don't do them well (or soon). In my youth, in my proletarian-near-idealization, I felt that Arthur Miller was right when Willy Loman says a man isn't a man unless he can do things with his hands. So I tried adult education shop courses and the like for a brief time. I went in a "klutz" and came out a "klutz." Now in a spirit of reactive arrogance or greater self-pride, I boldly assert the counter-position that I believe in the division of labor and prefer to pay for specialized labor. I do little around the house—and that usually long delayed. Since skilled labor is hard to get at any price, things are undone or my wife does them, but my principle of specialization (for me) remains unimpaired.

Similarly, I have been relieved of the task of paying bills. With my usual speed and disdain for trivia, I did this job very rapidly and made mistakes. Now my wife spends time doing this task. It is easier, in her view, for her to do it than to keep after me to do a competent job. Failure is its own reward: I have escaped another task.

Of course, I have been after my wife to have a part-time secretary and bookkeeper and have located several people for her. But she resists, as they do not provide enough help to make it worthwhile. The result is that my personal efforts reduce my feelings of guilt when she spends evenings writing out checks. After all, I did try to get her out of that function. But I am still irritated by her doing the checks—for that is another indication that she is failing me by not showing our true equality, by not spending more time on her professional writing and research.

I guess what dismays me and makes me see my marriage and family as unfortunately typically upper-middle-class, collegial, pseudo-egalitarian American—especially in light of my own continuing commitment to an equalitarian, participatory ethos—is that I assume no responsibility for major household tasks and family activities. True, my wife has always worked in her profession (she is a physician) even when our sons were only some weeks old. (I used to say that behind the working wife with young children, there stands a tired husband.) True, I help in many ways and feel responsible that she have time to work on her professional interests. But, I do partial, limited things to free her to do her work. I don't do the basic thinking about the planning of meals and housekeeping or the situation of the children. Sure, I will wash dishes, "spend time" with the children; I will often do the shopping, cook, make beds, "share" the burden of most household tasks; but that is not the same thing as direct and primary responsibility for planning and managing a household and meeting the day-to-day needs of children.

It is not that I object in principle to householding and child-rearing. I don't find such work demeaning or unmasculine—just a drain of my time, which could be devoted to other "more rewarding" things. Just as I don't like to shop for clothes for myself even though I like clothes. My energies are poised to help me work on my professional-political concerns, and I resist "wasting time" on other pursuits even when basic to managing a day-to-day existence.

The more crucial issue, I now think, is not my specific omissions and commissions but the atmosphere that I create. My wife does not expect much of me in order to let me work and to lessen the strain which I produce when I feel blocked from working. Even our sons have always largely respected my efforts to work while feeling much freer to interrupt their mother at hers. The years have been less happy than they would have been if I were more involved and attentive and my wife had not lowered her ambitions.

Outstanding academically from an early age, a poor girl scholarship-winner at a prestige college and medical school, excelling in her beginning professional work, she expected and was expected to do great things. But with children, she immediately reduced her goals. Of course, medical schools don't pay much attention to faculty members who are part-time or female. The combination of both is powerful in getting offhand treatment.

She is now coming out to fuller professional development, but I have always felt guilty that she wasn't achieving more. So I nagged her to publish, while not providing the circumstances and climate which would make serious work much easier. I had the benefit of feeling relieved that I was "motivating" her by my emphasis on her doing more, while I did not suffer the calls on my time and emotions that making more useful time available to her would require. In the long run, I undoubtedly lost more by limited involvement because she was distressed by the obstacles to her professional work. But the long run is hard to consider when today's saved and protected time helps meet a deadline.

What are the lessons of this saga of a well-intentioned male? One is that equality or communality is not won once and for all, but must continually be striven for. Backsliding and easy accommodation-to-the-male-is-less-troublesome are likely to occur unless there is, at least occasionally, effort to bring about or maintain true communality rather than peaceful adjustment.

What follows is that women must struggle for equality—that it will not easily be won or re-won. A male is not likely to bestow it—in more than surface ways. Some women are arguing that it is not worth the effort to have equality with men in close personal relations and not to bother with men, but equality and communality among women will not be automatic either. The struggle does not necessarily mean nastiness but the perceptiveness and willingness to engage issues not only of prejudice and discrimination but also of subtle practices requiring female accommodation to males.

I know that this point is often misused and will open me to much criticism, but let me try to make it. A third lesson is that bringing up of children must be changed and that many women are lagging in this respect although present-day concerns suggest a possible change. For all of male reluctance, resistance, and avoidance, many women, particularly when they have young children, end up structuring life so that it is difficult to make a collegial life. Indeed, the concentration, nay absorption, with children makes even a low-level decent relationship difficult, let alone an egalitarian one. Yes, I realize that the subordinate group is never the main source of difficulty, that men make women embrace the mother-housemother syndrome, but cultural and personal history are involved as well as direct or more covert husbandly pressure and unwillingness to be a full partner. Overinvolvement with children may operate to discourage many husbands from fully sharing because they do not accept the ideology of close attention to children.

A fourth lesson is about sex, and I am rather surprised by it. It turns out that the most easy acceptance of equality is in bed—not in the kitchen. Few middle-class men, except those regarded as crude or brutes, would assert that women do not have a right to enjoyment in bed equal to that of their partner. (I doubt, however, that female extramarital affairs are treated as casually by men as they think their own extramarital adventures should be regarded.) Even if the male does not generally assume great responsibility for a female's difficulty in achieving orgasm, he is expected by himself and others to try to help her gain at least some measure of fulfillment. "Biff, bang, thank you, ma'am" is more of a joke than ever before.

This suggests that the most delicate of human relations—sex—isn't that central. Men are adjusting to new requirements and incorporating them in their definition of maleness. But the other elements of equality are not so easily absorbed into the definition of maleness. The "male-ness" of many young females' attitudes to sex—ready to go to bed without much emotional involvement with the partner; sex as kicks, not love—may be misleading them. "Good sex" doesn't necessarily mean real equality. I suspect many young women are being exploited by men just as my generation exploited women with the notion that true freedom, both political and psychological, was demonstrated by an "uninhibited" attitude toward relatively casual intercourse.

The phenomenal and depressing success of *Love Story,* as trite and sentimentalized a story of romance and sexism as has come along in a long while—truly a 1950-ish romance—indicates that many young women, even when they use four-letter words, dream of the everlasting and all-satisfying flame of love, including the purity of death as authenticating it. And, I fear that they think that equality in bed means equality in other things. They are much less liberated than they think and are probably sexually exploited by their male friends. Both young men and women seem unlikely to sustain untraditional forms of bedding and wedding, which is one of the reasons that I think my experiences still have relevance.

But all these "implications" are minor, except for the importance of struggle. What strikes me as the crucial concern, at least for the occupationally striving family, is the male involvement in work, success, striving. It is the pressure around which the family often gets molded. Accommodation to it is frequently the measure of being a "good wife"—moving when the male's "future" requires it, regulating activities so that the male is free to concentrate on his work or business. It isn't sexism or prejudice against women which is at work here—although these contribute—but the compulsive concentration upon the objective of achievement and the relegating of other activities to secondary concern. Egalitarian relationships cannot survive if people are not somewhat equally involved with each other and if the major commitment is great to things outside the relationship but which inevitably intrude upon it.

As long as success or achievement burns bright for the male, it is going to be difficult to change drastically the situation of the family and the women. While I am strongly of the mind that success drives should be banked and other more humanitarian urges encouraged, I don't accept that all of the drive for success or achievement is pernicious or undesirable. This drive is exciting and can be fulfilling. It is a great danger to be avoided when it becomes all embracing or when it is a success without a content that is both personally and socially satisfying or beneficial.

It should be made easier to do interesting and useful things, to feel a sense of accomplishment. As in military strategy, a "sufficing" level of achievement rather than a "maximum level" of security or position should be sought. Being "number one" should not be the goal; rather, high competence should be enough for both men and women. I have seen many talented people blighted in their work by number-oneism when they probably would have done outstanding and useful work by adopting a high-competence performance criterion.

And if women accept "success" to the same extent and in the same way that many men do, the problems will be enormous. If women simply adopt the number-oneism which dominates the workplace, the achievement drive will probably lead them into the same narrowing and unpromising obsessions which destroy many men.

A more egalitarian society in terms of the distribution of income and social respect, of course, would make it easier to escape number-oneism. But meanwhile we shall have to struggle with the values which surround us and which corrode true equality in the home.

Finally, men have to feel some gains in the growing equality in their relationship to women. Over the long run there may well be greater satisfactions for the males in egalitarian relationships, but in the short run the tensions and demands may not lead to enjoyment and satisfaction. Some short-term gains for males will be important in speeding up the road to equality. But such gains are not easy nor automatically forthcoming. Substitute satisfaction or gains for the male are needed to push out sexism. That is why I made the first points about the inevitability of struggle. But successful struggle requires modes of living and relationships to which the male can accommodate without total loss. That is hard to do without falling back again to women accommodating to men. Hopefully, what is needed is not accommodation but the growth of new or deeper mutual satisfactions arising from an easier exchange of ideas and a more profound expression of love and affection.

I recognize that I concentrate upon the upper middle class and upon the experience of one male. I don't think either is the world—I really don't. But I do perceive that some of my experiences and interpretations are not solipsistic pieces of life. And that with things changing, others are experiencing similar shocks and stresses. I wonder whether the egalitarian changes I see in some young families will mean permanent changes or "lapsed egalitarianism" once again. My hope is that the seventies will be different.

3

MEN AND CHILDREN

Of all the areas where we are beginning to examine ourselves and go beyond the limits of the traditional masculine role, perhaps the one to bear the most sweet fruit will be our relations with children. Robert Fein, in "Men and Young Children," describes the rewards some men are getting in being with children. For some of us, being with children and joining in the immediacy of their emotional life may be a route toward reclaiming the spontaneous emotional awareness that our own masculine training drove into hiding so long ago.

In the past, men's feelings about children have ranged from fears of inadequacy as a father, to a distant, shy pride and loving; from relief at not having to do much of the real work of child care, to believing that, in other ways, they "do everything" for their children. For years, it was asked whether maternal employment was harmful to children. No one ever asked whether or how *paternal* employment limited or distorted our relations with children.

The masculine role has clearly restricted our ability to relate to children. Our drive toward getting ahead means we often find little time or energy for being with children; moreover, we may project our own strivings for success upon them. Our unemotionality may make us think we have no skill or interest in relating to children in their everyday life; it may show up in a discomfort with children's direct expression of feelings. In "Being a 'Father'" one man tells how his desire not to reproduce the distant judgment he felt from his father required struggling with his own moralism and his feeling that he didn't "have time" for the kids.

If children of both sexes are to grow up to develop their full potential, rather than to exaggerate one side of themselves and suppress another, sex-role programming must be reduced. Sex roles are transmitted in two ways. First, different behavior is directed toward boys than toward girls. Second, when children look at adults and at older children, they see that what males do differs from what females do.

We can, if we try, reduce our tendency to relate differently to boys and to girls; mainly it takes the consciousness of relating to a person rather than to a role. We can also, by our own examples, reduce the extent to which certain activities are invariably associated with one sex or another. Ben Cannon offers such a counter-example to sex-role stereotypes; he tells of his experiences as a single father raising his son. Kelvin Seifert, from his experience in a child care center, observes how men there demonstrate that males need not act in some special "manly" way.

Paternity leaves and regular part-time positions are two work arrangements, increasingly frequent, which permit men more time with children. Today, institutions and individuals are changing in ways that will help re-establish contact between men and children, and permit each to reap the rewards of being with the other.

Men and Young Children

Robert A. Fein

ROBERT FEIN *has been exploring questions involving relationships between men and young children. He has recently completed a study of men's experiences before and after the birth of a first child and is teaching and writing about men's lives and maleness.*

Noontime in busy Boston. A tall, suited man walks down Beacon Street holding hands with a small girl. She stops and insistently pulls on his sleeve. Bending, he listens attentively to her ear-aimed whisper. And with a whoosh and a giggle, she is whisked onto his shoulders. They continue down the street together, his hands firmly gripping her knees, her face showing delight at being "bigger than the big people."

A classroom in a day care center in Salt Lake City, Utah. In the middle of the tousled room, a bushy-eyed, rumply-looking young man sits reading to the little boy and girl nestled in his lap. Around him an ethnic salad-bowl of four-year-olds are engaged in block-playing, crayoning, book-looking, and truck-riding. Each child seems aware of

---

the man's quiet presence: it is as if he is the hub of their activity. A small, teary boy comes over for comfort, his feelings hurt in a spill. The teacher soothes him gently with a hug, then sends him back to his play.

A small town in rural Colorado. A spare, middle-aged man with weathered western features is making his weekly visits to families in the Parent-Child Center Program. He worked for twenty-five years on the railroad, then retired at the age of 50 to take a job working with children and families because, "I figured there was more to do than juggling numbers in an office." Three small children spot him heading toward their house and, shouting excitedly, run to his open arms. He will take them on an "outing" to show them the trees on a nearby farm, then spend an hour talking with their mother about the nutrition and health care of her infant.

Three nurturant moments in a 1973 American day, each with a gracefulness that gives it a life of its own. Men with young children. Relationships long ignored and abused by the media, social scientists, politicians, teachers, clinicians . . . and mothers and fathers. Relationships being rediscovered today, often with a richness born of exile, by men who are coming home, to themselves and to their loved ones.

The circumstances that are leading men to become more involved with young children vary from man to man, and from family to family. An editor recently changed jobs because "I got tired of the loneliness of travelling all the time. I thought that if I didn't come home soon my kids would grow up without knowing their father, and I wanted to get to know them." He wonders if his situation was unique. "I listened for four years to guys who bitched about being locked into their jobs, and finally figured that there had to be more room for change in my field than everyone said. I was right."

An administrator tells of lunching twice a week with his five-year-old son. "I blocked out Tuesdays and Thursdays on my calendar and simply said I was having lunch with Michael. The first few weeks I got some funny looks from people who dropped in to see me as I was on my way out and some 'Who's Michael?' comments. Pretty soon, though, people realized that they could see me just as well at other times."

An expectant father who works in a metal parts factory tells of his conversations at work. "Two other guys are also expecting children, so we talk a fair amount about kids, our wives, and fatherhood. You know, in the last few years, even the travelling salesmen have started talking about their children. It's almost like a guy seems more alive when he talks about children."

What may account for the increasing number of men who are choosing to spend more time in caring contact with the youngest generations? There are two related social changes that help explain the renewed attention men are paying to young children: one in the economy, the other in people's consciousnesses.

First, the percentage of women in the labor force has jumped from 18% in 1948 to over 39% in 1973. Women who used to spend their daytime hours in child care and homemaking have chosen or been forced to find paid employment outside the home. These changes in labor-force participation rates have resulted in an increased demand for child care at the same time as the supply of child carers has been reduced. Many women have realized, under these pressures, that they can no longer afford to waste one-half of the potential suppliers of child care by branding them unfit to care for children, leaving them locked into stereotyped "breadwinner" roles, or by letting them avoid responsibility for regular child care. And many men, though shy and sometimes scared, are glad to be asked to take care of the kids.

Second, the women's movement of the 1960's and 1970's, in both its institutional and intimate manifestations, has thrown men back on their own resources and led to often-painful and often-rewarding re-evaluations by men of their lives. Men, spurred by wives, sisters, and female friends who have come to view themselves through feminist lenses, are examining the nature of masculinity—and finding society's image of the "real" man to be wanting.

Changes in men's lives are usually quiet ones, so far unheralded by the media, savored privately and many times passionately. These changes, particularly in the depth and extent of men's relationships with young children, have no large-scale economic or institutional forms: they are not generally recorded in national economic- or social-trend data. Increasingly, however, men are speaking of their inner journeys and wishes.

"We, as men, want to take back our full humanity," asserts the Berkeley Men's Center Manifesto, an at-the-edge articulation of hopes and concerns that touch the thoughts of a growing number of American males. "We no longer want to strain to compete to live up to an impossible oppressive masculine image—strong, silent, cool, handsome, unemotional, successful, master of women, leader of men, wealthy, brilliant, athletic, and 'heavy.' . . . We want to relate to both women and men in more human ways—with warmth, sensitivity, emotion, and honesty. We want to share our feelings with one another to break down the walls and grow closer. We want to be equal with women and end destructive competitive relationships between men."

The pressures against men who seek to rediscover their caring selves through closer and more satisfying relationships with young children are considerable. American society presents few models of nurturant manhood to guide its boys and girls and men and women. To some, it seems that only in insurance advertisements (where young men are tempted with pictures of the joys of fatherhood and admonished to "take care of your family now while you can"), on television doctor shows where periodically during crises bright young men save the lives of desperately ill children, and in articles and advertisements celebrating the glories of Father's Day, are men shown nurturing young children.

For every newsnote published or broadcast that highlights a caring experience between a man and a child, the media still trot out five situation comedies or horror stories that show men who are tyrants, or incompetent, or plain uninterested in nurturing young children. A recent program on CBS's Saturday night "Bob Newhart Show" portrayed an immature divorced father who was panicked into childish helplessness ("he doesn't love me any more") when his young son talked with another man at lunch. Ads for Pampers show a man carrying a puppy greeting two women holding infants. Women care for babies, is the message, men take care of dogs.

The disciplines of psychology and psychiatry, with their obsession with and reification of mother-child relationships and their virtual neglect of father-child (let alone man-child) relationships in the past fifty years, have contributed to the social atmosphere that has excluded many men from close relationships with children and has forced men to become "exceptions" when they express and dare to act on needs and desires for emotional involvement with the young children in their lives. In many quarters, British psychoanalyst John Bowlby's 1951 statement is still the guiding wisdom: "fathers have their uses even in infancy. Not only do they provide for their wives to enable them to devote themselves unrestrictedly to the care of the infant and toddler, but, by providing love and companionship, they support her emotionally and help her maintain that harmonious contented mood in the aura of which the infant thrives . . ."

Myths about men causing harm to little children are still disturbingly prevalent. (How many men have been warned while teaching elementary school never, never to touch a child?) Boys who have younger friends are viewed as strange in many neighborhoods ("how come he's not with kids his own age?"), whereas it is "natural" that girls are attracted to young children. Men who play with children they have not fathered (not their "own"), and who may not even be fathers at all, are viewed with suspicion by some ("what's *he* doing with that kid?"), while it is assumed and demanded that women like and be comfortable with children.

But despite past and current absences of visible social support, increasing numbers of men are finding time and energy to care for children and are learning to share with children the specialness of every day. "I want to meet my wife's needs," said an expectant father three weeks before the birth of his first child, "and I want to be actively involved with the baby, too. I want to hold the baby and have a lot of physical contact with him or her. I want to carry our baby on my back and take walks with it. I want to change it and do as much as my wife does, except breastfeed which I can't do."

Often-rigid social norms, established in nineteenth-century, industrializing America, that order men to "be competent" and women to "be nurturant," are increasingly recognized as personally and socially limiting by those who realize that twentieth-century organizational America needs men and women who are both able and caring. An androgynous model of human well-being, suggesting that men and women can both work and love, may be emerging, as society allows women to explore the reality of competent adulthood and men to touch parts of their emotional lives buried or hidden in a "boys don't cry" childhood and to become caring adults.

With the rediscovery and recognition of the validity of their inner lives, many men are choosing to nurture. Men and women are sharing the birth of their children ("We got into this pregnancy together, we'll get out of it together."), and many men are following up their inclusion in the delivery room tumult and joy with efforts to share the trials, tribulations, and rewards of caring in the nursery. In 1973, it is increasingly accepted that it is good for children to have caring time with men. And more and more parents, child care workers, clinicians, and teachers are realizing that it is good for men also to have time with children.

Caring for young children, as any new mother soon learns, is no Eden of sweetness and bliss. Men who have experienced the boredom, frustration, and occasional pain of ministering to the needs of the young are sharing and accepting both the bitter and the sweet. With knowledge of the hours of humdrum and knowledge of the moments of gentle ecstacy, men are choosing to care for young children, often bringing with them a combination of warmth, imagination, and willingness to dream that daily distinguishes the special times from those merely routine.

Mark, 31, rides the subway at 7:30 in the morning, with daughter Kristen, three and a half, firmly gripping his hand. They ride into the Bronx so Kristen can stay each work day with the woman who has cared for her since Jean, Kristen's mother, returned to her nursing job when Kristen was six months old. The family has since moved to New Jersey but Mark and Jean feel strongly about Kristen's need and right to her relationship with her family day-care mother. On the subway this morning, with Kristen's small hand tucked in his overcoat pocket, Mark is roused from his office thoughts by her insistent question, "Daddy, where do shoes come from?" Streaks of early morning irritation twist across his mind. Shoes, dammit, don't compare with his 10:00 meeting with the vice-president for marketing. Then a fathering pause. But this day shoes mean something to her. "Hmm, Kristen, where do you think shoes come from?" The beginning of a quiet adventure. Mark and Kristen look at people's shoes the rest of the way into the Bronx and before he leaves for the ride to his office, Mark has planned with her a Saturday trip to a shoe store and to the zoo. Mark arrives at the office with Kristen's small voice still in his ear, "Daddy, I love you." A voice that doesn't go away.

Mack is a truck driver and father of a four-year-old son, Brian, who goes to nursery school because his mother feels that "Brian needs to have a chance to play with kids his own age, rather than hang around all day with me and the baby." At school, Brian loves to play with trucks, especially those he says are like "my Daddy's truck."

As part of the nursery school's program to encourage fathers to share their lives with children in the school, a male teacher visited Brian and his family at home. After suggesting that there might be a relation between Brian's love of trucks and the fact that Mack was a truck driver ("Naw," said Mack, pleased despite himself, "he doesn't like me, he likes trucks."), the teacher invited Mack to come to school to play with the children. Mack, a bit taken aback and gruffly shy, muttered that "he wouldn't want me to come to school. School's for kids. Wouldya, Brian?" Brian, playing with a truck in the corner, obediently said no.

Several days later, Mack called the teacher and said that he had been able to find a morning when he could come to school. "But what'll I do there?" he worried to the teacher. "They're just kids." "Let's play with trucks," said the teacher.

On the appointed day, Mack showed up nervously at school, a library book about trucks tucked under his arm. "What are they going to do today?" he whispered anxiously. Brian, who had been glowing for four days with the news that his daddy was coming to school, played quietly on the other side of the room, ignoring his father. While a female teacher showed Mack the toys and equipment in the room, the male teacher began building a road out of blocks and moving around some trucks and cars. Several children started playing with the toys, and soon Mack came over, first to watch, then to "drive" a truck. After half an hour of make-believe engine "brrmms" and car "beep-beeps," and driving trucks and autos around and through the block city they had built, Mack read his truck book to eleven captivated boys and girls who sat circled up on the rug.

Mack emerged from the classroom at the end of the hour slightly dazed. "Thanks," he mumbled to the teacher, "that was . . . uh . . . really great." Then going down the steps, the young father turned with a puzzled, almost anguished look. "What'll I tell the guys at work about this?"

Many American men, in their childhoods and early manhoods, have little or no contact with infants or small children. Man after man, in a recent doctoral study of men and women's experiences before and after the birth of their first child,* reported that he had never held, or fed, or changed, or played with a baby. Unlike some non-Western societies in which boys have major caring responsibilities for younger children, American society has effectively blocked opportunities for boys and men to care for and learn about young children.

"I feel in a bind," said one expectant father. "When I was little my father never really took care of me. He was the breadwinner, and I guess he demanded respect more than he gave affection. But now the norms seem to have changed. Men are expected to take care of children. I feel like I want to care for our baby, and I feel that I ought to care for the child, but, frankly, I don't really know how. I'm afraid I won't be a good father." His comments point up the fact that it is not easy for men who have been divorced from children all their lives to suddenly become nurturers when they are presented with the realities of fatherhood.

The remarks of a successful executive about his four-week-old son typify the confusion of the transition to fatherhood for some men. "It's just not rational for David to behave that way. After all, why should his needs be met first all the time just because he's a baby? But somehow what's rational has nothing to do with it. He's little and we take care of him."

Sometimes caring for children can trigger a bewildering and disturbing range of emotions in men who long ago blocked off parts of their childlike selves. One male nursery school teacher found himself angry at little boys who cried when they felt hurt or sad. His anger was so upsetting to him that he withdrew whenever little boys needed consolation or support. Under the careful and supportive probing of the head teacher in the school, who sensed his conflict, he exclaimed that "I never was allowed to cry when I was little and they shouldn't cry either." Further talking suggested that when little he had very much wanted to cry and be comforted and felt he rarely got what he needed from the grownups in his world, particularly his father. Aware of some of the reasons why he got so angry at little boys who felt sad, he was better able to respond to their individual needs.

While the risks in caring for small children—the fears of loss, the difficulty with separations, the realizations of the gravity of parental responsibility, the needs to delay gratification of one's wishes because a little one is more helpless—are sometimes severe and painful, the joys of nurturance and the pleasures of giving and receiving love with children, are deep and plentiful.

A young father talked of what children mean to him. "Little kids just

* Robert Fein, "Men's experiences before and after the birth of a first child: dependence, marital sharing, and anxiety," Ph.D. thesis, Harvard University, 1974.

give so much without asking. They can sense when you like them. And they in turn like you back. And they're sensitive and aware of changes in mood. They'll come out and ask, 'Why are you so sad and unhappy today?' And then you just can't stay unhappy or sad. They can communicate very honestly on a simple level that's very direct, and it's just great. You can't really stay mad when a little kid comes up and asks you what's wrong."

Emotional honesty. Simplicity. Directness. Three paths to a man's buried soul. Men are finding that contact with children leads them back to themselves, allowing them to integrate their childlike selves with their grownup selves. "I guess I was told so often to stiffen up and be a man when I was little," reflected a child-care worker, "that I decided there was something wrong about being a child. So I practiced hard to be a man, always afraid that I wouldn't make it, that the scared little boy hiding underneath would pop out at any moment and give me away. Caring for kids has led me to see that I'm like the kids in some ways and I'm different in others because I'm a grownup. Working with children has helped me locate myself as an able, caring adult. I'm liking what I'm learning about the strength of nurturance."

A rising lawyer, forced to spend several weeks at home recuperating from an operation, found himself playing each day with his four-year-old son. "Billy really took good care of me," he mused to a friend. "He knew when I felt sad, and when I wanted to be alone. And I learned a little of what the world looks like through his eyes. It's a different world than mine, and it's pretty nice. You know, I had no idea what's on the underside of a parking meter. And I'm not used to watching people's faces the way he is. I really like my work, but I'm considering trying to change my schedule so I can spend more weekday hours with my son."

Society provides little support—either financial or emotional—for men who want to spend regular time caring for young children. Economic pressures and the press toward a successful career often force a man to choose between his work life and his family life, an anguishing choice that some men now are refusing to make.

A growing number of men are changing their career plans to allow them greater control of the ways they spend their time. Others, watching older men at work who have "broken their backs" for the kids, and who go home at the age of 42 to discover that their adolescent sons and daughters are strangers to them and are actively rejecting the values of the "old man," are anxiously but determinedly resolving to find ways to avoid abandoning their families to a career.

The concept of paternity leave is slowly gaining acceptance, symbolizing a gathering recognition that fathers have needs and rights to participate in the care of their children. Some men and women are considering the feasibility of legislation that would guarantee part-time job options and the desirability of tax laws that would give incentives to corporations who support men and women in their finding balances of work life and family life that are appropriate to their family needs.

The issues involved in relationships between men and young children are, at the same time, clear and complex. At one level, they are obvious, mundane, simplistic. Of course, some say, men can and want to care for children. At another level, they are more confusing. How many men, in fact, does the average person know who spend regular time nurturing the young children who touch their lives?

In a society where it is increasingly possible for a child to grow to adulthood without being given a single opportunity to take care of a live creature (let alone a small human), newly found relationships between men and young children are both valuable in and of themselves and as a means toward larger ends.

For an America daily confronted with physical and emotional brutality at home and abroad, caring contact between men and young children may provide one way to relocate the heart and soul of the often fearsome technological giant. Growing awareness of the "sandpaper existence" of many American men (the pervasive loneliness, the frantic competition, the prevalence of ulcers and heart attacks, the premature dying) propels some to seek new ways to order the structure and meaning of their daily lives. Relationships between men and young childern, long awaited homecomings, may lead toward a more caring society.

Being a "Father"

Anne has two kids. When I was first going out with her I was living in the City and the kids were staying at a commune in the country. We would regularly visit up there and I liked the kids, but they were no particular problem—or even a reality—to me. There were several kids up there and Anne's were just part of the group. But as Anne and I got closer together, I was forced more and more to face the kids' existence and their implication to me; I was now a "father!" Far out.

From *Unbecoming Men: A Men's Consciousness-Raising Group Writes on Oppression and Themselves,* Times Change Press (c/o Monthly Review Press, 62 W. 14th St., New York, NY 10011, $1.75 plus 35¢ handling), 1971, pp. 26–28. Reprinted by permission.

I was just beginning to be at all sensitive to Anne and responsive to her feelings and needs. She had to practically club me along every inch of the way—throwing things, getting hysterical, giving me "logical" arguments, threatening me and making unavoidably correct demands —just to get me to wake-up and move. But as for the kids, Ollie and Celia, they couldn't club me along. If anything, Anne had to defend them against my bullshit. So I'd been able to resist responsibility to the kids' feelings for a long time. But in finally facing that irresponsibility, I've had to see what a pig I am, how much I'm like *my* father who I hated for the same reasons, and how hypocritical my professed communism and Summerhillianism is.

When Ollie or Celia spill something (again!) I cringe and get rigid and up-tight. I hate them, the dumb, clumsy kids. And all these very heavy, disapproval vibes radiate out from me. As a step in the right direction, I've learned not to say anything hostile or come out with a condemning moralism. But I still stew, silently, and the kids feel it. I'm just like my father and all the other old, rigid, authoritarian bastards that fucked me up.

Also, I don't "have time" for the kids. I'm always compulsively busy at my desk or doing the dishes or reading and I don't like being interrupted. Relating to the people I live with doesn't seem to be as important as "getting my work done," and without interruptions. Also, my pacing is compulsively fast. When I do break down and agree to build a plane, for example, with Ollie, I soon get impatient with his pokeyness or with his susceptibility to getting interested in other things. "All right Ollie, we started this, and don't you think we should finish it?"

Ollie has this particularly irritating habit of snacking a lot. He especially seems to go through the refrigerator or shelves, taking the only can of dark cherries or nuts or something like that, which I always consider a luxury and like to save (for what, I don't know). This bugs me to no end and I use my rational adult privilege to stop him, when I can. I'm always saying, "No, Ollie, that's too expensive just to eat as a snack." Or, "No, Ollie, wait until we can all divide it up evenly." Whenever he goes into the kitchen I get all tense listening to what he's opening, thinking about having to go in and watch him. I'm constantly on guard-duty, at attention. Ollie has helped me a lot to see the uptight Puritan in me.

Anne and I let Ollie and Celia work out their arguments and fights by themselves. They do a very good job of it, but I still find myself wanting to sometimes intervene against Ollie. He's bigger and usually causing the fuss, and that grates against my moral sense of Fair Play. Although I know it is always better for them to work their problems out alone between themselves, I still want to yell at Ollie and make him leave little Celia alone. God-damn he gets me angry!

I love Ollie a lot, especially more and more as I am able to shake off more of my rigidity and superiority. I love him because he's been in a large part responsible for my growing in this way. I also love him because of guilt at the way I used to treat him and come down on him, and also just because he's a beautiful person. But how can I show him? How can I just be gentle and sensitive and close to him? That's a big, big problem for me now. I still have a long way to go in learning to relate to Anne better, but at least she can directly help me in this. But with Ollie, it's much more up to me. He's at the age when society tells him he's too big of a boy to be into hugs and kisses—even with Anne, let alone me. And Lord knows I have big problems relating warmly to anybody, let alone a boy. Ollie has his own limitations too, so that makes it doubly hard for us to communicate.

From noticing the vast differences between Ollie and Celia, I've learned quite a lot about sex-role stereotyping and about my own hang-ups. Ollie is already, at nine, very much into the accomplishment- and thing-oriented male trip. He places a high value on acquiring numerous and high priced possessions and big-shot skills and knowledge, which he tries to use to gain status. It's competitive as hell already for Ollie. His worth in the eyes of the world, and hence his self-worth, is dependent on his accomplishments and his acquisitions. It's tragic how he's got to compete and prove himself all the time. Not that he (or his friends) have a choice—their very survival in boy/man culture makes it *necessary*. Celia on the other hand is already, at age seven, very much oriented as a female. Her energy goes toward interacting with the people around her; toward psyching-out people, finding out their likes and needs, and then relating to them. (But this conditioning for a little girl has its own liabilities too—so much of it is preparation for her future woman's role of "taking care of" other people.) She responds to people's feelings, whereas Ollie responds so much to their status and possessions. The only real "toys" Celia likes are stuffed and real animals, whereas Ollie consumes as many cars, rockets and guns as possible. Celia likes talking *with* you about *yourself* and *herself,* whereas Ollie talks *to* you about *things*. And Celia is very oriented in the present, to what's happening right here and now. Ollie always has big plans for the future—things he's going to do or get.

I'm afraid this contrast between Ollie and Celia comes off a bit exaggerated. Of course it's not so simplistically polarized, but the cultivated distortions are there and pronounced. And the same distortions that cripple Ollie have crippled me into becoming, like *my* father, a crippler of others.

Michael and Me

Ben Cannon

BEN CANNON *is 36 years old. He is black, tall, thin, thoughtful. He lives with his six-year-old son Michael. The house they share is small, immaculate. The livingroom has just enough space for one armchair, a couch, coffee table, a formal photo of Michael, a T.V. and, directly opposite the couch, a large fish tank with various kinds of tropical fish. Spare as a bone. The house is in the rear of another home, one-half block past a clapboard church on the corner, in an older residential neighborhood; a stone's throw from South Central Avenue, Watts, Los Angeles.*

Michael's mother died in childbirth. Ben decided to keep his son and even though his decision was contested by the grandmother, Ben was awarded custody by the court. In order to be with his baby through infancy, Ben went on Welfare, and was then trained in the WIN program as a nursery school teacher. He has been teaching for the past four years at the Second Baptist Church Day Care Center. Michael went to Second Baptist pre-school and now goes to public school. Ben has been married and divorced once since Michael was born.

Ben Cannon says of himself: "Since writing this article I have become the director of a nursery school. It has been a very rewarding experience for me and my son to accept the challenge to operate a nursery school. I realize now what most directors go through and why their hair turns grey overnight. I have been on both sides of the fence, since I was once a teacher and now I am the director."

Slowly and matter-of-factly, Ben talks about his life.

I like working with children, although my job is a challenge. It's like a woman trying to go into the construction field . . . you've got a lot to learn. I enjoy being around kids, getting involved with them, going on trips, answering their questions.

I bring home $560, so I don't go out and buy a brand new Cadillac. I know I have a range to live in. After I get the Cadillac, I can't pay for it. Right now, I don't owe nobody. I pay $55 a month for rent, $20

From *Momma: The Newspaper/Magazine for Single Mothers* (PO Box 567, Venice, Calif. 90291), May 1973, *1*(5), 6–7. Reprinted by permission.

a week to the babysitter and that leaves me enough for other things, like my fish. I've got $300 tied up in my fish.

Mothering is better done by women. It's a mother's instinct. Michael's mother died in childbirth, so I've had him since he was an infant. He would start to cough at night, or holler. The first thing I did was to get up and give him a bottle. Maybe he don't want the bottle at that time. Maybe he just wants somebody to hold him. I go get the bottle. He don't want the bottle. A woman knows these things, she knows what to look for in a baby. A man has to learn it.

I give in more to Michael than a woman would. Say you were Michael's mother. "Can I go outside?" You say no. Then you go about your housework, or cooking or whatever. With me, if I say no, he keeps on saying, "Can I go out? Can I go out?" I give in. Even when it's raining, he wants to water the grass. I say, "No, Michael, you can't water the grass, the rain just watered the grass." A few minutes later, "Can I water the grass?" So I finally give in. The hose is out there, so, O.K., go water the grass. A woman, she says no, she means it. I let it all build up then I spank him. He'll do something he really shouldn't do and he gets a spanking for all that he did before. I took him to buy a hat. He picked it out himself, most of the clothes he picks out himself. That's the way I was raised. Not that Michael dictates to me what he could do or what he shouldn't do. I feel that he should have a mind of his own, too. And he ought to know that in the morning when he gets up he picks what he wants to wear to school, not me. I might decide, O.K., Michael, wear Levis today and he knows at school they have a program or something and he wants to wear something nice. I let him have his way about most things. But this time I said, "Michael, don't lose the hat. It cost me $4.98. You wear it to school and bring it back home. Michael goes to school and gives the hat away. O.K., so I bring him in and I spank him. Bought him another hat, and he's still got it.

After he was born, my family turned their back on me. I wanted to keep Michael but I needed help, so I went on the County. I didn't know what to do.

If it hadn't been for his babysitter, I probably would have been crazy. She took Michael like he was her own child. It's like a big family over there, she keeps her own grandchildren. Michael goes from my house to her house in the morning, then he goes to school. When he gets out of school, he goes over to her house because I'm still at work. He stays there till I come home and she gives him his dinner. I give her $20 a week and sometimes I don't give her anything because she says Michael is just like hers. I was over there this evening and tried to get him to come home but he didn't want to come. The fact is he has a lot of kids over there. Here the kids come in, play with him, then bam they go home. All he has is me to play with, and when I get off work I'm kind of bushed. I help him with his homework and then he goes in and watches television. He has his own television and I have mine. He likes to watch all those Mickey Mouse things, and I like to watch sports. We share the same bedroom, which isn't nice, but it's the best I can do. He likes it over here. I have my fish and he has his puppies and his cat. We're good together. I like to take him places, to the zoo. The weekend before last, we went to Disneyland in the rain. I went looking for Michael because I thought he was getting wet out there. He went into the penny arcade and stayed 'til it stopped raining. I went all over the park looking for him. He's dry as a bone and I'm the one soaked.

Michael don't ask about his mother. He asked when I'm going to get married again. I married a woman with two kids, 5 and 4, when Michael was 2. The kids got along real well. We got along good, too, until her ex-husband got out of jail. She had gotten a divorce from him but evidently the feeling must have still been there because when he got out, we got into a couple of arguments. She asked if Bobby could come by and see the kids. I said O.K. I didn't mind the man coming around to see his kids. I would never stop a man from seeing his kids. I thought she meant when I was home or during the daylight hours because I was going to City College at night. The guy would come by at 8:00 or 9:00 at night and the kids would be in bed. Or he'd come by during the day, they're either at school or outside somewhere. Come by and see your kids, but do it at a reasonable hour. Don't make me feel that you can't come by and see your kids if I'm at home. Respect me as well as respect your kids.

When he was in prison, I did for his kids. There wasn't no difference made. Everybody got shoes. Everybody got a coat. There wasn't I buy for Michael, you buy for your two. When he got out of prison, he bought his two kids stuff, then Michael wondered why those kids had things and he didn't. How can you explain that to a 5-year-old kid?

I came home from work one day and she was gone. Took everything. All this was mine. All she left was two plates, two glasses, two spoons and two forks. And a bed for me and Michael to sleep in. Sometimes now I see her. I don't cry over spilled milk. When it's done, it's done, you can't undo it. I didn't leave no hard feelings. She left me. If she's with him, I still speak. See, because I look at it this way, a man can't make a woman do no more than she wants to do. Now that man can't twist her arm to tell her to leave me and come back to him. She did it because she wanted to. There's too many women in this world to argue over one woman. It hurt, sure it hurt. But why argue about it?

Michael was heartbroken for a good four or five months. "When is Derek and Brenda gonna come back and see me? When can I go over and stay with Derek and Brenda?" When after almost two years kids grow up together, a kid's not going to forget that easy.

After they left, I told him that Jerri was going back with Bobby, and that they had a house, and Derek and Brenda could come over here. If Jerri feels her nerves ain't on edge and he wanted to go over there, he could. Her kids have come over and visited me and Michael; her kids even spent the night. But Michael has never spent the night over at their house. I don't know why. Like I told her, "Whatever went between you and me shouldn't reflect on the children, because the children don't know from Adam and Eve what happened. All they know is that you and Bobby got back together. I never say anything disrespectful to Michael about you, and I hope you feel the same way about your kids and me."

I don't have a girlfriend right now, just associates. A girlfriend is somebody you later contemplate getting married with. I'm not in the right frame of mind to get married again, not right away. Most of the women I associate with know Michael. Most of them enjoy being around him. They like to take him places, things like that. But they don't spend the night here. With a one-bedroom house? Michael's a light sleeper, like I am. He might decide to get up, and little boys do talk. I feel that Michael shouldn't be . . . he's gonna learn about sex soon enough anyway. Why should he see me?

Someday I'd like to get married. For companionship, to give Michael a mother and me a wife. But it has to be somebody who not just wants me but wants my child as well. You got a lot of women out here that would accept me, but won't accept Michael. And I don't want a young woman. I want no more young women. Their minds ain't settled. I'm 36 years old; my wife was 22 years old when we got divorced. Let's say she was in her early 30's; I think she'd have thought twice before she went back to her ex-husband. An older woman is more mature. And some of these young girls out here . . . everything looks pleasing to them in the beginning, and as you progress into marriage, it ain't like a bowl of peaches and cream.

Let Michael be whatever he wants to be as long as he's not a hoodlum. I'm not going to sit up and say now I'll help Michael go to college. Michael's going to have to help himself as well. It ain't all gonna be just Daddy. When I got my first car, my daddy helped me. But I had me a part time job and he matched me. I put $50 in the bank, he'd put $50 in the bank. I made $6 a week. I gave my mother half, I kept half. As I grew older, the value of money meant more to me. I wasn't just handed everything. I got out and earned it. I finished high school on my own. I went in the service. Been around six foreign countries and 16 states in the U.S. I've seen America and I'm ready to settle down. I would like to have my own nursery school. I went through all the procedures to get one for our church. But then President Nixon started cutting all the poverty programs. I was given the runaround by Nixon, Yorty and the EYOA. I don't know if I'll ever get one.

Some Problems of Men in Child Care Center Work

Kelvin Seifert

A male teacher in a child care center faces special problems relating to his own behavior and the reactions of the children and his staff colleagues. A major contribution can be his countering of sexual stereotypes.

KELVIN SEIFERT *is a head teacher at the demonstration preschool at San Jose State University, San Jose, California. He has written several articles on the role of men in working with young children, the problems they have in doing so, and the strengths they bring to such work.*

Parents and teachers often comment that more male teachers are needed in child care centers. Their reasons for saying so have often not been clear. One person might say that young children need a male image; another, that young boys in particular relate better to male teachers; still another might say that with a male teacher, children learn that men can be nurturing and loving, just as women can. These assertions are hardly ever made from personal experience, since full-time male child care workers are still virtually nonexistent. Nor are they made from objective studies of men in child care centers, since such studies have not been made. At best, the comments represent application to the classroom of the research and knowledge about men in other settings, especially the home. Even more commonly, the "need" for men is simply taken for granted. Little evidence seems to be necessary for such a widely accepted idea.

The writer believes that men should involve themselves in child-care programs, but also believes that child care educators generally have failed to understand some of the problems in working with men who choose a traditionally "feminine" career such as child care. This lack of understanding is evidenced in my informal conversations with

Kelvin Seifert, "Some Problems of Men in Child Care Center Work," *Child Welfare,* March 1973, *102*(3), 167–71. Reprinted by permission.

other child care workers. On another level, it is reflected in the paucity of writings about men in child care. A handful of kindergarten teachers (not all men) have written personal accounts (8:132–135; 4:293–299; 10:139–147; 6), but they have not detached themselves enough from their individual experiences to consider how maleness per se affects young children and staff relationships. Some research studies are finally under way (9:5), but the rudimentary state of knowledge about male child-care workers may make these findings tentative. Even without verified knowledge, some ideas about male workers emerge from experience; if better understood, they might increase and enhance the participation of men in the care of young children.

THE SEX STEREOTYPE

The most important fact about a successful male child-care worker is the extent to which his work contradicts sex-role conventions. Although most male social workers try to free themselves from sexually stereotyped behavior, the male in a child care center must do so to an unusual extent. In general the male worker must like, or learn to like, "feminine" activities. He must like painting and drawing; like to cook simple foods, like to give a gentle hug when it is needed. No matter what he does, his gender makes most of his classroom behavior seem unconventional.

Although his peculiar position can be expected to affect his work, it may not do so in the ways commonly supposed. Examine, for example, three areas of child-care activity and the expectations in each: the worker's behavior with a roomful of children, their behavior with him, and his relationships with his female colleagues.

Oddly enough, his gender probably has little systematic effect on his behavior with his children. By his own preference, the male child-care worker might tend to choose "manly" activities a little more frequently—playing with trucks, roughhousing, playing ball. But the "masculine" flavor of his program would necessarily be overshadowed by the major objective in the group child-care situation: to provide a variety of activities to meet a variety of social and educational needs. It seems likely, then, that successful child-care workers would provide similar programs, no matter what their gender. The male's special contribution would consist not in "acting like a man" for the children, but in disproving the idea that men need act in some special, "manly" way.

THE CHILDREN'S REACTION

His problems begin with the children's behavior toward him: To some extent the children may treat a male teacher as if he were "odd." Considerable child development research suggests that children acquire sex-role stereotypes early and pervasively. Their stereotypes have been documented by behaviorists (7), Piagetans (3) and by psychoanalysts (1). When confronted with a man doing "feminine" things, therefore, children can be expected to express varying degrees of surprise, disbelief and mistrust. It is hoped that they soon will give up their sexual stereotypes and learn to like their odd (that is, male) teacher; he is there, in fact, to help them do so. But in the process of disproving the children's sex-role stereotypes, the male teacher may have to endure a bit more rejection from them than will a female teacher of comparable talents and temperament. If the male worker also has personal doubts about his ability to handle such "feminine" work, he may find the children's fleeting rejections especially painful.

The male child-care worker can expect his biggest problems in staff relations. In sociological terms, he clearly suffers from "status inconsistency" (2). He is a man, but he is doing work usually considered "feminine." The women who work with him may experience some discomfort in reconciling these facts. In forming their impressions of him, they may try to understand his reasons for working with children. The more conservative female colleagues may doubt his initiative, courage or intelligence: Since he presumably had a chance for a "real" career, why didn't he take it? The more liberal colleagues may perceive the arrogance of this attitude, but still feel troubled. Surely, the liberal ones may think, a man eventually will be bored by working with children; he must not really feel much personal investment in preschool teaching. They may not want to burden him with too much talk about the children and about programming. In any case, his presence will be, at the least, puzzling to everyone and, at the most, upsetting. The man who causes these staff problems can expect to be treated somewhat awkwardly at first, perhaps even ungraciously. Relatively unimportant incidents may be taken as confirming preexisting attitudes about male incompetence or boredom with children. To counteract these tendencies, the male worker must be extra capable and extra interested in children.

THE "EXCEPTIONAL" SOLUTION

Everyone's sex-role stereotypes can be preserved, of course, by deciding that the particular male in the center is "exceptional." Most men, it can then be argued, do not like working with children, but *our* man is different. This kind of thinking is widespread in dealing with the presence of minorities, but it confronts the male child-care worker with a new dilemma. If he insists that he is a "real" man, he may unconsciously imply that he is incompetent (because in this field all men supposedly are). He may thereby consign himself to minor roles in the child-care center. But if he decides he actually is different from other men, he gives up his chance to demonstrate the falseness of sex-role stereotypes. In addition, his professional relationship with any new male worker may suffer if one joins him on the staff. If the new man is not "exceptional," he therefore is incompetent.

Eventually, of course, the entire staff may make a new "exception" to their preconceptions to accommodate the new male. If enough such exceptions are made, the problem of working with men may be considerably reduced. Individual differences among the men will become more apparent, and conflicts among staff members may then center on important behaviors and issues, rather than on minor behaviors used to support major stereotypes. Sex-role stereotypes, even when consciously believed, will lose their force as more and more "exceptional" men have to be recognized.

For the time being, the male child-care worker must work alone, at least psychologically. No doubt this keeps many interested men from trying to work with young children. Those who do try must contradict sex-role conventions that run far deeper than the child-care professions. Even though social forces may be undermining these conventions somewhat, preschool child-care work remains one of the most "feminine" occupations in the world. Whether or not the male worker is consciously troubled by sexual stereotypes, he must navigate in a world full of them; and at almost every step he must contradict them. In doing so, he somehow must not feel like an occupational failure or like a pet rabbit, "the (exceptional) male at the child-care center."

On top of all this he must plan and carry out interesting activities with a group of young children and gradually build up sensitive relationships with them. In view of his special burdens, it should not surprise anyone that so few men enter child-care work as a full-time occupation, and that even fewer stay in it long. It should also not surprise anyone if further research finds that male child-care workers tend to prefer part-time positions, rather than full-time ones; and that once in the classroom, they tend to play relatively minor teaching roles. The entire staff, as representatives of society, prefer them to take these roles.

REFERENCES

1. Brenner, Charles. *Elementary Textbook of Psychoanalysis*. Garden City, N.Y.: Doubleday Anchor Books, 1957.

2. Hughes, Everett. "Dilemmas and Contradictions in Status," American Journal of Sociology, L (1945).

3. Kohlberg, Lawrence. "Cognitive-Developmental Analysis of Children's Sex-Role Concepts and Attitudes," in Maccoby, Eleanor (editor). *Development of Sex Differences*. Palo Alto: Stanford University Press, 1966.

4. KYSELKA, WILLIAM. "A Young Man in a Nursery School," Childhood Education, XLII, 5 (1966).

5. MCCANDLESS, BOYD. Personal communication.

6. MENDELSON, ANNA. "A Young Man Around the Class," Young Children, XXVII, 5 (June 1972).

7. MISCHEL, WALTER. "Social Learning View of Sex Differences in Behavior," in *Development of Sex Differences.*

8. MURGATROYD, RAYMOND. "A Man Among Six-Year-Olds," in Childhood Education, XXXII, 3 (1955).

9. SCIARRA, DOROTHY J. "The Behavior of Male Volunteers in Child Care Centers." Unpublished doctoral dissertation, University of Cincinnati, 1972.

10. WILLIAMS, BRUCE, and JOHNSTON, JOHN. "Men in Young Children's Lives," Childhood Education, XLVII, 3 (1970).

4

MEN AND MEN

The masculine role permits only certain types of intimacy among men. While some of us find that our relationships with other men as teammates, co-workers, or as participants of male social groups are supportive and meaningful to us, others of us feel deeply unsatisfied, and want stronger relationships with other men than the traditional masculine role allows.

Why have our relationships with other men been so limited? One reason lies in the masculine need for getting ahead. It is in the eyes of other men that we are judged to be a success or a failure. Most of us are in real or imagined competition with other men for the rewards society offers. For most of us, it is important to know what other men think of us—how competent a worker, how good a friend, how responsible a family man we are. In almost everything we do, male culture encourages us to compare ourselves with other men, and to see them as a standard showing what we should be able to do. No wonder we are so often uneasy with other men. The hierarchical or authority relationships among men, which reflect this process of comparison, make intimacy even more awkward and uncomfortable.

Another barrier makes it difficult for us to be open with each other even when we want to. The masculine role, which suppresses emotional expression generally, especially limits the expression of feeling among men. Touch, for example, is acceptable among men in only a few special ways—a handshake, a pat on the back, an arm around the shoulder. Most men in the United States do not feel comfortable hugging another man. In general, we do not feel comfortable expressing our emotions with other men. Often, we simply do not realize or pay attention to how we feel about each other. "About a Month Ago" tells of two men on a camping trip who could only relate easily after a woman joined them—a common enough pattern in men's relationships with each other.

For many of us, feelings of warmth toward one another are particularly difficult to express. Much of this reluctance relates to fears about sexuality among men. Because of our fear of homosexuality, we sometimes react negatively to close friendships in other men, as Joseph LaBonte describes in the response of others to his relationship with another man in prison. These negative reactions often have to be dealt with by men who are seeking closer intimacy with each other. But in addition to these reactions, we must also deal with the fears inside ourselves about what it means for other men to be important to us, and for us to be important to them.

Don Clark has found confrontations with feelings about homosexuality useful in the all-male personal growth groups he has conducted, and notes that "it would be a strange men's group in which they did not surface." Some of us, in overcoming the traditional barriers in male relationships, are exploring sexual sharing with other men. Jeff Keith, describing his own emotional and sexual relations, asks "How to love those around me, both men and women?" Many of us are still working out in our own lives just what degree of emotional and sexual intimacy we want with others, both male and female. However each of us works this out, many of us already know that the traditional masculine role allows much less emotional expression with other males than we want, and that we must seek more.

About a Month Ago

Michael C.

About a month ago a brother and I spent two weeks together in an isolated mountain cabin. We had been casual friends for a few years, and we shared an apartment for about six months a year ago. I never felt very close to him emotionally. There had been a few occasions when we tried to talk to each other about what we were feeling. Those

---

"About a Month Ago," from *Brother: A Forum for Men Against Sexism* (P. O. Box 4387, Berkeley, Calif. 94704), April 1971, #1, p. 3. Reprinted by permission. This article by itself should not be considered representative of the politics of the staff of *Brother*. Each issue was meant to be seen as a whole.

were always times when there was some kind of crisis in one of our lives, like breaking up with a lover. Those conversations never worked out to much. We had grown apart over a period of months, but then this idea to go to the country came up. I really wanted to get away for a while, and I welcomed a chance to spend some time alone with another man. I wanted to try to break down some of the barriers which kept us apart. We would have a lot of time to work and play, and I thought that our closeness would probably develop spontaneously out of the situation.

We went to the cabin, but it didn't work out that way. We had a really good time, but I didn't feel any emotional kinship growing up among us. We remained very individualistic. There was a certain amount of competition over who had the best knack for building fires. We never built them together. Each of us took separate responsibility for parts of the meals. When we built an outhouse a conflict developed over the proper way to do it. I thought I knew the logical way to build it, and he had a very strong image of how he wanted it to be. In these discussions the disagreement was greater than the issue of construction. It was a conflict of dominance.

We played cards a lot at night. I was really into winning. When we talked we spent a lot of words exchanging information. When we started to get into our thoughts and ideas and feelings, I never felt like I was all there, and I felt a similar kind of restraint or repression in him. It wasn't really much different from our previous relations. It wasn't all that different from most male friendships I know.

During the last weekend we were there a woman joined us. We both knew her well. The situation changed. I reacted very strongly to a suggestion he made while I was rebuilding the fire one night. It brought to the surface a lot of low level antagonism that had been building up during our stay. We were able to talk about that: where it came from, how it got repressed, why it came out. Why didn't we build fires together?

We got into an argument about collectivization. She thought it was ridiculous to impose an act of will on such petty behavior. Tensions between her and me coming out of our particular relationship made me want to drop out of a very antagonistic kind of argument. But she and my other friend continued. I started listening carefully to what he said, where he was coming from, who he was. In the course of that discussion I felt much closer to him than I had the whole time we had been there. Something about the situation brought him out, and brought us together.

As long as it was just the two of us, two men, we remained distant. We were unwilling to put out much energy, or attention, or emotion to each other. We were unwilling to expose ourselves in much of a real way. We were unable to put enough of ourselves into an interaction to really feel each other's presence. But then, when the woman was present we both changed our whole way of being. We became involved in what we said. We were committed. I could feel his presence. I could see him much more clearly.

In the course of the next few weeks I started to reflect upon what this incident meant more generally. In my life I find I look to women for virtually all my close relationships. I am much more willing to commit something of myself to a relationship with a woman. I look to women for the impetus to grow and change emotionally. When I meet two new people, when one is a man and one is a woman, I invariably seek out a friendship with the woman. I put a great deal of energy into cultivating her friendship. I feel very good if she responds.

Conversely, I tend to ignore the man. I put very little energy out to get to know him. I don't care whether he responds to me or not. Not only does this way of living put an incredibly distorted load upon relationships with women, but it also causes me to completely ignore relationships with other men. This is the behavior that has kept us apart. I feel that I don't know how to talk to men except on a very superficial level. I think this arises out of the situation of not trying very hard, not being able to be close to men, and not feeling much growth or satisfaction from relationships with men.

I need a new context in which to be with men. We need to struggle together. Just struggling with women is not enough for me. That perpetuates the same habits that keep me distant from other men; habits which cause me to always return to women for succor and warmth. I have found that meeting regularly with other men is helping me to grow and survive. The group can become a commitment of time and energy and emotion that is devoted wholly to brothers. I am paying attention to men for the first time. It feels great.

Peaches and Me: A Story from Prison

Joseph LaBonte

JOSEPH LABONTE *is now twenty-three years old and has been out of jail for three years. He was born in Beverly, Massachusetts, where he still resides. He comes from a family of seven children, six of whom are*

Joseph LaBonte, "Peaches and Me: A Story from Prison," *Boston Phoenix*, May 22, 1973. Reprinted by permission.

now living. His father, though, has been dead six years. He is painting in oils as well as other media, but intends to continue his writing career. He now assists in running a rooming house called The Mackerel Cove Lodge.

It all started in early May, 1970. I was serving a six month sentence for breaking and entering into a house. One afternoon about one o'clock a new inmate came into the jail at which I happened to be, to await an appeal of a two-and-one-half-year sentence for using a motor vehicle without proper authority and various other charges. After he had changed from street clothes to prison dungarees and striped shirt he was put on the tier directly above me; that is when I found out his name was Ray.

When he was in jail prior to this time he said everyone called him Peaches. I couldn't understand why a person in jail would be called Peaches, but I found out why after talking to Ray, who was 18 years of age and very good looking. It seems that Ray has very soft skin (just like a peach). A person like that has to be very careful in jail. He told me that he had just been in another jail in Salem ten days before he arrived here. During his three-months' stay there other inmates tried to force him into homosexual acts; he refused, naturally. He was finally released into his own custody, but once again he was in trouble with the law and he went back to jail.

It turned out that when they put Ray above me it was really a good thing, for when we got together we started to become friends. Of course, Ray hesitated at first because of what the other jail inmates tried to do. After talking to him for a week he got to trust me some. He told me his father was in a state prison and that his mother did not really care about him, so Ray didn't have anyone. He seldom received letters or visits from anyone. Seeing this, I felt sorry for him; it's hard enough doing time without being alone. I said to myself, "I'm going to help Ray as much as I can." But the most I could do was talk to him as often as possible and see to it that he had cigarettes and enough books to read. I told him I would try my best to get him a radio. It wouldn't be easy because usually you would have to buy one from another inmate. I happened to be lucky. I got one off a friend of mine who was going home, and gave it to Ray. He was really happy. He trusted me after that, and finally realized that I wanted to help him and be his friend, and was not seeking sex acts. After that our friendship increased. At first I wasn't sure if Ray cared for me or not, or if he was using me to satisfy his wants and needs. He told me many times that he really cared but I still wasn't sure.

I was asked to work in the kitchen which would mean moving to another part of the jail, plus being away from Ray all the time. I was hesitant in answering but I wanted to go in the kitchen and try and cook. It would keep me busy and out of trouble but taking the job proved to be a mistake because after I was in the kitchen for about a month I got wind of a story. It seemed Ray started getting bothered by some inmates about doing some homosexual acts, but I never found out if it really happened.

The next week, Ray was working in the kitchen with me; of course it took a lot of talking to the right people but it paid off. It was fun working in the kitchen, eating all we wanted and keeping busy working about 13 hours a day. At night Ray and I would talk for an hour or so about what we were going to do when we got out. I told Ray I would be going home with my mother and he said he was going home for a while but he didn't think he would stay there, because his mother did not really care about him. But about 3 weeks after talking about going home we both came out of the kitchen and went back on a tier to just hang around.

A day in jail could be very boring. You couldn't do anything, so we talked most of the time and we played cards together. A regular day in jail starts at 7 o'clock for breakfast in the dining room and then we are locked back in our cells until 9. At 9, we get unlocked for work which would mean sweeping, mopping tiers, washing bars or really any kind of cleaning. After work, we hang around till 11 and time for dinner. After dinner, it's back on the tier until shower time which is any time between 12 and 1. After showers we hang around until 4 and then back in the dining room. After supper we stay on the tier and watch T.V., play cards, ping pong or just read until 8 and then it's lockup time. Usually when I get locked in, I read or listen to my radio until they tell me to shut off my light which would be 10 at night. We had plenty of time for ourselves, which with Ray and myself is taken up by talk. People probably wonder what two men can talk about every day. Most of it is about the jail, but we talked about sports, girls and getting out which for me was to be soon. One day after the mail was passed out, I found Ray crying in his cell and I didn't know why. I tried to talk to him but to no avail, except that he showed me a letter he had just received from his mother. After reading the letter I found out why Ray was so upset. It seems his mother didn't want anything to do with him. She told him not to bother writing or coming home when he got out. I tried to comfort him. After a while he stopped crying and we started talking about the letter. There wasn't much I could tell him except that it might turn out all right and maybe I could talk to my mother about the possibility of Ray coming home to live with us and become part of our family. I told him not to count on it but that I would talk to my mother next time she came up to see me and that I would try to explain the situation to her and find out if it was possible. Two weeks later, I received my visit. I was never happier in my life to see my mother as I was that day and she really couldn't understand why I was so happy. I explained to her all about Ray being my closest friend, in fact he was more of a brother to me and it would mean a lot to me to have Ray in the family. After she thought for a while she said she didn't want to say yes or no just yet, but that she would think it over and I agreed with her. I asked her about visiting both of us next time she came up so that she could meet Ray and find out what kind of person he was. I said, "I think you'll like him. I do. In fact without any doubt in my mind I can say I've grown to love him very much and I'm very fond of him."

To me it's very hard to put in words how I feel emotionally about Ray. He always brightened my day whenever I was with him and it made him happy when I was happy so we had a good friendly relationship. I hoped it would never end. I don't want to give the wrong idea. This was not a homosexual relationship but more of a brotherly relationship because we didn't have any kind of sex. I didn't want any sex and Peaches didn't either so we're both happy.

But, good things don't last. After being together for so long, the jail master thought that something was going on as far as sex between Peaches and myself so he separated us. I went to talk to the jail master to find out what was going on and he told me that he had heard stories about Peaches and myself and that it would be best to keep us apart, for the benefit of the jail. In what way he meant "for the benefit of the jail" I'll probably never know. I didn't give up though. I kept trying to get moved back with Ray but to no avail. Every time I talked to the master he said, "I'll never put you back on the same tier for as long as you're here." Every time he said that I felt like crying because I couldn't see how a man with so little understanding or knowledge of any kind of needs of a prisoner could get the job he has. Everyone in jail has a friend that he can tell anything he wants to without it getting back all over the jail. I think you know how I feel. There are some things you can tell a person and he understands and other people wouldn't or couldn't. This is how Ray and I were. We could tell each other anything without worrying about embarrassment or it getting back to the wrong people. I talked to a lot of the inmates and most of the guards about the way the master kept Peaches and me apart; most of them felt the same way I do about the need of a friend, especially Ray because he didn't have anyone on the outside and he depended on me to be with him when he needed me. For one man to stop Ray from being with the one person that really cares for him was a crime in itself.

Don't get me wrong, I really care for Ray. I love him very much and I'm going to help him in any way I can to become a good citizen, but I can't help thinking that what happened between Ray and me is probably happening in other jails, to other kids, young kids that need help, who need the love from a friend because they never got the love from their family. They are asking us for help and love, and the judge and probation officers put them in reform school or jail; and when they get there a lot of them find a friend they can trust and a friendly, brotherly love that everyone needs but the masters keep them apart because they think sex is involved. I know that in some cases sex is involved but to condemn everyone for a minority of the friendships is wrong. And it's about time someone told people about how politicians run our jails and guards and masters of our penal system. I don't think they care about our young people. I don't want you to think I'm a radical or something but I'm only 20 years old and this was my third time in jail—and it will be my last. I found the love and trust I need in a fellow human being and I thought that even if Ray and I didn't get back on the same tier it would not really matter because we would always have the love and trust for each other no matter where we were. But what about the rest of the kids left in reform schools and jails? Will they have a chance to find their friend and the love everyone needs to survive or will they end up in state prison for most of their lives because no one would help them?

I was lucky I found Ray and he found me and we became good friends before the master could stop us.

My Own Men's Liberation

Jeff Keith

JEFF KEITH, *age 29, has been a Quaker freak active in the radical peace movement since 1963. Raised in Louisville, Kentucky, now living in Massachusetts. Gentle, intense, and introspective. His father died not long ago and he felt relief. This article was written soon after the final breakup of his marriage, which caused him great pain. Now he's fairly happy and gay. Loves apple trees and gentle radical men. Joins his feminist sisters in a common struggle.*

I feel a real need to express some of my thoughts on men's liberation (liberation from male chauvinism and oppressive dehumanizing sex roles).

I have always felt a very strong opposition to differentiating people along the lines of biological sex—that is, according to people's having

---

Jeff Keith, "My Own Men's Liberation," *WIN Magazine,* September 1, 1971, pp. 22–26. Reprinted by permission.

been born male or female. I suppose this was because I saw myself as somewhere in between: not identifying with the male stereotype but certainly not feeling feminine, either. My opposition to sex roles came in large part from my own psychological make-up, and caused me a lot of pain and alienation. Only later did I discover that a lot of people were uneasy and unfulfilled fitting into the stereotyped masculine role, and that I am much better off being outside it.

In the early patterns of my parents and the adults around me, I saw men as being cold disciplinarians and women as being warm, loving, nurturing people. I knew I wanted to be a loving person who was liked by others, and not a cruel disciplinarian on one hand while being a "good socializer" when drunk on the other hand. This was how I saw my father.

However, there were some things about being a boy that I liked—especially being given more freedom than girls got, and not having to be constantly afraid of getting raped by strange men. I also got to see as time went on that some women were very domineering and aggressive (like my mother's mother) whereas some men were kind and fairly gentle though still "masculine." It was this latter type that I hoped I would be like, although it was a sharp difference from what my father was like.

Maybe it was having both sisters and brothers that made me learn to treat both sexes equally. I never related very well to all-boy games, but instead was much happier in sexually mixed situations. I was pushed around and oppressed both by my older sister and by a cousin who was older.

I didn't want to be dominant and pushy because I learned at an early age (probably from my mother) that domineering people may get their way on a superficial level but they don't get love or acceptance on any deep level. I wanted to have friends and be well-liked by girls, and so I knew I shouldn't let myself be identified very strongly with "those dirty nasty boys."

> "Little girls are made of sugar and spice and everything nice.
> Little boys are made of snips and snails and puppy dogs' tails."

Sexual ambivalence never got me in very much trouble until I was in junior high and began discovering my own awakening sexuality. Now I was no longer sexually dormant but I was one of those nasty, aggressive things called a boy (and soon to be, horror of horrors, a man). I had a girlfriend that I liked a lot and saw very often for over two years but was afraid to touch in any way. Genital stimulation was something filthy that I did with a couple of friends or else did, much to my own shock and shame, in dark corners when I was alone. Having an orgasm certainly had nothing to do with love or any of the good and warm aspects of life.

Eventually I found that girlfriend to be too simple-minded and boring, and I broke off the relationship. During my three years of senior high school, I had crushes on several girls, but I couldn't picture touching them or having any sort of sexual involvement. After all, sex was filthy. One did it only with prostitutes and later, magically, felt like doing it with one's wife.

Many guys I knew did get involved in things like "going steady," necking, taking girls to drive-ins, and so forth, but I always saw the men in those situations being in the superior, aggressive role which I wanted no part of. I found a couple of friends who thought as I did, and we privately ridiculed all the sex games going on around us.

Sex with women might be wicked, but sex with men was unimaginable and mysterious. If two men wanted to be sexual with each other, obviously one would have to be more feminine, a "fairy"—that's what I picked up from my reading somehow. I knew I didn't want to imitate a girl—after all, I was a boy of some sort even though a very alienated and unhappy one.

I was very interested and curious about my own developing body and those of my close friends. Any close male friends I had were ones I had no sexual feelings toward. Homosexuality was dirty and perverted, something done by "fairies" and I didn't want to be "perverted" since I was so different and alienated already.

I had always done a fair amount of very lonely and ashamed masturbating. I loved the feeling and was intrigued by my male body. I wanted to see if other guys felt similarly to me, but I was afraid to ask. Premarital sex with girls wasn't "nice," and I wanted to be a nice person, gentle and friendly towards women. Friendships come between equals *not* between a superior and an inferior or between a hunter and his prey. I wanted to be a friend of women, not a hunter.

In the twelfth grade, after some incredible unhappiness, loneliness, and switching of high schools, I began somehow to get out of myself and make some genuine friends, both male and female. I felt really close to three friends—Dick, Holly, and Justine.

With Holly and Justine this was all right because they were female, but with Dick it was very confusing because he was male. A further complicating factor was that I could spend the night at Dick's house but not at Holly's or Justine's. By this time I was really getting overwhelmed with the desire to be loving and sexual with someone. Society seemed to be conspiring to throw me together with Dick constantly, whereas if I had been with Justine or Holly that much, I would be identified with all those dirty jokes and unspeakable sex games.

Both Dick and I desperately wanted to have some sort of physical contact with each other, and that was completely impossible for me to imagine. Since I was not "feminine," I must be "masculine" and he must be "feminine." But he wasn't any more feminine than I was. What gives? I had always been taught that everyone was either feminine or masculine, dominant or submissive, a leader or a follower.

Wanting to be neither a masculine-aggressive-leader nor a feminine-passive-follower with my friend Dick, and being very confused by the sexual potential of our relationship, I broke off this very precious friendship and talked to him almost none at all for a year and a half. Both of us remained close friends with Justine, Holly, and our other mutual friends, so I saw him frequently although I was afraid to talk to him.

After a few months, we all graduated from high school and went to different colleges, where we had to begin all over again to make new friendships. At Reed College, I felt constant urges towards reaching out sexually to both men and women, which frustrated me tremendously. I did succeed in having interesting but disappointing relationships with a few girls. Since I didn't want to be aggressive or dominant, the sexual relationships were kind of unusual and confusing. Luckily none of them went as far as intercourse, or I would have gotten even more confused.

I had long-distance relationships with a couple of girls, seeing them only at holiday vacation seasons. One, Georgeanne, was very interesting and free of dominance-submission roles, but she was engaged to be married. The other, my old friend Justine, was extremely dissatisfying to me because I hated that leader role and could not get her to keep relating to me as a human being once we got into the habit of "making out" with each other. I hung on to her a long time because I was becoming very afraid of my "inadequacies" in the sexual area.

At the end of the year, I dropped out of college and worked in a couple of different situations in Eastern cities. I made several close friends but was confused about how to include sex in the friendships. I was again in touch with my friend Dick, and I had a sort of non-sexual infatuation for a guy named Jay whose long-distance girlfriend I also felt close to. After a while I began having sexual fantasies about Jay, since he had such an extremely handsome and graceful body. He was very kind and warm to me, but warned me that if I ever tried to be sexual with him our friendship would end. Needing the friendship so much, I never thought of touching him, although our emotional closeness was really wonderful. At one point someone referred to me as a "dirty little faggot" for the way I acted around Jay.

My friend Dick had some sort of one-night-stand homosexual thing once, and really liked it but wouldn't talk much about it. I really loved him, in a non-sexual way. I wanted to relate physically with women, but emotionally I treated all my female friends similarly to the way I treated Dick and Jay. Many women around me felt that I was not interested in sex since I was so unaggressive about it.

I got into Quakerism and pacifism and developed an awareness of how nice gentleness and patience were. But how did these relate to getting sexual fulfillment? The society around me was constantly telling me that the only way to find a sexual partner was to be aggressive —"masculine"—a hunter. But I knew that both aggressive and helpless submissive people were really upsetting to me and not what I wanted in a friend and a lover.

A girlfriend, Janie, was the first one I had intercourse with (I was 20 and she was 22). She enjoyed sex a lot and pursued it rather vigorously though not too much so for me. We were very attached to each other for a few months but then something went wrong— I felt she was getting too dependent and weak. That relationship was very intense, but it was sorely tested by my going to prison for draft resistance, and it didn't pass the test.

I got very emotionally involved in the prison world and could not handle an intense, very exclusive relationship with someone who wasn't there with me. I made several close friends, but of course I never imagined having sex with them, since the prevailing prison ethic said that all sexuality was either extremely aggressive or extremely passive. Many of the other inmates told me I was attractive to them sexually, but I couldn't imagine getting involved in sex in prison throughout most of my year there.

As time went on, I met two guys in prison who openly said they were homosexual but were neither very feminine nor very masculine. I became fairly good friends with one of these just a month before I was released, and I felt very attracted to him in some undefinable way. A couple of years after I was released, I had quite a few dreams about having sex with him.

After prison, I went to Antioch College, which I felt was a wonderfully free and open environment. I wanted very much to find a heavy girlfriend, and after a few months I met J. I had always felt that I was incomplete unless I was relating sexually to a woman, and now that J. and I were together, I felt really good. I was no longer expected to relate sexually to womankind in the abstract, since I had a specific lover to focus myself on. How can I describe that feeling of being so much in love? We were really good for each other, so open and candid.

Neither of us was exclusively a leader and neither was a follower. We sometimes fought like cats and dogs over who was forcing whom to do something and who was robbing the other of spontaneity. She was always resentful of the fact that during intercourse I seemed to be taking and never giving—no matter how much I wanted to please her, it seemed impossible through the pattern of conventional sexual intercourse.

Her resentment and my uneasiness in sexuality naturally spilled over from the bedroom into the rest of our life together. She was less used to making decisions for herself than I was, and she would often hesitate so long that I would get impatient and finally do something decisive myself. My ideal was that all decisions should be mutual agreements arrived at through discussions. I didn't believe in insisting on my own way, but somehow this seemed to be what was constantly happening. J. likewise resented the pattern, but was not willing to be quicker at making decisions. This went on and on and was a real problem.

J. and I lived together in Ohio and then New York, and after nine months of this our sex life was really a mess. I really enjoyed intercourse and was quite upset when she continued not to enjoy it and to accuse me of being only out for my own gratification. I had this incredibly strong feeling that I could only be fulfilled if I was having a sexual relationship with a woman. When sex between J. and me began to go bad (or, when I began to become aware of how messed up it was), I felt again unfulfilled, angry, and confused, and I began having more homosexual fantasies.

I found a very explicit homosexual novel that, although romantic, unreal, and almost pornographic, appealed to me a lot. J. and I decided to be apart for a month and I went to visit the Pacific Northwest, where I had several friends. It happened that my friend Dick was then living in Seattle. When I visited him, we had a week-long sexual affair which I enjoyed very much but which confused me a lot. We had known each other for almost six years and agreed that our relationship should have been sexual long before this.

Losing my "homosexual virginity," I panicked and went rushing back across the continent to my messy relationship with J. Lately she and I had been having serious hassles about contraception, with her refusing to take pills which she knew were causing weird changes in her body chemistry. Very soon after we got back together—almost before we knew what was happening—she was pregnant. Since I had a very strong urge to be a parent and she didn't want to raise the baby alone, we got married.

In getting pregnant and then married, J. was again indecisive and let my stronger feelings determine how she made up her mind. I didn't fight against this very strongly except to say intellectually that she should take responsibility for her own decisions. On one hand she would find it very hard to deal with me in any kind of equal way, when I wanted to make strong decisions by mutual agreement. Thus I felt forced to dominate sometimes, for my own sanity. But then on the other hand she would resent my leadership and argue and fight with me about it.

Eventually, as sex continued to be messy, she decided she wanted no more sexual intercourse for an indefinite period. She also said she wasn't sure she had made the right decision of who to marry, and had only been pressured due to the pregnancy. With her now taking all these heavy, aggressive actions, I reacted by becoming weak, getting passively overwhelmed by her and resentful of the whole situation. Somehow we were both sick and tired of cooperating with each other, and we just wanted to sort out our own heads without interference from our supposed marriage partner.

We struggled on unhappily for over a year, being thought of as married by the world but not feeling really "married" in any sense of the word. The superficial structure of our life was wonderfully free of sex roles: we tried to split up the care of our daughter half and half, as well as the earning money, cooking, cleaning house, and getting firewood for winter. She fixed and drove the car while I didn't know how to drive but was willing to go shopping and do the laundry.

Our life looked really beautiful, except for the fact that we had very little real love or understanding for each other. She continued to be domineering and I continued to be weak and resentful. As time went on, I was away from home more and more, and had closer friends on my own than I had near the home where I was supposedly married to J.

My friend Dick lives several hundred miles away from me and he lives in the city while I really enjoy living in the country. We had a very sporadic sexual relationship for a while during my hard times with J., but finally we gave that up since we lived so far apart. Then I had a relationship right near home with a guy named Joe, who was physically very fine but emotionally extremely unsatisfying to me. Finally through Dick I made contact with a movement called the Gay Liberation Front which I really liked.

As my marital relationship continued to break up, I tried to find women to get sexually involved with, but eventually I decided that was a very unnatural thing for me to do. The more natural thing for me to do was to get into homosexual relationships where I could finally be free of the sex roles that were so oppressive to me. Eventually (Spring, 1971), J. and I decided to stop calling ourselves married and to live apart. I decided to be exclusively homosexual and see how I liked it. It is a tremendous relief now to be no longer trying to relate sexually with women.

A drawback to saying I am homosexual is that I have supposedly said I would not relate sexually with women. But I am aware that intense, loving friendships can lead to sexual involvements, and I am certainly not prepared to stop being very close friends with women. Thus it seems that the label "homosexual" is a very inadequate one to describe me (but it is certainly better than the label "heterosexual"). Although I feel that in the past six weeks I have been honest about my sexual/emotional desires for the first time in my life, I have felt drawn to some of the women I have met during that time, too.

The Gay Liberation Front has a saying, "Free the sister in ourselves." I really like that. There is so much inside me that has been repressed and bottled up for so long due to my trying to be "masculine." Inability to cry or show my emotions very strongly, feeling that I am somehow better off if I stay cool and aloof, feeling inferior if I am not loud and aggressive, and very self-assertive in public. Being expected not to relate well to children, to be always "dignified" and never to play or be uninhibited. To be cool, uninvolved, in control of certain people (with others in control of me); and a firm believer in the system of leaders and followers, dominance and submission, male masters and female slaves.

Free the sister in myself! How to liberate *all* of myself? How to fit sexuality into the framework of my whole life, to be proud of myself and glad for what I am? How to love those around me, both men and women?

Homosexual Encounter in All-Male Groups

Don Clark

DON CLARK *is a writer, teacher, and clinical psychologist in private practice in San Francisco and Menlo Park, Calif.*

Sex is a pale, undernourished part of self for most Americans. We live in a culture that is phobic in its fear of and obsessive attention to sex. We have learned to feel most comfortable when the sexual aspects of self develop in darkened areas of our being where the light of awareness, understanding, and acceptance rarely penetrates. And of this neglected and distorted part of self called sex, those facets that might be called homosexual are the most carefully hidden.

In working with all-male groups, it has become increasingly clear to me that men need more from one another than they believe they are permitted to have. Expression of positive affect, or affection, between men is seriously inhibited in our culture. Negative affect is acceptable. Men can argue, fight, and injure one another in public view but they cannot as easily hold hands, embrace, or kiss. When emotions in any

---

From Don Clark, "Homosexual Encounter in All-Male Groups," in L. Solomon and B. Berzon, eds., *New Perspectives on Encounter Groups* (San Francisco: Jossey-Bass, 1972), pp. 368–82. Reprinted by permission.

area are blocked in expression they seek other outlets, in distorted form if necessary. Affection between males finds outlet with only mild distortion in such forms as competitive body-contact sports. Some war behavior is probably an outlet for extreme distortions of these feelings.

Encountering homosexuality in all-male groups can be helpful in recovering awareness, understanding, and acceptance of male-male affectional needs. The scarecrow of homosexuality can be appreciated for what it is in the accepting warmth of brotherhood. Uncontaminated homosexuality is nothing more than a sexual expression of affection. Taking other needs and the context of his current life style into consideration, a man can choose whether or not he wishes to express affection sexually. It is one of many possible means that can be used to express affection between men.

Work with real and presumed homosexuality in all-male groups is a constant reminder of the ancient wisdom that in order to be yourself, you must first know yourself. And knowing yourself involves friendly acceptance of all the basic ingredients of self no matter how unattractive they appear when first compared to current community manners and morals. Affection for other males is one basic ingredient of self. Homosexuality is one possible way to express that affection. Fear and misunderstanding have led us to view homosexuality as pathological and have made most expressions of masculine affection seem homosexual. The all-male group is a suitable place for a man to stop running in fear, to search for full awareness of his affection for other males, and to consider all personally satisfying forms of expressing that affection.

I began conducting all-male groups in a college setting in 1968. These groups were for young men who were teaching in disadvantaged urban schools as an alternative to participation in the Vietnam War. They were fondly called "draft-dodger" groups, and when they began no one knew what would happen. I knew only that I would use encounter techniques in conducting the groups and hoped that these inexperienced teachers would get on better terms with their feelings about themselves and their pupils so they could give more energy to the job and not be too separated from their students by barriers of guilt, insecurity, and resentment.

What happened is not very surprising with the wisdom of hindsight. A room full of males paying attention to the here and now began to sort negative and positive feelings. As positive feelings were differentiated, someone mentioned the unmentionable with words like, "You're good looking. I mean, I guess what I'm saying about my feelings is that you're sexy looking to me, and I guess that means you kind of turn me on!" This kind of revelation in turn led to even finer distinctions, such as sometimes wanting to sit next to a particular man or wanting to touch hands, or hug, or put a weary head in his lap.

Sometimes the feeling was relatively nonsexual; sometimes it was obviously sexual.

The group gained skill in differentiating various feelings that have to do with affection and that would ordinarily be lumped together as homosexual and therefore dealt with in hidden ways. In the early weeks a lot of attention was paid to sexual and other affectional feelings, then, gradually, attention went more often to other subjects. Male-male affection remained a matter of concern, however, and the group's acceptance of these feelings accomplished something special.

It seemed to me that the open exploration and acceptance of man to man affectional feelings acted as a catalyst. It was as if, having faced the unmentionable and having made friends with it, we were afraid of nothing. Anything could be brought up in the group, any feelings could be said aloud, anything could be tried. We viewed ourselves as close to emotionally fearless. I had seen some of these same ingredients at work in other encounter groups, but what seemed different in the all-male groups was the pace. We usually met only two hours a week but things sped along. Barriers to communication were unusually weak. Bonds of mutual support were unusually strong.

We spent a lot of time examining male roles. We were aware of cultural definitions for man, teacher, husband, brother, son, father, lover, and friend. Each of us had had those cultural definitions reinforced daily for years. Now we paid attention to self-satisfying definitions of those roles. I remember someone saying, "I don't want to be John Wayne. I want to be the man that is me, but I've been so busy trying to squeeze into the right categories that I don't even know my personal wants."

I began to offer general male groups at various growth centers. These groups were titled *On Being a Man* or *Natural Man.* They were not attempts to immerse participants in consideration of homosexuality but were more an outgrowth of the early draft-dodger groups in the college. They were designed to facilitate a kind of male liberation, where a man could consider the difference between cultural definitions of various male roles and his own needs, expectations, and satisfactions in those roles. It was also a natural place to take a good here-and-now look at male-male relationships, and the inevitable talk of homosexuality performed its usual catalytic magic for the group.

With more experience in these groups, I became aware of how much damage is done to the average male by the fear of homosexuality and by the complex misunderstanding of the phenomenon in our culture. Many men who think of themselves as homosexual or bisexual are not liberated by their ability to make sexual contact with other men. They have been told repeatedly that they are abnormal, sick, depraved, wicked, perverted, handicapped, immature, disgusting, and generally not up to expected human standards. Some of this negativism is incorporated into self-concept and distorts relationships with other men and with women. Men are apt to be treated as sex objects and women as objects of fear and complex fantasy. (One man said, "My wife never knew she was sleeping with an enemy alien all those years.") But we have all been taught to expect anyone with admitted homosexual interests to be damaged, so these kinds of observations were not so surprising even when they emerged in the mixed (gay and straight) groups.

The big surprises came with clearer understanding of the straight or supposedly nonhomosexual men. With saddening regularity they described how much they wanted to have closer, more satisfying relationships with other men: "I'd settle for having one really close man friend. I supposedly have some close men friends now. We play golf or go for a drink. We complain about our jobs and our wives. I care about them and they care about me. We even have some physical contact—I mean, we may even give a hug on a big occasion. But it's not enough."

In one group, a huge, soft-spoken Texan who had described himself as a Little League father asked an aggressive middle-aged businessman if he could give him a back rub during the group break time. Half an hour later the businessman was sobbing loudly. When he had gotten to a point where he wanted to talk he told the rest of us that he had flashed a rapid set of mental pictures: his father giving him a nightly ritual back rub in bed that ended abruptly at about age ten with no explanation; a "you hold mine and I'll hold yours" sex play scene with a playmate at about age six; comforting a close Navy buddy in his arms a few hours after he had been wounded and a few days before he died; and sitting in the living room at home looking at his eleven-year-old son and not knowing how to touch him.

His face fell into a mask of mourning as he said, "I've pushed away the wanting because of a scared feeling that it was wrong. Now my dad's dead, my buddy's dead, I never even got to know that kid back home, and my son and I are afraid to touch each other." He started to cry again, turned to the Texan, and said, "If you don't think I'm crazy already, you sure will now, because all I want to say to you, Bill, is 'thanks.' Things may turn out different for my son."

An ex-star of college football turned long-hair dropout asked for six volunteers who would be willing to stand nude in a small circle around him. He said, "I want to shut my eyes and really get into it and see if there's any part of me that wants to get it on with men."

Later he was laughing and saying, "Far out! You know when I was playing ball there was always the locker room fooling around, but all we ever did was slap one another on the ass sometimes. For the last year I've gotten really close to some dudes and wondered what it would be like to make it with one of them—you know, just to give him pleasure because the vibes are good between us. But just now I flashed how important and at the same time absurdly unimportant it all is. I really got into touching you guys, and I didn't turn to stone, man. I got turned on once or twice and it was a groove. I didn't have to do anything and I didn't have to stop myself from doing anything. I could just be there and let the feelings flow back and forth."

He closed his eyes for a quiet moment and a smile spread on his face. "It's beautiful. I can be me with you, and with you, and with you, and whatever is between us is there and we can just let it be. That skin over tight muscle is a whole different trip than a chick. It's like with guys I've been walking around with my eyes tight shut with all kinds of 'should' and 'shouldn't' in my head because I was afraid that if I got into my feelings with dudes I'd find out I was queer or that I had no feelings at all. It's far out! I learned it so long ago with chicks—you know, that you only have to listen to what's there between you and flow with it and not hassle about it and nobody gets hurt."

The theme, sounded time after time, is: "A large segment of my feelings about other men are unknown or distorted because I am afraid they might have something to do with homosexuality. Now I'm lonely for other men and don't know how to find what I want with them."

The spectre of homosexuality seems to be the dragon at the gateway to self-awareness, understanding, and acceptance of male-male needs. If a man tries to pretend the dragon is not there by turning a blind eye to erotic feelings for all other males, he also blinds himself to the rich variety of feelings that are related. If he offers himself up as victim to the dragon by owning awareness and saying "therefore I am queer," he plunges into a type of homosexuality that may be physically gratifying but keeps him occupied with the dragon at the gate (usually compulsively searching for sexual contacts) and just as estranged from the self-awareness, understanding, and acceptance that await him on the other side of the gate.

The dragon need not be at the gate. It is a monster that has been created by our society. Homosexuality is a reality but it need not be a monster. Since it is firmly chained to the gate at this point in the evolution of our culture, however, a man has few choices. He can blind himself to the dragon and be blind to what lies beyond the gate. He can stand far back from the dragon and settle for awareness that there is a barrier between himself and the gate that he is unwilling to confront. He can compulsively interact with the dragon. Or he can confront the dragon—find strength to admit homoerotic impulses, admit that he is a beautiful and impressive dragon (valued along with other things life has to offer, in addition) and pass through the gateway to self-awareness, understanding, and acceptance. The man who has confronted the dragon and tamed him with honesty admits to the dragon's power and beauty and explains that he is also interested in the riches that lie beyond the gate.

All-male groups, whether gay or mixed, question basic assumptions about masculinity. Each man is offered help in finding what he has to give and what he wants to receive from other men as a way of increasing his understanding and acceptance of self. He is offered support in tracking down his homosexual feelings and separating them from other masculine affectional feelings so that they can be experienced in perspective. To some men, a surprising by-product is more satisfying interaction with women and children. The most obvious probable reason is that he comes to each relationship less disguised in restrictive he-man roles and is thereby less likely to encourage reaction in equally restrictive roles.

Apparently, homosexual self-understanding (which is accompanied by understanding of a wide spectrum of male-male affectional needs) is a necessary facet of male liberation. (My work in mixed groups of females and males leads me to suspect that the same is true for women.) It is a necessary step in throwing off the yoke of society's voice saying, "If you want to be a man you must . . . you should . . . you dare not." Such self-understanding is a necessary step toward manhood if that state implies having all parts of emotional self intact and available. Homosexual encounter is useful in any all-male growth group, and it would be a strange men's group in which it did not surface.

5

MEN AND WORK

"What do you want to be when you grow up, little man?" The right answer, as most boys know, is not "happy," "healthy," or "a husband." School, parents, the media, and others tell us clearly enough: what we are supposed to be when we "grow up" is a worker of one kind or another. Having a good job is the way to have a good life, and we can't start too soon to prepare.

Work is the institution that most defines the majority of adult males. Many of us look to work for our basic sense of worth. If we are lucky, we may find the work satisfying in itself. Or we may have pride at holding a position that is respected. Or we may simply take satisfaction at earning the money a job provides. On the other hand, we may, as many do, find the work not meaningful, the position not esteemed, and the wages not satisfying—and suffer accordingly.

As men, the desire to do good work, hold a respected position, or earn good money follows from learning as boys that it is important to get ahead. The physical, social, and academic skills on which we assessed ourselves as boys translate into jobs that line us up in the adult hierarchy of worth. Our need to take a place in this work hierarchy serves the institutions of society well. The welfare of an economic institution, and most others, depends upon having people to produce something and people to consume it. Men's work meets well these institutional needs. But to what extent does the work of men promote men's own real needs, and how much does it simply fulfill a masculine image?

Money appears the most compelling reason to work. But the fact is that we do not know how much money we really need. Our notion, in the United States, of a "proper standard of living" is greatly inflated by desires created by institutions with something to sell. Institutions use the masculine image to help create desires. Our learned need to get ahead makes us vulnerable to the appeals of advertising to buy our way to a better life. Getting ahead comes to be defined as having more things, and so we desire more, not necessarily because of actual need, but partly to fulfill a masculine role expectation. A man should be "a good provider." To provide more goods, which may or may not make for a better life, requires more money. So money itself—regardless of real need—comes to be a symbol of success as a man. In "Measuring Masculinity by the Size of a Paycheck," Robert Gould tells some of the price men pay for this symbolic success.

The need to work goes beyond material or psychic satisfactions of the paycheck. Masculinity is also measured by the prestige and power a position bestows. Academic, business, and political positions often serve, through their influence and status, to enhance the self-esteem of the man who holds them. Michael Silverstein tells how in the university the masculine need to get ahead is turned to intellectual competition and bureaucratic maneuvering for power. Whether for money, prestige, or power, we men work as hard as we do because we have learned that is what we are supposed to do—and learned it so gradually, so subtly, and so long ago that we do not remember we once did not need to work just to feel worthwhile.

At the same time that jobs exploit men's desire to get ahead, they also take advantage of our capacity to stay cool and unemotional. On most jobs, as Fernando Bartolomé notes in his study of executives, "feelings are considered a nuisance." Emotions only get in the way of doing the job. To the institution, of course, the job is the important thing; the welfare of the individual is necessarily secondary to getting the job done. Institutions have defined jobs so as to generally separate our work and our emotional lives.

Some of us are searching for new ways to work that will more fully express ourselves rather than our learned desire for masculinity. We are reducing our material standards of what it takes for a good life while raising our nonmaterial standards. Needing less money gives us more choice with our time and effort. We *can* find ways to work with involvement, with cooperation, and in emotional contact with self and others.

Measuring Masculinity by the Size of a Paycheck

Robert E. Gould, M.D.

Is Bobby Murcer a $100,000 ballplayer? Did Tom Seaver earn a raise above his $120,000 off his 21–12 record? How much is rookie Jon Matlack worth on the open market?
—Lead paragraph from a *New York Post* news story, January 10, 1973.

DR. ROBERT E. GOULD *is Professor of Psychiatry, N.Y. Medical College and Director of Out-Patient Psychiatry, Metropolitan Hospital. His research, articles and special areas of interest include problems of adolescents such as suicide, drugs, delinquency; cultural and social class influence on the individual; preventive and community psychiatry programs.*

Currently Dr. Gould is studying changing sexual and sociocultural roles of men and women and their effects on the individual and society. He leads mixed (male and female) consciousness-raising groups as part of his private work.

In our culture money equals success. Does it also equal masculinity? Yes—to the extent that a man is too often measured by his money, by what he is "worth." Not by his worth as a human being, but by what he is able to earn, how much he can command on the "open market."

In my psychiatric practice I have seen a number of male patients through the years, of all ages, who have equated moneymaking with a sense of masculinity. Peter G., for example. He was 23 years old, very inhibited, and socially inept. Raised in a strict, religious home, he had had very little contact with girls and virtually no dating experience until his second year of college. He was sure that no woman would find him attractive unless he was making good money. In analysis it became evident that he was painfully insecure and unsure of his abilities in

---

Robert E. Gould, M.D., "Measuring Masculinity by the Size of a Paycheck," *Ms.*, June 1973, 18ff. Reprinted by permission.

any area. Money was his "cover": if he flashed a roll of bills, no one would see how little else there was to him. He needed expensive clothes, a big sporty car, and a thick wallet; all these were extensions of his penis. Money would show women he could give them what they needed, and thereby get him what he thought he needed, "a beautiful girl with big boobs." His idea that women were essentially passive and looking to be taken care of by a big, strong male demanded that he "make" good money before he could "make" the woman of his dreams.

This kind of thinking is often reinforced by both men and women who have bought the myth that endows a moneymaking man with sexiness and virility, and is based on man's dominance, strength, and ability to provide for and care for "his" woman. We have many cultural models of this unrealistic and frequently self-defeating image of masculinity. Hollywood has gone a long way to reflect and glorify it in such figures as the John Wayne-style cowboy, the private eye, war hero, foreign correspondent, lone adventurer—all "he-men" (a phrase that in its redundancy seems to "protest too much") who use physical strength, courage, and masculine wiles to conquer their worlds, their villainous rivals, and their women. *Money* rarely has anything to do with it.

But in real life in the 1970s, few women have much concern about men like that. After all, there are few frontiers to conquer, or international spy rings to crack, or glorious wars to wage. All that is left for the real-life, middle-class man is the battle for the bulging wallet.

This measure of one's "masculinity quotient" becomes a convenient fallback to those who have a weak sense of self and who doubt their innate ability to attract women. Because it is hard for these men to face their inadequacies and the anxieties that would follow, they strive for money as a panacea for all their personal ills.

For them, money alone separates the men from the boys. I have even seen youngsters drop out of school to make money, just to prove their manhood.

For their part, women have been taught that men who achieve success are the best "catches" in the marriage market. Women have also been taught that the right motives for marriage are love and sexual attraction. Thus, if a woman wants to marry a man with money, she has to believe she loves him; that he is sexually appealing—even if the real appeal is his money. She has to convince herself—and him—that it's the man behind the money that turns her on. Many women *learn* to make this emotional jump: to feel genuinely attracted to the man who makes it big, and to accept the equation of moneymaking power with sexual power.

There are many phenomenally wealthy men in the public eye who are physically unattractive by traditional criteria; yet they are surrounded by beautiful women and an aura of sexiness and virility. A woman in the same financial position loses in attractiveness (at least if she is *earning* the money rather than spending an inheritance); she poses a threat to a man's sense of masculinity. As I once heard a sociologist say: men are unsexed by failure, women by success.

Yet why is it that many men who have met the moneymaking standards are still not sure of their masculinity? Quite simply because money is—and always was—a pretty insecure peg on which to hang a masculine image.

Take Jerry L., a stockbroker. He lost most of his money three years ago during a very bad spell in the market. Distraught as he was over the financial loss, he was devastated over the sexual impotence which followed in its wake. This direct one-to-one relationship may seem awfully pat, but its validity can be attested to by many men (and "their" women) who have gone through serious financial setbacks. Even a temporary inability to provide properly for his family and to justify himself with his checkbook makes such a man feel totally "worthless."

When Jerry L. recouped most of his losses in the course of the next two years, he did *not* regain his previous sexual potency. The experience had made it impossible for him ever again to rely *solely* on money as proof of his masculinity.

The most extreme and dramatic reaction to personal financial loss is suicide. I have seen several men to whom great losses of money represented such a great loss of self, of ego, and ultimately of masculine image, that life no longer seemed worth living.

The situation becomes even more complicated when "the head of the house" is competing against his wife's paycheck as well as his own expectations. Recently, economic realities have made the two-paycheck family respectable. This is tolerable to Jack as long as he can provide for his family and Jill only earns enough to make all the "little extras" possible.

Given current salary inequities, it is unlikely that she will threaten his place as number-one breadwinner. But if she does, if she can make *real money,* she is co-opting the man's passport to masculinity (thus the stereotype of the successful woman being too masculine, too competitive, too unfeminine), and he is effectively castrated.

Thus it is vital that the woman be "kept in her place," which is classically "in the home," so that her second-class status assures him of his first place. Many divorces and breakups that are blamed on "conflict of careers" often mean nothing more than a wife who would not give up her career (and earning ability) in deference to her husband's.

I know plenty of men who are sufficiently "enlightened" intellectually to accept the idea that a woman has as much right (and power) to make money as a man does. But in practice emotionally—when it comes to *their* wives—these men often feel threatened and emasculated. Because he is unable to see this in himself, such a man expresses his anxiety by forcing a "conflict" with the woman in some other area of their relationship, like dealing with in-laws or running the house, where there is, in fact, no conflict. In this way he deflects attention from his problem but also precludes adequate resolution of it in their relationship.

There is one other common male defense against the income-producing woman. No matter how much she makes, he still maintains she doesn't "understand" money, calling upon the stereotyped image of the cute little wife who can't balance the checkbook. He doesn't have to look further for reassurance than the insurance company, for example, that appeals to a husband's protector-provider definition of himself with pictures of helpless widows and children, and the caption "What will happen to them after you're gone?"

Marty B. was caught in this bind. A successful doctor, he divided his time between research, which he found enjoyable but not very rewarding financially, and the practice of internal medicine, which was more lucrative but not so enjoyable. Marty felt it a strain to deal with many diverse people; he was more comfortable with animal research, which also fufilled his creative talents and led to his writing a number of solid scientific papers. So far, so good. But then Marty's wife, Janet, an actress who had had only middling success, became an actors' agent and clicked right away.

Soon, Janet began to earn more money than Marty. At first he joked about it with her and even with close friends, but, as it turned out later, the joking was uneasy, and laden with anxiety. Marty decided to increase his patient practice at the expense of his research. He forced himself to make more money—when he actually needed less, thanks to Janet's high income.

They began quarreling about many small things—arguments without resolutions because they had nothing to do with the real issue: that her new money-making powers were a threat to his masculinity.

Marty and Janet came to see me because they were considering separating after eight years of a happy marriage. After a number of sessions, it became clear that Marty felt that Janet's success meant she didn't need him any more; that he had been diminished as "the man of the house." This was not easy for Marty to admit; he had always claimed he was happy to see Janet doing what she wanted to professionally. But this was the first time he had to face her actually succeeding at it. Marty agreed, with some ambivalence, to go into psychoanalytic therapy. As therapy evolved, his problem with "masculinity" emerged even more clearly. He had never felt comfortable competing with men; this was a contributing factor to his going into animal research. He really received very little gratification from his medical practice, but he needed to make a lot of money to feel competent as a man. He resented Janet's success but since he was not aware that his manhood was threatened, he found "other" things to complain and argue about. After three years of therapy and six months of a trial separation, Marty worked through his problems. Their marriage and Janet's success both survived.

There are many marriages with similar tension that don't survive. Often neither husband nor wife is aware of how profoundly money and masculinity are equated, or of how much a husband's financial security may depend on having a dependent wife.

But are the old rules working as they once did? Increasing numbers of men making good money are not feeling the strong sense of masculinity it used to provide. A man can buy an expensive car and still get stalled in traffic; how powerful does he feel then? Money seems in danger of losing its omnipotence. In a complicated world, the formerly "almighty" dollar has all too few magical properties.

As a result, we may have to begin dealing with the fact that money has been an artificial symbol of masculinity all along, that we invested it with power and that, like brute strength, it can no longer get us where we want to go.

I suspect we will have to give up the whole idea of "masculinity" and start trying to find out about the real male person. We may find that masculinity has more to do with a man's sensitivity, with the nature of his emotional capacity to respond to others, than it has to do with dominance, strength, or ability to "provide for" a woman materially —especially if she isn't pretending to be helpless any more.

Some day soon virility may be the measure of how well a man relates to a woman as an equal, and masculinity will be equated not with moneymaking prowess but with a man's power to feel, express, and give love. That might just possibly be worth much more than money.

Executives as Human Beings

Fernando Bartolomé

MR. BARTOLOMÉ *is Assistant Professor of Business Administration, specializing in organizational behavior, at the Institut Européen d'Administration des Affaires (INSEAD) in Fontainebleau, France. While*

From Fernando Bartolomé, "Executives as Human Beings," *Harvard Business Review,* Nov–Dec 1972, pp. 62–69. Reprinted by permission.

a doctoral student at the Harvard Business School, he conducted the study that forms the basis for this article.

Since man's only possession is his life, or rather his living, man's most fundamental question is, "How will I do my living?" So the search for a meaningful way of being alive should be a central aspect of man's life.

Man should be free from stereotypes, self-imposed or otherwise, and rigid role definitions that limit his existence. The American business executive is, in my opinion, a man caught in a stereotype. He is limited by a role definition obliging him to be super-masculine, super-tough, super-self-sufficient, and super-strong. It allows him very little freedom to be that mixture of strength and weakness, independence and dependence, toughness and tenderness which a human being is.

When one thinks of the executive's situation, several questions come to mind:

How does he relate to himself, to others, and to the world?

Does he conceive of different ways of living his life, different ways of relating to himself, to others, and to the world?

Does he want to live his life differently? Is he tired of being the strong and reliable one, the one who is always on top of things?

The executive, I suspect, has great difficulty conceiving of alternative life styles in realistic terms. But only when he understands and is "tuned in" to these alternatives can he be in a position to choose his own life style.

Not long ago I conducted a study dealing with these questions. At great length I interviewed 40 young executives and their wives. The executives' average age was 37 and they had been married an average of 13 years. Nearly half (19) were employed by large or medium-sized companies, 5 by small companies; 7 were entrepreneurs, and 9 were managers of organizations other than business.

EXPRESSION OF FEELING

In the interviews I conducted, nearly all the men (36) described themselves as seldom experiencing feelings of dependence. While unable to confirm it, I believe they experienced these feelings more often than they acknowledged to themselves. Also, the great majority (32) admitted great reluctance to reveal to their wives their feelings of dependence when they experienced them.

"It's difficult for me to express dependence," said one executive. "Feelings of dependence are identified with weakness or 'untoughness' and our culture doesn't accept these things in men."

With respect to feelings of tenderness, the executives (with one or two exceptions) acknowledged having them often. Nevertheless, they recognized some difficulty in expressing them and great difficulty in full experiencing and sharing of these feelings.

Most of the men acknowledged that their expressions of tenderness were usually limited to members of their families, especially young children. And even displays of tenderness to their children, particularly boys, were inhibited by fear of "smothering" them or making them too dependent on their parents. "Doing things is more important than people," said one executive during an interview. "I want my children to learn to ski well. In skiing one only needs man and hill; nobody else is needed."

With few exceptions, the women I interviewed shared their husbands' reticence in expressing feelings and desire to encourage children's independence. The wife of the executive I just quoted said, "I'm trying to make my children stand on their own feet. I wouldn't express openly my affection for them because I don't want to smother them. I'm quite cold."

During the course of many hours of interviewing and many purely social occasions, I observed little physical contact between couples and their children, although the parents seemed to love them a lot.

To my surprise, I heard very few complaints on the part of husband or wife about the other's inability to express tenderness, even in those cases where I perceived displays of affection to be rather meager and not very rich in form.

Expression of tenderness to outsiders, including friends—especially a man's display of affection or even regard for a male friend—was very difficult for the men. One of them said, "I consider myself a sentimentalist and I think I am quite able to express my feelings. But the other day my wife described a friend of mine to some people as being my best friend and I felt embarrassed when I heard her say it."

On thinking about what these men and women had told me, I emerged with some ideas about the factors that seem to influence their expression of feelings of dependence and tenderness. They include cultural beliefs and job characteristics, which I discuss in the sections that follow.

CULTURAL BELIEFS

All the persons I interviewed mentioned that the Anglo-Saxon culture discourages open and rich expression of emotion—any kind of emotion. Only the four couples of Irish extraction described themselves as experiencing less difficulty in expressing their feelings.

The men interviewed considered character traits such as strength, self-reliance, and "keeping a stiff upper lip" as both masculine and conducive to success. The picture of an executive one gets from one couple's remarks was typical.

WIFE: My husband is very self-reliant, secure, self-sufficient. He never expresses his needs.

HUSBAND: At work one gets accustomed not to express dependence and one does the same at home. As a matter of fact, at work I never think in terms of asking for help or expressing my needs but rather in terms of making good use of the available human resources. When I get home, I don't want to talk about any big problem; I just want to rest.

In contrast, the executives considered such characteristics as dependency, a need to be cared for, enjoyment of passive things, and tenderness as unmasculine and leading to failure—except for persons such as artists and "people of that kind." One gets a flavor of this point of view from what one executive said:

> I group my friends in two ways, those who have made it and don't complain and those who haven't made it. And only the latter spend time talking to their wives about their problems and how bad their boss is and all that. The ones who concentrate more on communicating with their wives and families are those who have realized that they aren't going to make it and therefore they have changed their focus of attention.
>
> The top executive really enjoys himself; he has the company plane and a lot of staff and has it easy. The ones who get the ulcers are those who are trying to get up there.

In some cases the men seemed to agree fully with the cultural beliefs and were intent on inculcating them and developing those culturally desirable characteristics in their children. In other cases, however, I saw indications that these men and women were becoming aware of the relative value of those cultural norms, and I got the impression that they had started to explore the worth of different value systems.

But even in those cases where the process of reevaluation had started on an intellectual level, the executives still appeared to be willing to conform to societal values even if they opposed them. Their conformity influenced what feelings they revealed to their wives and others.

The values of strength and self-reliance remained unquestioned, while the values of toughness and controlled expressiveness were starting to be reconsidered. Often I heard these couples criticize the excessive competitiveness of the American elementary and high school systems, while at the same time they indicated they valued highly the development of the child's strength by facing life without returning to ask for shelter. They wanted to make their children more sensitive but also strong and with equally big needs for high achievement.

With respect to themselves, they were quite conscious of the difficulty of abiding by the values they had adopted. But at the same time they seemed unable to move in another direction. An example of what I mean is their relationship with friends. Their restraint is typified by one executive's remark: "A very good friend of mine, a school roommate, came to visit and grabbed and hugged me. I felt very uncomfortable and awkward."

Many of the men acknowledged that they felt more affection, and with more intensity, than they were able to show, and they would like to express affection more fully. Yet none of them manifested any intention of exploring ways of establishing new and more open forms of relating to their friends and expressing their feelings to them.

JOB CHARACTERISTICS

Most of the executives seemed quite satisfied with their work, though they complained that their jobs left too little time for family and other activities. Some of them were indeed putting in a lot of hours.

The consequences can be inhibiting for both husband and wife, as illustrated by the candid remarks of one couple.

HUSBAND: A lot of executives are seduced by their jobs. They become fanatical about their jobs because they like the work and because their companies reward their fanaticism. But as a result they have very little time to be at home and talk about their feelings. When they come back home, there are a thousand things to do or take care of before they have time for themselves.

WIFE: When he goes away because of his job, I'm left alone and I have to take care of things. When he comes back, I resent him for abandoning me and it takes some time to unwind, to relax, and be able to feel and express tenderness.

Those who seemed to be most involved in their work described how it took not only most of their time, but also nearly all of their energy. So when they returned home, they felt "drained" and able to communicate very little with their wives and children.

The competitive atmosphere, the premium placed on success, and the great value given to self-reliance on the job obviously affect the way an executive feels about himself when he leaves the office for home. And his attitude toward his performance affects his ability, once at home, to "unwind," let his needs be known, and accept affection from his family. As one wife put it:

"When they don't achieve what they think they should, they don't like themselves. And when they don't like themselves, how can they let others know them, how can they believe that others love them?"

RESTIVE ACHIEVERS

Most of the men I talked with seemed to have abandoned any romantic views they once had of their marriages. They had seen their marital relationships turn from being in love to loving each other. They had come to realize how marriages change, mature, and lose their original charm and intensity to become partnerships in living. The observation of one man reflected this pragmatic realization:

> It's much riskier to express tenderness and dependence when you're married because you can't interrupt the relationship. Therefore, if your needs are not satisfied or your tenderness is rejected—if the other person doesn't accept what you have to give, or doesn't fulfill your needs, or doesn't understand you and rejects you—there is very little you can do about it. You are rejected and yet you can't abandon the boat you share with the other person.

These men, being very competent and doing interesting work, I felt had learned to examine their jobs for rewards as important as those they received at home—for a sense of work accomplished, objectives achieved, and something built. In their jobs these men sought and often found their creativity, a limited transcendence, and sometimes a way of spending their lives without being aware of too much pain.

Why do they devote so much of their lives to their work and so little, comparatively speaking, to achieving awareness in living and experiencing their feelings? It seems to me there are two reasons:

1. While we train men to become "doers," to succeed in the world of action, we do not train them to explore the world of emotions. As the testimony of executives and their wives in this article has shown, feelings are to be controlled, channeled, repressed, or forced into acceptable molds. Not only are men told how they should express their feelings—big boys don't cry—they are also told what and how to feel.

In the world of business, feelings are considered a nuisance that must be coped with or a possible threat to the effective functioning of the organization. The research of Chris Argyris has amply demonstrated the practice in organizations of denial of feelings and the maneuvers of people in those organizations to avoid situations where emotions might come into play and to smooth over situations where deep emotions have been expressed.[1]

The result is a vicious circle: the less we recognize our feelings and

[1] See, for example, his article, "Interpersonal Barriers to Decision Making," *Harvard Business Review,* March–April 1966, p. 84.

learn to relate to them, the less chance we have of developing skills to deal with them—our own and others'. And the less skillful we are, the more threatening feelings seem, and the more vehemently we deny them or avoid dealing with them.

Men's lack of skill in relating to their feelings exists not only in the business milieu but also in the home environment and in their personal relationships. If you are skeptical of this, stop and think for a minute about the means that you have available to express your tenderness or your needs or your joy to your wife, children, and close friends. Then reflect on your ability to express richly these feelings to people who are close to you.

2. One always falls frustratingly short of gaining complete satisfaction of one's needs. In our personal relationships we often search, in vain, for somebody who will fulfill us completely, give us all we need.

On the other hand, at work we can complete something—reach our goal. (The goal being usually modest, achieving it may give us a sense of being let down—and perhaps we will feel the shadow of death that is present whenever anything ends.) For an instant we touched our work and it gave us a good feeling because we had created it.

So, men seem to learn to enjoy their achievements as they have learned to give up the search for "everything" in a relationship. Their more or less meaningful world of companionship and work is enough for them.

It should be kept in mind that executives are people with high achievement needs, and one of their characteristics is the desire to measure accurately and unambiguously the extent of their achievement. This is not difficult in the world of action, but indications of achievement in the unstable world of feelings and personal relationships are hard to perceive and measure.

The principal purpose of this article is not to offer solutions but to present the landscape of an exciting territory to explore: the land of our own feelings. I could try to incite you to explore this territory by saying that, when you know it better, you will have become a better administrator or a better father and husband. But nobody can guarantee you that.

All I can tell you is that in the process of getting more in touch with our own feelings, we become more fully ourselves and we live more fully the only thing we have, our own lives.

The History of a Short, Unsuccessful Academic Career

Michael Silverstein

MICHAEL SILVERSTEIN *is part of the Gay Men's Collective of the Berkeley Free Clinic, and is active in the gay movement in the Bay Area. He lives in a gay men's house in Oakland, California.*

PART I

The usefulness of a history is to show the operation of process. In this case, the process is the development of an identity. By using my experiences as an example, I hope to show the experiential reality of the one-dimensionality of this society in determining an individual's identity. This is done through the key institution of sex roles. What I must grow up to be, what it must mean to me to be a male human being, was presented to me as inevitable and unquestionable. Masculinity was defined for me by the social world I was part of as a set of personal characteristics that must become a part of my identity. I, like all male children, was taught that my value as a person depended on my power over others. I was taught that I must compete for personal power, and that to be successful I must conceal feelings of weakness, tenderness, and dependence, and present myself to other men as self-sufficient and insensitive.

In spite of the all-pervasiveness of this lesson, I finally found myself in full rebellion against manhood. The source of this rebellion was something that seemed entirely external to the reality of the world I was taught about—the fact of my Gayness. To those of us who identify with the Gay Liberation movement, Gayness has come to mean far more than the original fact of our homosexuality. The description of how I came to reject the definition of myself as a man is also a description of how I came to understand the concept of Gayness, by

From Michael Silverstein, "The History of a Short, Unsuccessful Academic Career," *Insurgent Sociologist,* Fall 1972, *3*(1), 4–19, and reprinted by permission. Reproduced by special permission from the *Journal of Applied Behavioral Science,* "Power and Sex Roles in Academia," by Michael Silverstein, *8* (5), pp. 536–63, , where it also appeared.

coming to an understanding of the political reality of the psychological characteristics of manliness.

Our lives are lived in the context of social institutions. In my case, these processes worked themselves out in the context of Academia. This was not accidental. I found myself in Academia because it had been presented to me as a less masculine milieu than most social institutions. Yet it turned out that success in this sphere is as much dependent on those personality traits defined as male as it is in any other part of the society. Thus in describing my academic career, I believe I can show how the social needs men are taught to act upon are essential to the functioning of even the less masculine-appearing social institutions.

Ultimately, this assertion leads to the generalization that the masculine personality, man's learned drive for interpersonal dominance, is the psychic engine required for capitalist society to function. Those with real power, ruling-class white males, in order to perpetuate the existing social structure and thus ensure their continued control, use their control of the educational, communicational, entertainment, and religious institutions to create men who seek a positive self-image in their power over others. Thus they have at their disposal middle-class men motivated to operate the organizational machinery of capitalism by a desire to achieve power, and working-class men who can be reconciled to their real powerlessness by personal power over their women and the possibility of successful competition for personal power with rivals of their own class. In addition, white working-class men are given at least a vicarious power over third-world peoples. Similarly, those in power also require women to learn to evaluate their self-worth by their success in emotionally and materially supporting a man in his struggle for power, rather than acting as competitors themselves. The present paper illustrates how the masculine drive for power is the essential motivating force in the functioning of academic institutions.

But these abstractions can only define the argument; they can never advance it. My experiences aren't abstractions to me; my life depends on them. Manhood now appears to me not as a sociological concept, but as a Procrustean bed the society would force me into; my struggle against it is a struggle to keep from being mutilated out of all human shape. My academic career was a life-and-death struggle I just barely survived. It is the reality of this struggle I want to communicate. It was well under way by the time I was ten years old.

PART II

By the time I was ten, the central fact of my life was the demand that I become a man. By then the most important relationships by which

I was taught to define myself were those I had with other boys. I already knew that I must see every encounter with another boy as a contrast in which I must win or at least hold my own. School was the major arena of this contest, especially the playground and P.E. The same lesson continued everywhere, after school, even in Sunday School. My parents, relatives, teachers, the books I read, movies I saw, all taught me that my self-worth depended on my manliness, my willingness to stand up to the other boys. This usually didn't mean a physical fight, though the willingness to stand up and "fight like a man" always remained a final test. But the relationship between us usually had the character of an armed truce. Girls weren't part of this social world at all yet, just because they weren't part of this contest. They didn't have to be bluffed, no credit was gained by cowing them, so they were more or less ignored. Sometimes when there were no grownups around we would let each other know we liked each other, but most of the time we did as we were taught.

So I knew what I had to do to be a man. One could only succeed at establishing his manliness or be a failure, a sissy, someone who couldn't stand up and fight. One didn't choose to be a sissy, a loser—one lost. Since manliness was, of course, what everyone would want, the unmanly must be those who were too weak to make it as a man.

By the time I was in junior high, I defined myself and was defined by the other boys as a loser, as the class sissy. Largely this meant that I saw myself as a failed man. Yet (I now realize) the beginning of my Gayness was the beginning of my attempt to choose to be what I was. I began to redefine myself positively, to redefine what it meant *not* to be a successful man. In so doing, I was moving outside the social reality I had been born to.

My first attempt at self-affirmation was to insist to myself that I didn't really want to be a man anyway. Much of this was sour grapes, of course, and I knew it. But there really was a part of me that, in opposition to everything I had been taught, really didn't want to be a man. I didn't know anything about homosexuality then; I didn't even know about sex. But from the time I was five years old, I had wanted to touch and hold the bodies of other boys, and when I had done so I had felt warm and comfortable, and affectionate toward them. By the time I was eight or nine I had learned how bad and dirty, how unmanly, this was, and I was so scared of being caught at it that I stopped. But the desire remained, a gigantic thing always there. It was totally outside the reality of what it was to be a man. Yet it was so real, so undeniably a part of me, that it forced me to see myself as outside the world of all the other boys I knew. It was not just that I couldn't be a man, it was also that I knew about this part of me that could never be satisfied by manhood, because it wanted something that no man would ever want. For the reward of success as a man is power over other men—and I understood that this need I had could never be satisfied by power. I wasn't exactly sure what I wanted, what I actually wanted to do with another boy. But I knew that whatever it was, it required that we both want it, that it was only itself if given freely. All sorts of fantasies were going on in my head, completely dominating my consciousness. They were all rather vague, but they all involved relating to other boys in very unmanly ways, ways that had nothing to do with power.

So although I tried to be a man, I could never entirely put my heart into the contest when the reward for success seemed incompatible with what I really wanted. This may seem rather abstract for a 13-year-old, but I believe I understood the reality of the world far better at 13 than I did for a long time thereafter. It was at this time that I set out to find an alternative to manhood, something else that I could grow up to be. (Ultimately, this would lead to the goal of Gayness, the rejection of the whole dimension of masculinity–femininity as a scale on which people find their proper status, and the attempt to create a new concept of peoplehood. But that came later.)

I didn't feel ready yet to take on the world in junior high, so I started looking around in the world as it had been presented to me to find a place for myself. One choice I could have made was to decide that since I wouldn't be a man I would be like a woman instead. Many young Gay males make that choice. I thought I saw another alternative, something else I could be, which was a recognized part of the world I knew, yet wasn't a man. In fact, this alternative turned out to be a 20-year-long detour into a blind alley, the blind alley of an academic career. But at the time I thought I saw an escape route: I would grow up to be a Brain.

Intellectual abilities and attainments had always been presented to me as essentially unmasculine, something a real man wouldn't take seriously, because they weren't practical (that is, they didn't lead to power). Thus they were an escape from masculinity into asceticism and the source of the only positive self-image I could imagine. I had hoped that by graduate school, with the Big Men On Campus off to the professional and graduate business schools, I might find myself among other people like myself, and that as unmanly intellectuals, we might find some new way to relate to one another.

Instead, now that all the Big Men were gone, it seemed that all the other Brains wanted to play at being men. Only now they'd play their way. But their way was my way. My sanctuary from manly competitiveness had become another one of its arenas. And the weapons being used, words, were something I was accomplished in the use of. For the first time in my life I could be a Big Man, a winner. Moreover, I started doing this without even knowing it. I just went on as I always had. Suddenly I started finding myself being proclaimed a winner in a contest I never knew I had entered.

My perception of myself had changed, but I wasn't aware of having deliberately changed myself. Rather, it seemed as if the world had changed around me, so that by remaining as I had always been, I now found myself in a very new position relative to the social milieu.

The graduate Sociology Department at UCLA was as masculine as any locker room. The female graduate students were self-effacing, weren't taken seriously in the competition, and didn't seem to take themselves seriously. (Of the three exceptions I can remember, two are now radical feminists, and the third killed herself.) But I didn't recognize the games being played, because the main way I had recognized them in the past was from the perspective of a loser. Suddenly finding myself in the middle of the game as a winner, I didn't know where I was for quite a while. But I knew that I was one of the bright young men of the department. I was awarded a Special Research Training Fellowship of the National Institute of General Medical Sciences. I talked more than anybody else in all the seminars and could keep the other men from getting in a word edgewise. And I found myself enjoying the hell out of doing it.

For the first time in my life I had some taste of power over others. While I still appeared to my teachers as rather naïve and erratic, nonetheless I was finally treated like a man. Even my family decided that college professors did pretty well after all. For the first (and last) time in my life, my family regarded me as a success. I just about forgot about being the sissy of my junior high, and I started believing that I was just a late bloomer, that now I was coming into my manhood at last.

At least I tried to believe this. But to do so I would have had to totally repress what I knew to be the truth about myself, that I was a homosexual. I could never succeed in doing this, so I could never believe in the reality of my masculine power. I could use it only as a defensive façade.

Even in academic circles, being a successful man means more than just success as an academician. The successful man doesn't just succeed in his career; he uses that success to win all the rewards common to a successful man. This requires that he achieve recognition as a prominent member of his community. And part of this is being a householder, the head of a family. Even an academician has to get himself at least one woman and a child or two. I was still an outsider to this world. I felt neither the desire nor the ability to become the head of a household. Thus although I had access to masculine power for the first time, I still didn't want what this power must be used to purchase if it is to be actualized in this society. And I was sure that as soon as this became apparent, people would realize that I wasn't a man after all.

Thus the power I started to attain in the academic world never meant the same thing to me as it would have to a heterosexual man. I believe this power was typical of that wielded by "successful" homosexuals, in that I experienced it as essentially defensive. It was not a weapon to win for myself that masculine prize I still didn't want, but a shield to hide my failure from public view. No matter how powerful I might appear to others, the most I could ever hope from this power was security, safety—never gratification. If this is true of apparently powerful homosexual men, then no matter how much they appear a part of and committed to the society, their attachment is based on fear and defensiveness; their only hope of gratification lies in abandoning their power and abandoning their commitment to the society in which it is the greatest possible gratification.

(None of this is to deny the objective reality of the power actually wielded by middle-class, white, male, educated homosexuals, such as myself. From the perspective of the students I would teach, of third-world people, of women, I had the power to act as their oppressor. I would have this power by virtue of my academic position, my credentials, and the "expert" skills I had been taught. All of these are rooted in class and male privilege. I am only saying that the benefits I got from such power were not meaningful to me.

But this does not mean my exercise of power would be any less real or oppressive to my subordinates, and implies no obligation on their part to accept the legitimacy of my power. The tendency of powerful men to ask oppressed people to feel sympathy for their feelings of inauthenticity and powerlessness seems essentially hypocritical to me. What I expect from those I have power over is nothing but the demand that I relinquish such power. Similarly, when more powerful men tell me that their power is of no benefit to them, my only response is to point out that this should make them more willing to relinquish it.

This brings me back to my point. I believe that homosexual men such as myself can give up class and sex privileges more easily than straight men, because the benefits we gain from them are not so real. Only then can we assert any solidarity with other oppressed peoples.)

At this time in my life, I wasn't willing to give up my privileges, because I saw no alternative way I could live. So I set out to be a success after all. Academia might just be another masculine cage, but at least it was one where I found myself on one of the higher perches. Just to be confident I could pass for a man, especially with my family, was something to be grateful for. I had even picked out a specialty: I hoped to make it as the Big Man in alienation theory.

But now, just when I was ready to play at being a man and strive for success, the game changed again. As I reached the end of graduate school and started looking for a job, the most important arena of competition moved from the polemics of the classroom to the use of entrepreneurial and managerial skills within the bureaucracies of academic departments. Success was now determined by the sale of your products and future products: writing and research projects. These were to be sold to academic departments, publishers, and agencies that funded research grants. While the polemical skills that let me argue successfully for the correctness of my analysis of things were relevant to this kind of competition, other skills were more important, such as the ability to write long, formal, highly structured, and bureaucratically sound research proposals. I first ran into this new set of required skills in applying for fellowships. Then came applying for a job. I was already getting scared by the prospect that a successful career would require a concentration on these things. I could do them if I had to, but they didn't bring even the spurious gratification of power in the classroom. They didn't seem to be any fun—only drudgery, alienated labor. They were the means to a successful career, but the end never seemed worth it.

Again the world seemed to have changed around me. Without any self-conscious change on my part, the gratification I could draw from my environment began to lessen. By this time I had gone to my first sociology convention, and any hope I had left that I might find some other non-men around was smashed by the sight of all the bustling young executive-types, drinks in hand, buttonholing one another to sound out prospects. Seeing this, I realized why my family had decided that it would be all right for me to be a college professor.

PART III

Nevertheless I got a job at C.C.N.Y. Arriving in New York in the fall of 1967, I had a whole personality ready for presentation, down to a bushy beard. By now I knew that as long as I kept things on an abstract and intellectual level—and we men kept them there—I could be articulate to the point of glibness, and self-confident to the point of smugness. I was distantly friendly and impersonally cheerful to everyone. I was pretty sure I could pass as a man now.

But I still knew that passing as a man wouldn't help. And thus the dirty, ugly, angry city of New York pounded into me every day I spent in it—I was too lonely to give a damn about making it, too lonely to take seriously anything as meaningless as a successful academic career. I'm still grateful to New York for this. When I got there and felt what it was like, I needed people so badly I wanted to die most of the time. This forced me to get down to the real business of living and start finding out how to get in touch with other people, and with myself.

So, once in New York, my most urgent need was other people. Looking around me, I saw two groups of them: my colleagues and the students. Since my colleagues were the group from which I was supposed to draw my friends, I turned to them first. What I found should not have been surprising: they were not so different from me as I had thought. But somehow the differences were such that they made the similarities between us barriers.

A lot of my colleagues looked as if they had been pretty lousy at sports as kids, and had had a hard time hustling up a date. And I wasn't the only one who had read about the "Absent-Minded Professor." Plenty of them had ended up in the academy for reasons similar to mine, but they were still very different from me, most importantly because as adults they had finally found that they could make it as men, if they worked at it, and they certainly were working at it. The rewards of manliness were real goals for them.

My colleagues could not meet my needs for friendship. So I turned to the students. My first encounter with them had been the first morning of the semester. At 8:00 A.M., I found the first of three groups of 80 persons staring at me. As a promising graduate student, I had been continually groomed to do research, and to define myself as a researcher. Teaching was a minor chore I'd pick up on the side. Consequently, I had never been in front of a class before in my life, and I was very scared. I stammered through the first day, but made it somehow. By the end of the week it was much easier, though there were occasional flashes of panic. By the second week I was starting to get into it, and by the end of a month, I was home. The endless, effortless flow of words that had made me the terror of the graduate seminar would still turn the trick. In a class of 30 graduate students, I had kept the other men from getting a word in edgewise; with undergraduates, inexperienced and already accepting my right to speak as much as I wanted, it was all my show. This was just opposite to the pattern of most of my colleagues. Since they tended to shy away from verbal encounter and argument, from masculine competition on that level, they were generally intimidated by any direct contest with students. Their ability to compete was exerted at a distance, by paper proxies; their victories were in endurance contests in the production of paperwork evaluated by weight. They were particularly afraid of young people, who represented an enigmatic and possibly hostile force to them. They knew young people so little that they feared they were on the edge of revolution. In the social sciences, there is an additional reason for defensiveness: The faculty suspected the students regarded both the ideas of the social sciences and the methods by which they are arrived at as trivial and irrelevant to an understanding of the real world around them, thus calling into question the faculty member's authority as expert. Most students regard the kind of concepts and analysis found in social science texts as obtuse and pretentious, and they are right.

Consequently, most of the faculty needed to use their power as teachers to force students to acknowledge the legitimacy of their authority as experts (and thus the truth of the conceptual system within which their expertise lies). This is how our system of higher education works. All the requirements—texts, tests, papers—are designed so that the student's success or failure depends on her/his ability to understand, interpret, and work within the teacher's definition of reality. Of course academic freedom requires that the student have the right —be encouraged in fact—to evaluate ideas independently. But only after understanding the official interpretation thoroughly. And given the pressure of requirements, students usually can't budget any time to do anything more than understand the teacher's ideas well enough to pass. Moreover, the amount of effort invested in understanding the official line gives the student some commitment to accepting its reality. Thus, even with all the academic freedom in the world, all the power is on the side of the teacher. And her/his own insecurity in dealing with students on any basis other than that of power assures that she'll/he'll use it.

Thus, the connection that men learn to make between self-esteem and power works as the psychological underpinning in the operation of such capitalist institutions as the educational system. Even the most independent student can only be on the defensive, since she/he has to work within the teacher's conceptual world, and the teacher has not the slightest obligation to understand the student's perspective at all. The most independent response most students can make is a sullen resentment, and an anti-intellectual skepticism denying the relevance of any abstract analysis, while meeting requirements as superficially as possible. This well describes the attitude of most of the students I've known.

As a teacher, I didn't have to resort to any of this. I didn't need to use my formal authority to have power over my students. First of all, I didn't find them particularly intimidating. As a vicarious hippie, and a vicarious radical for years, I understood the youth culture as only an envious outsider could. (Neither hippies nor radicals have much use for queers.) Most importantly, I didn't see students as an outside threat to an establishment of which I was a part—I saw myself as far more outside it than they were. I was defending neither a system of analysis in which I believed—I'd considered the practice of American sociology garbage for quite some time—nor my authority as an expert in the understanding and teaching of these concepts.

In fact, my real power over students lay just in my ability to give up formal authority. By abdicating my sole right to define the situation I seduced the students into speaking up, presenting their own ideas, disagreeing with me. Then I'd smash them. I put on quite a show. But I was intimidated by students, too (male students at least —I was just starting to see women as people); I was intimidated by them as men, usually men who were bigger, stronger, better-looking than I was. But in class they were on my home ground. I was more than eager to give up all external power, professional authority, and fight on a man-to-man basis. I was finally getting back at the kind of man who had always beat the shit out of me. This was far better than just making him study hard for tests.

And on top of all this I was loved. For I could afford to be generous. I didn't actually humiliate students. I just wanted a general acknowledgment that I was smarter than they were. The atmosphere was one of easy informality, with an undertone of benevolent paternalism, typical of the classroom of the "radical" teacher. Since this is about the freest atmosphere any student is likely to find in a classroom, I was appreciated. Within a few months I had a reputation as one of the grooviest of the hip, young, radical teachers. By the second year, I could depend on all the Big Radical Men of the school being in my classes, considering me an ally, or even something of a guru.

Soon, most of my close friends were students, former students, and other people I met through them. They were generally younger than I was, poorer than I was, and didn't have their lines down nearly so well as I did. I was guru, father-figure, and host. My apartment was a meeting place for young, hip radicals. Usually a few of them were crashing there. In my office or the cafeteria, I usually had an entourage of half a dozen students or so.

(Some of this was real. Sometimes I did manage to establish real human contact. There are people—students and colleagues—whom I love, and who love me, whom I met while I was teaching. I'm still in contact with some of them. We've talked about the past, and have gone on to more authentic relationships. To dismiss the four years of experience I've just come from is not only unfair to myself, but to many other good people. In spite of everything, there was some real human contact, some authentic friendship, some little love.)

But with so much game playing, so many power trips, I came close to being a man after all. Finally, though, with all the gratification, victory, power, and recognition, it still wasn't real; I still couldn't believe in it. For what I got from people still depended on the power I had over them—that was all society would ever offer to me as a professional success, and it wasn't enough. I could make it as a teacher, guru, advisor, but I never believed I was any of these things; they were never real enough to satisfy me. Outside these roles, my friends who were straight men would never give me what I really wanted from them. Sex was part of it, of course. In fact, at the time I believe I experienced it as the major part, since I lived in a seemingly eternal state of sexual tension and frustration. The whole atmosphere of the milieu I'd built up for myself reeked of sublimated sexuality. But looking back on it (from the perspective of having had a lot of sex, and finding out that didn't help much either), the real reason I couldn't settle for the kind of life and relationships I had was less direct. My friends were the most important people in the world to me. My relationships with them were the most important part of my life. But for them, no matter how much they liked me, no matter how much they looked up to me, even, their relationships with me were of secondary importance. Their most important relationships were with women—wives or girl-friends. Our time together was when they didn't have dates, or when their wives had something else to do. Or I was a guest of the family, or was dragged along on a date.

This wasn't due to any personal failure either on my part or theirs. They were part of a society in which a man's real intimacy and commitment can be expressed only toward a woman. That is, he can reveal himself and make himself emotionally dependent only on someone who is not a potential rival, but who, on the contrary, has been trained to be emotionally supportive of men rather than competitive with them, and to expect a position of dependency. Before another man, a rival, display of emotional commitment is an indication of weakness. Masculine solidarity, male bonding, is a real phenomenon in this society among straight men. But it is a coalition of equals against inferiors for the maintenance of power. The personal relationships within such coalitions are a grown-up version of the armed truce that has existed among men since boyhood. Such relationships are satisfying to straight men who are interested in maintaining power and can turn to subservient women for emotional support, but they were not satisfying to me at all. And these were the only kinds of relationships with other men that my straight male friends were really comfortable with. I needed close emotional relationships with other men; my straight friends did not. Such relationships are threatening to the masculine façade of self-sufficiency; this threat is behind much of the straight man's revulsion from Gayness. Even the best-intentioned, most liberal straight male friend is not going to place the same value on a friendship with a Gay man that the Gay man places on it.

So as I got over being grateful for what I had, I started to panic at the thought that this was the best I could ever expect if I continued to live life in the only way that seemed open to me. The best I could look forward to within the straight world was to be a friend of the family, to depend for my emotional needs on people to whom I was a pleasant, but superfluous, relationship.

My life didn't change at this time, but the level of desperation I felt began to build up. Later, when the possibility of change did appear to me, this desperation would be the motivating force that would push me ahead.

But even with all my desperation, I still couldn't see any space for change, any place to go. Until then, everything I had been taught about Gay men had made it totally unthinkable for me to accept myself openly as one of them. Ever since their existence had been admitted to me, I had been taught increasingly sophisticated reasons why they were not to be taken seriously as people. For years the only knowledge I had of the category of people in which I was included came through dirty jokes. Later I learned that Gay people were to be pitied as cases of arrested development. The message that came across was that they were pitiful, crippled, tormented creatures, always good for a laugh. But in any case, Gay people could not be taken seriously. Since it was tremendously important for me that I take myself seriously, I was completely unwilling to see myself as part of a group depicted as vain, frivolous, childlike, foolish—or as a tormented, mutilated metaphor for human loneliness.

My fear of this image was so great that it prevented me from having any real contact with Gay people, which might have shattered the image. The only way I saw open to me to avoid self-hate was telling myself I must be different from the rest of those fairies. Thus the image of the homosexual presented in this society not only teaches all men to be afraid of, to hide their own Gayness; it teaches those of us who cannot hide our Gayness from ourselves to avoid and be contemptuous of other Gay people. Even when our sexual needs bring us together, there is often a mutual distrust and contempt based on our early internalization of the society's stereotypes, and this works against any real solidarity among us. Then the isolation of Gay people from one another can be pointed to by the society that creates it as evidence of the neurotic inability of homosexuals to relate to one another.

This describes my life up to my twenty-eighth year. But I was desperate enough now so that very little was necessary to break me out of the pattern I was in. Gay Liberation did it. The Gay Liberation movement is a very complicated thing; it requires extensive analysis. But for me, in 1969, there was nothing complicated about it at all. I went to the November Peace March in Washington, and I saw five Gay men with a Gay Liberation banner. I don't think I can ever communicate how important a thing that was for me. Nothing would ever be the same again. I saw five people with a Gay Liberation banner. People. They didn't look ridiculous, silly, or grotesque. They were talking to one another like friends; they didn't seem tormented, lonely, miserable. They were people, like me, at a peace march, and proud of being Gay. They looked like people I could talk to about serious things, about my life.

As before, the change seemed not so much in myself as in the world around me. This time a new part of the world seemed to open up to me, a new space, the space to be Gay without conforming to the stereotypes that I had rejected. The motivation to move into such a space was provided by the desperation that had been inside of me for a long time.

Nothing happened right away. But all sorts of things were going on in me. For a while I was extremely depressed. Some time around the middle of December I reached the decision that I wanted to be Gay. In the middle of January, I went to my first meeting of the Gay Liberation Front. I started becoming a different person, and the world started appearing to me as a different kind of place. Before, my homosexuality had made me an outsider, alienated from society. But the social reality I had been taught still gave me the terms in which I defined myself. I had seen myself from the perspective of the dominant society as a tiny isolated satellite revolving around an immense social universe. Now I had contacted other people out there, and suddenly it appeared that what I had been taught about such people wasn't true. There were people like me, and I didn't have to be isolated. I didn't understand at first why I had been lied to. But now that I could talk to others like myself, it gradually dawned on us that the lie was essential for the ruling class to keep American running. Men, if they are to be driven to function by a need to prove their masculine power, have to believe that anyone who chooses not to be a man is a failure or a fool. As we understand this, all the self-hate of our isolation started to turn outward in a growing torrent of rage. I had never really hated anything before—except part of myself. Now I began to hate this society, and I began wanting to destroy all of it. It was this wave of rage that finally broke through the conditioning of a lifetime, and what had seemed true and unalterable before now appeared as something monstrously evil that must be destroyed. I hated what this society had done to me, then what it had done to us.

And that led me to really see what it had done to still others. I had always been against racism from the usual liberal perspective of paternalistic altruism. Now I could connect it to my own experience in having been taught that I was less than human. This didn't make me sympathetic toward black people; it made me look to them and the rest of the third world as people who might be willing to join with me in the destruction of America. I was able to listen to women now and understand something of what they are saying. All oppressed peoples, all the people whom the ruling class has defined as incapable of determining their own lives, share the same need to destroy the present reality of this society, if they are to assert their right to determine how they will choose to live. This is getting ahead of myself, because all of this happened gradually—in fact, it has just begun. But the Gay Liberation Movement set this process in motion for me. For me all of it became inevitable when I saw five Gay men carrying a banner in a Peace March.

Meanwhile, my academic career was quietly dying of neglect. My emotional life was the focus of all my energies. Teaching was very much a part of it; the rest of the package wasn't. I applied for no grants, set up no research projects, and served on no committees in more than a perfunctory way. The only thing that still meant anything to me aside from teaching was writing. But as my conception of sociology became more subjective and problem-oriented, it became harder and harder to write about something that didn't touch on my personal experience as an extremely alienated closet Gay, and I wasn't ready for that yet.

More and more, I felt detached from the motivational system that was supposed to keep me functioning in the academic context. An academic career had never seemed to me to be more than a *faute de mieux* excuse for a life. With the possibilities that Gay Liberation offered, I didn't feel any need for settling for academic life any more.

Now I was up for tenure, and the alternative to tenure was dismissal. The sociology department faculty committee, much to my surprise, recommended me for tenure. Perhaps it was because they wanted one "experimental teacher" around, who had rapport with students. Also I believe they liked me, since I was the least manly of the radical teachers. I didn't try to bully them personally, and I wasn't trying to take over power in the department. I was seen as radical, but not as personally threatening. They, like the radicals, perhaps sensed they didn't have to take me seriously as a man. However, the real Big Man of the department voted against me, higher authority supported him, and I was fired. The reasons, as tradition dictates, were kept as obscure as possible, but one official suggested to the student newspaper that my behavior was "unprofessional." Quite a number of radical faculty were fired that year, eight in the sociology department alone. I got to be one of the Sociology 8, and a building was taken in our honor and held for several hours. In any case, I was out.

PART IV

My academic career was now drawing to a close. I had finally stopped being a Brain and had become a Gay person working at being a teacher. I was out of the closet and working actively in the Gay Liberation Front. The whole academic world was becoming increasingly peripheral to my social reality, as I struggled to redefine myself within a new Gay community we were and are struggling to create.

But being a "good teacher" still seemed meaningful, and was still an important source of gratification for me. And I still felt too isolated, too cut off from the support of a community, to live without a job. So I looked around for another place to teach. Several senior colleagues who liked me helped me. I wanted to stay in New York, to continue working with the Gay Liberation Front, but I could not work it out.

So in the fall of 1970, I found myself starting the second and last job of my academic career, at California State College, Hayward. It was essentially an epilogue. Teaching there was never the central part of my life that teaching at C.C.N.Y. had been. My life was in adjacent Berkeley, and in the Gay community there. A whole new set of struggles had begun for me, including my first real attempts to define and explore my sexuality. But that is another story, outside my academic career.

In any case my experience at Hayward was brief, a smaller-scale replay of events at C.C.N.Y. I found it more than ever impossible to associate with my colleagues without getting quite depressed. There was an almost metaphysical air to the unreality with which they viewed the world. They were equally out of touch with the social and historical events proceeding around them, and with their own emotions, desires, and weaknesses as human beings. To be in the same space with them was to be sealed in a crystalline little world, out of time, out of space, where all the world, for all eternity, was precisely determined by clearly specified guidelines, set down by the appropriately designated authorities. They drew about them a world without creativity, without passion, without morality.

In such an atmosphere, far more bureaucratic and technocratic, far less intellectual than C.C.N.Y., I nonetheless felt more free to teach and act as I felt I should, since I now had so much less commitment to survival in such a world. Consequently, this time I was fired at the end of one year. The suggested reason was that I had failed to develop a professional self-image and tended to identify with students. That was the end of my academic career.

PART V

Well, where does that leave me now? Coming out of the blind alley of Academia I had been led into by my faliure to see that Brains turn into men after all, trying to get back to where I was when I was ten. Back then I had decided I didn't want to be a man. I never entirely gave up that decision. Defensiveness, a desire for security, and the surprising fact of my masculine competence in an academic setting—all of this led me into being a male impersonator for far too long, and I got so used to it that it was very hard to stop. But I am not now, nor have I ever been a man.

When I was ten, what I really wanted to be when I grew up hadn't been invented yet. It does not—cannot—exist within the capitalistic social system. Those of us who are now trying to create it call it Gayness. Being Gay means relating to other people without a need for power over them, or a fear of revealing yourself to them. It is the ability to love equals, like other men, or women defining themselves as equals, without being humiliated by the exhibition of unmasculine interdependence. Gayness is revolutionary because it requires the end of capitalist society and the creation of a society in which Gay people can live.

The concept of Gayness has come a long way from homosexuality, but it grew out of the efforts of the people defined by this society as homosexual to redefine and recreate themselves. What Gay people will really be like none of us knows yet. We have had to survive in America, and that has made it impossible to be really Gay. We cannot even entirely renounce power yet. We must be able to defend ourselves against a society that will increasingly attack us as it comes to perceive the danger we are to it. Thus we talk about Gay Power. But this must not be power for its own sake. We must not define ourselves in terms of power. The first step we can take toward Gayness, the first concrete thing Gay people can do now, is to relate to one another without a reliance on power.

That's the theory. It becomes reality only as it becomes a real part of one's life. Right now my life is learning what it means to be Gay. At the moment I'm living in a big old house in Oakland, California, with five other Gay men. We've been living together for a year now, supporting ourselves with savings and various odd jobs, and trying to learn to relate to one another. We are breaking up soon. We didn't make it. We are still too frozen in the old patterns, still too much men. But we learned something in the process. Two of us are working at setting up a new collective, and we'll try again. There's no turning back; there's only a void behind us. And what's ahead of us only begins to exist as we create it.

I also have to decide what to do with all the knowledge and skills I've learned in my life in the straight world—with the resources and power these give me access to. Now that I don't define myself as an intellectual, I have come to terms with intellectualism. When I was a Brain, things of the mind were the source of my sense of self-worth and a consolation for loneliness. Now I have other, less alienated sources of self-worth, but it will be a long time (if ever) before I can live without such consolation. As an academician, I learned to use ideas as weapons to establish my power over others. Now I reject a self-concept based on power. Yet I am involved more than ever in a struggle against all the power of this society; in this struggle, it is only through the use of ideas that I can feel I am fighting back against my oppressors. Thus this paper.

Finally I have no answers. I don't know where I am going, only the direction in which I must proceed. I often feel alone and isolated in this journey, but that is changing. Slowly, with many false starts, we are coming together. We are frightened because we are leaving all of the world we knew behind us, with whatever security it provided. It is still very hard to trust one another with our lives. But there is no going back, and we are building the future as we go. We must create a new world, if we are to be able to go on living. We are determined to live, so the future is ours.

6

MEN AND SOCIETY

The masculine role not only oppresses us individually as we strive to fulfill it, but also encourages us to lend support, through our work, to institutional goals that may oppress others. Many of society's institutions actively promote the masculine role and at the same time use it toward their own ends. The military uses masculinity to help prepare men to do what is deemed necessary to protect American interests abroad. "Be a man," a trainee is told: "Be able to take it, and be able to dish it out." In "Life in the Military," one man reflects on what he did in Vietnam to be the "real man" the Army wanted.

The masculine role motivates not only physical violence in battle, but also the decisions back home that direct it. Men at the top do not deal first hand in individual violence; instead they make decisions that involve life or death for thousands. These men often rationalize their actions with masculine imagery from sports, war, and hand-to-hand fighting. I. F. Stone, in "Machismo in Washington," tells how a "small boy mentality" guides government thinking in military and foreign policy. He quotes one Pentagon official who describes how the rationale of escalated bombing "is much like the tactics of two boys fighting."

Senators speak of a "test of our national will" and of the danger of a "weak-kneed, jelly-backed attitude." Gloria Steinem, in "The Myth of Masculine Mystique," relates President Johnson's fear that McNamara and other ex-Kennedy men would think him "less of a man" than President Kennedy if Johnson did not carry through with Vietnam. She notes also that "Nixon's statements are full of concern that the United States may become a 'pitiful, helpless giant,' 'a second rate power.' "

There is good reason that the men at the top make as much use of masculine imagery as they do. They are men who, to an extraordinary degree, have fulfilled the masculine criteria of getting ahead and staying cool. These politicians, generals, and executives have worked all their lives at getting ahead—*and have succeeded.* They have done what the masculine role tells us all we are supposed to do—only they have done it better.

In the process of getting ahead as well as they have, and in doing the jobs this requires, they have also had to be unusually cool. Being at the top requires making "tough decisions"—decisions which may cause some people to suffer. Not everyone is so capable of making decisions that—even though judged "necessary"—inflict pain upon others. The process of getting to the top, however, tends to select men who are sufficiently unaffected emotionally that they can more readily make these "tough decisions." Steinem notes how those who deal with national security must "demonstrate toughness . . . accept the use of violence as routine." "To be 'soft'—that is, unbelligerent, compassionate, willing to settle for less—or simply to be repelled by homicide, is to be 'irresponsible.' It means walking out of the club."

"Tough decisions" are made not only in the Pentagon and the White House, but also in Wall Street and Detroit. Business executives succeed on their ability to make decisions that promote the interests of the corporation. Their masculine need to get ahead is validated by such measures as profits, prestige, and power. But the goods and services that return the best profit may not be the ones that people most need.

As one executive, in an unguarded moment, confessed to Leonard Silk, a member of the editorial board of the *New York Times* (March 5, 1974, p. 33), "When a business statesman makes public speeches, he has to talk in terms of social responsibility and long-term profit maximization, but the truth—the deep secret he can never admit to anyone except the lady who shares his pillow—is that he is a short-term profit maximizer." The need to choose corporate profit over social need is made easier by an emotional insensitivity that permits men at the top who make these decisions not to feel too directly the pain of the people whose unmet needs they could but do not serve.

For most of the rest of us, not at the top, corporate profit is not what validates our masculinity. Our own masculine need to get ahead, however, may require the fulfillment, respect, or money some institutional job provides. As a result we may work for an institution whose actions we do not fully support, one that in some way perpetuates oppression by failing to serve people's real needs as well as it could. Our masculine ability to stay cool makes it easier for us to overlook this unfortunate side-effect of our employment.

Thus we, too, though perhaps ourselves limited by a job that denies our full humanity, may at the same time be involved—if reluctantly—in the oppression of others. Since the masculine role in the family calls for men to dominate women and children, ultimately, most men, encouraged by their role, end up both being oppressed themselves and contributing to the oppression of others. What oppresses us all is a hierarchy that, among other effects, implies control by men higher up over men lower down, by men in general over women, and by adults of both sexes over children. This hierarchy is usually either accepted as the natural order of things or rationalized by the presumed interests of all, including those over whom it is exercised ("for their own good").

Our training as males helps us to accept this hierarchy of oppression. From boyhood, we have learned to take orders from those above and give them to those below. In the playground rankings based upon physical strength and skill, we long ago learned the idea of hierarchy among males (or, more specifically, patriarchy). We learned that the more powerful or skillful are generally favored over the weaker or less skillful.

As adults, the bases for determining the ranking shift to mental and social skills reflecting "ability to do the job" that institutions require. There is concern that the ranking be "fair," by reflecting true "merit." But even the "fair" ranking based upon "merit" is used to justify more for those at the top and less for those at the bottom. How a man ranks in the patriarchy determines what society permits him to do and what share of society's wealth he gets. No wonder we males care about where we stand in it.

Physical strength and skill—though it actually affects the hierarchy among males mainly when young—remains important for the imagery it provides for adult masculinity. The memory, from infancy on, of the importance of physical strength, or its lack, furnishes a powerful imagery that influences adult thinking. The memory also exists of how our society once did require substantial physical strength, and this is preserved in movies, sports, and elsewhere in our culture. John Gagnon, in "Physical Strength, Once of Significance," relates the early basis and present form of both these personal and societal memories.

The mythology of physical strength helps provide a basis for identification and psychic gratification from a connection with the "winning team"—be it a man's college, his company, or his country. The result may be a loyalty to the institution based more upon filling a masculine image than upon providing real benefits.

Institutions make the most of whatever parts of the culture they can use to promote their goals. The masculine role is a cultural feature that institutions have exploited extensively: to motivate us to work as hard as we do, and for ends that are not our own. Accepting a masculine role that emphasizes personal achievement and discourages feeling lets us think it is strictly our own fault if we are unhappy with our situation. Rejecting "getting ahead" and "staying cool" as masculine requirements helps provide sufficient perspective to see how our own situation relates to a system of institutions whose function is not to increase general human welfare but to enhance the profit, power, and prestige of the few who control them.

Life in the Military

Many people have written about how the military turns men into savage murderers and rapists. Having been through the military I'd like to go beyond such vague terms and ideas. Enormous pressures are applied to men to bring about such transformations and it's important to me and my brothers who've been put through them and served as lackeys in Vietnam to understand ourselves and our actions, instead of trying to forget them as just an undesirable memory.

I went into the Army like a lot of people do—a young scared kid of 17 told he should join the Army to get off probation for minor crimes. At the time the Army sounded real fine: three meals, rent-free home, adventure and *you would come out a real man.* (It's amazing how many parents put this trip on their kids.)

In basic training I met the dregs of the Army. (Who else would be given such an unimportant job as training "dumb shit kids"?) These instructors were constantly making jokes such as "don't bend over in the shower" and encouraging the supermasculine image of "so horny he'll fuck anything." People talked about fucking sheep and cows and women with about the same respect for them all.

Not many 17-year-olds could conform to such hard core experience. You're told the cooks were gay (pieces of ass for your benefit). The "hard core" sergeants with all these young "feminine" bodies (everyone appears very meek, i.e., feminine, when constantly humiliated, by having his head shaved and being harassed with no legitimate way of fighting back) were always dunghole talking ("your ass is grass and Jim's the lawnmower").

These "leaders" are the *men;* that pretty much makes you the "pussy's"—at the very most "boys." You have to conform to a hard core, tough image or you're a punk. And I began to believe it because of my insecure state of mind, which was so encouraged in training. I was

---

"Life in the Military," from *Brother: A Forum for Men Against Sexism* (P.O. Box 4387, Berkeley, Calif. 94704), Summer 1972, #5, p. 4. Reprinted by permission. This article by itself should not be considered representative of the politics of the staff of *Brother*. Each issue was meant to be seen as a whole.

real insecure, so I wanted to be a superman and went Airborne, which, unlike most of the Army, is more intense and worse than basic training. The pressures of assuming manhood are very heavy.

Not only are you hard, you're Airborne hard—sharp, mean, ruthless. You have to be having an impressive sexual life or a quick tongue to talk one up. You've got to be ready to fight a lot because you're tough and don't take shit from anyone. All these fronts were very hard for me to keep up because they contradicted everything I felt. I didn't feel tougher than anyone. I was very insecure about my dick size and ability to satisfy women.

All I had was my male birthright ego. I stayed drunk to be able to struggle through the barroom tests of strength and the bedroom obstacle courses. The pressures became heavier and stronger, requiring more of a facade to cover up the greater insecurity. To prove I was tougher I went looking for fights and people to fuck over. To prove I was "cock strong" I fucked over more women and talked more about it. I began to do all the things I was most insecure about doing, hoping that doing them would make me that "real man."

Having survived the initial shock of such a culture I became very capable in such required role-playing as toughest, meanest, and most virile—the last meaning a cold unreproachable lover (irresistible to women and unapproachable by other men).

I first spent time in the southern US where only WAC's were available to fuck over and abuse. But being new to it all I felt I was too good to be dealing with such women, who were notorious as being either too ugly to make it on the outside or dykes. In Europe it was very different. There were numerous bars and many women quite willing to sell themselves or suffer manual manipulation just to get a GI to take them to America (land of opportunity).

Most of these women seemed to be bored talking to, being with, or fucking you. In defense against this role reversal of callousness I became even "harder." There were still remnants of "proper respect for women" (meaning you had to at least bullshit enough to get a woman alone somewhere before you could molest her).

Finally in Vietnam there was almost total freedom to abuse women and other people. The pressures were such that you couldn't possibly feel anything for a "gook whore," women so desperate to survive they would beg you and try to pull you into their beds for the money to live. Scenes like waiting in a whorehouse and seeing a woman come squat over and douche in a bucket then wink at you a supposed sexy grin did something to bring back reality. But it usually made me conceive of the Vietnamese as even less human and so less entitled to human respect.

For a straight man feeling a failure in the required he-man role, it seemed a fantasy come true. Housegirls wait on you hand and foot and if you beat or rape one and she complains she gets fired for making trouble. And many of these women are so in need of money that they are at your mercy. Whores were brought into field environments along with a mobile PX unit—if not by the Army itself, there were enough interested civilians. When I began to get close to a few women (talking to them I began to realize they were real people), all the fantasy was shattered and the contradictions began to get heavier.

Once to compensate for a dope burn I slapped around a young boy in order to show my buddies that no punk kid could fuck over such a tough man as myself. I spent the rest of the day repressing my fears and uptightness about inhumanly treating a "gook." "The only good 'gook' is a dead one" was my logical defense. The brutality that has to be daily suppressed in a combat situation is enormous. That, with all the fears multiplied by the pressures to deny those fears, made me ready to desperately take out my frustration on the most susceptible target, the Vietnamese people. The same macho bullshit was heavier here than in other assignments because it revolved around life or death situations and even the *men* (officers and NCO's) began to crack under the strain and became even more oppressive to cover up the increased fear.

There was virtually no one or no way to talk about my feelings of guilt and my doubts. Some of us began to confront the flagrant misuse of our lives and our bodies by the officers and NCO's and we were attacked as cowards. It became a constant struggle even until my last week in Nam whether I should still try to prove myself a man (I still felt unable to satisfy the role) or accept myself as a punk and leave. I hadn't grown the chest hairs I was so sure I would get in combat.

It's been years of real painful hassles with others that could have been avoided had I been able to talk with other men who had been through the same pressures and shit, and tried to understand and overcome them. Even now I don't feel I dealt with that part of my life.

Coming back from Vietnam I was desperate for *love and understanding,* and followed the "proper" way of getting it by entering a relationship with a white, sexy woman. With that comfort, and no guys around who had been through the Army, my memories were unchallenged and I didn't have to accept a struggle with that part of my life.

I no longer feel secure about that past. Help me, brothers. Help us to understand what happened to us. I wanted to write about three years of experiences to understand them more clearly. But what I need is response from others to help me be more honest than what I now accept as the story of my involvement in the Army and in America now.

Machismo in Washington

I. F. Stone

I. F. STONE *is Contributing Editor of* The New York Review of Books, *for which he has been writing since 1964. A collection of his essays,* The I. F. Stone Weekly Reader, *has just been published.*

I see by the New York papers that the Bronx, like Vietnam, is plagued by civil war. I feel for Congressman Biaggi, who has been trying to bring its rival gangs together. There was something more than faintly familiar in the *New York Times* account on April 22 of his peace efforts. One gang leader, Ted Gonzalez of the Seven Immortals, avowed that *his* gang's intentions were utterly peaceful, unlike its rival the Black Spades. "The Spades just want to fight while we want to make peace," he told Biaggi. "But I tell you, if fight we must, then we're prepared for a rumble too. No one's going to tread on our turf." This manly readiness to stand up against aggression, to face up to the test of will at whatever cost—this sounds like those who rallied to support Nixon's bombing of Haiphong in the Senate a few days earlier.

If we fail to stand up to the aggressor in Vietnam, Thurmond of South Carolina told the Senate during the bombing debate on April 19, "our nation will be regarded with justification as a paper tiger." "The invasion of Vietnam," Dole of Kansas said, "is a test of our national will." "Should we accept Hanoi's terms now and surrender," Tower of Texas declared, "the President would have to crawl on his belly to Moscow in May." "The President," averred Allott of Colorado, "will not be intimidated. . . ." And Goldwater promised that the actions taken by Nixon "will overcome the weak-kneed, jelly-backed attitude of Members of this body and citizens of this country who think you can end a war overnight by snapping your fingers. . . ." These Senators and the Bronx's Seven Immortals have *machismo* in common.

A related maxim of statesmanly behavior was reported by Terence Smith in the *New York Times* April 23. The day after the bombing of

I. F. Stone, "Machismo in Washington," *The New York Review of Books,* May 18, 1972. Reprinted with permission from *The New York Review of Books.*

Hanoi and Haiphong the President ran into an old friend as he was leaving a luncheon on Capitol Hill. When the friend asked about the bombings, Mr. Nixon punched him affectionately on the shoulder and said, "When they jump on you, you have to let them have it."

The small boy mentality is also visible in military pronouncements. Orr Kelly, the Washington *Star*'s Pentagon reporter, was given a "background briefing" on the tactics being pursued in the new bombings of the North. "US Following 'Classic' Script in Escalation," said the headline over his story of April 23. The military in the Johnson-McNamara years claimed that the bombings of the North failed because the escalation was too gradual. The theory now being applied by the Pentagon, Mr. Kelly was told, "calls for rapidly increasing pressure on the enemy until he gives up." The theory is certainly classic in its simplicity. The rationale, Mr. Kelly's Pentagon informant explained, in an unconsciously revealing simile, "is much like the tactics of two boys fighting":

> If one boys gets the other in an arm lock, he can probably get his adversary to say "uncle" if he increases the pressure in sharp, painful jolts and gives every indication of willingness to break the other boy's arm.

There are subtleties involved, as in any systems analysis. "Between each painful move," so Mr. Kelly was briefed, "he must pause long enough to give the other boy a chance to think things over and give up." But if the pressure is applied "slowly and with obvious reluctance," as under Johnson and McNamara, "the boy on the ground has a chance to get used to the pain." This is the mistake the Joint Chiefs of Staff under Nixon are determined to avoid. Why read Clausewitz or consult Herman Kahn, why drop more coins in the computers, when the military can draw upon so rich a store of puerilities?

The first rule of this small boy statecraft is that the leader of a gang, like the leader of a tribe, horde, or nation, dare not appear "chicken." This axiom is as old as the cave man, but it remains a guiding principle of international confrontation a quarter-century after the nuclear age began at Hiroshima. It still charts our course as, in the waters of the Tonkin Gulf, we may be drifting toward the world's second nuclear "crunch," if wiser second thoughts do not prevail.

In the first, world peace was saved because Khrushchev backed down. Khrushchev soon after lost his job. Kennedy, had he lived, would have found it hard to keep his at the next election if he had made the sacrifice for peace and "blinked," leaving Soviet missiles aimed at us from Cuba. Now again, as then, the desire not to appear a pitiful, helpless giant, a patsy in office, is predominant. *The risks to the leader's political future outweigh the risks to his country and the world.* Crunch may become catastrophe because the man in power would rather risk a nuclear showdown than lose the next election or his majority in the Politbureau. This is not a rational planetary order. But it would be too easy to blame this on the "politicians." Their calculus of political expediency rests on the existence within each nation's boundaries of a sizable population of small boy mentalities and primitives who still see war as a test of their virility.

The leaders of the superpowers look toward their coming meeting in Moscow in mutual suspicion and fear. Mr. Nixon, as Senator Gravel told the Senate in the bombing debate, believes "what is happening" in Vietnam "is part of a diabolical plan by Mr. Brezhnev to pressure him into going to Moscow in a much more humble fashion than he would be prone to." On the other hand, Gravel continued, "it has been said, and accurately so, that the situation that exists in Moscow today is not unlike the situation that existed prior to the political demise of Nikita Khrushchev." The present Kremlin leadership may be feeling the hot breath of the hard liners down its neck, too.

When Ted Gonzalez of the Bronx gang, the Seven Immortals, told Congressman Biaggi, "If fight we must. . . . No one's going to tread on our turf," Biaggi—an ex-policeman, swamped with complaints from all over the Bronx about chronic gang warfare—retorted angrily, "You shouldn't rumble—get that out of your heads. It's not your turf. It's the community's. And you aren't laws unto yourselves." But who is to say to Washington and Moscow that the planet is not their turf—"You aren't laws unto yourselves"? When, indeed, they are.

Had the Cuban nuclear crisis erupted into nuclear war, Western Europe would have been doomed, too. But Kennedy did not consult our allies in NATO, much less the United Nations. Acheson was sent, after the decision was made, to inform de Gaulle, not to ask his consent to the showdown. Should the Vietnamese confrontation erupt into nuclear war, Japan, the Philippines, Taiwan, and South Korea, our allies in the Far East, would all suffer gravely, perhaps irremediably, even if only from radioactive fallout. But Nixon is not consulting them either.

No doubt Moscow and Peking are terrified of a nuclear confrontation. Nixon's strategy of spreading terror by unpredictability recalls Hitler. I do not compare the President to the Fuehrer, but in this respect their tactics are similar. Hitler won one Munich-style concession after another by them, but at a cost Germany and the world remember all too well.

In the Tonkin Gulf we are again entering treacherous waters. The other day an American guided missile frigate, the *Worden,* was badly damaged by what appeared at first to be enemy planes. It turned out later that the ship was hit by two air-to-ground missiles from American planes assigned to bomb Haiphong. What if an American ship, what if a carrier, should be sunk with heavy loss of American lives? What if the headlines proclaim it an enemy attack? And we do not find out until too late, or perhaps ever, that our own bombs did the dirty work?

If we move toward blockade, if we mine the harbors, if Moscow sends protective vessels and minesweepers, if the havoc done to Haiphong and Hanoi becomes unendurable even to the most appeasement-minded in Moscow and Peking . . . ? The chances of the situation getting out of hand, through accident or loss of nerve or design, will multiply swiftly, the flash point at which neither side can back down may pass much too quickly for anything as archaic as the Congressional right to declare war.

Secretary Rogers told the Senate Foreign Relations Committee that reintroducing US combat troops and using nuclear weapons were the only options excluded in escalating the war against North Vietnam. How easily these limits could be swept aside by some unexpected catastrophe! It is time again to "Remember the *Maine*," whose mysterious and still unsolved sinking precipitated the Spanish-American war.

The simple fact is that the world as now organized lives on the edge of destruction. Everyone knows it but everyone tries to forget about it. Most of the planet can be incinerated within less than a day should a crunch get out of hand. This didn't happen over Cuba, but it may happen over Vietnam. If it doesn't happen over Vietnam, it may happen over the Middle East. If it doesn't happen there, there will be other flash points—Bangladesh was the first flicker of the lightning over the Indian Ocean, the newest theater of confrontation. With each crunch, the probability—by sheer arithmetic—of its getting out of control will increase. The safety of mankind depends on somehow finding a way to a new world order in which no nation is so "sovereign" that it can press the button that may mean planetary extinction.

And what if Nixon "succeeds"? What if he escalates the bombing of the North *without* precipitating a third World War? What a price to prove that he and America are not "chicken." How many must die in the smaller countries, how many millions elsewhere must be placed in jeopardy because a superpower suffers from an inferiority complex?

The Myth of Masculine Mystique

Gloria Steinem

GLORIA STEINEM *is editor of the new journal* Ms., *dedicated to liberating mankind from irrational prejudices against women.*

It has been culturally assumed that men are by nature more aggressive and more violent than women, and are therefore better suited to politics. This assumption of man's nature was based on no evidence at all in the beginning—only on an observation of the status quo, which, of course, was thought to be sacred.

Later, scientists discovered some isolated facts they thought justified this status quo, and the socially impotent position of women. The most provable of them had to do with hormones. When given large doses of the male hormone, individuals tended to become more aggressive or irritable. When given the female hormone, they became more calm.

Thus, men and women, the leaders and the led, were said to be locked into their roles by nature.

In fact, if hormones really were the chief dictators of behavior, women could now turn that bit of science to our own advantage. In the atomic era, after all, it would be equally logical to insist on women as chiefs-of-state precisely because we are supposed to be innately more calm, less aggressive.

But women are not trying to prove the innate superiority of one sex to another. That would only be repeating a masculine mistake.

The truth is that hormonal difference between the sexes is much less great than our similarities as human beings. A recent study by the World Health Organization could find no marked differences between men and women in intellectual or emotional capacity. More surprising, the study found that the much touted difference in physical strength was marginal and transitory; that it was evident in child-bearing years but tended to disappear thereafter. The forces locking us into so-called masculine and feminine roles turn out to be cultural, not biological.

Gloria Steinem, "The Myth of Masculine Mystique," *International Education,* 1972, *1,* 30–35. Reprinted by permission of *International Education,* and by permission of the Sterling Lord Agency, Inc.

The brainwashing comes from all sides—parents, peer groups, art, education, television—and it is very effective. So much so that a boy and a girl may live in almost separate cultures, though they go to the same school and even come from the same family.

According to the California Gender Identity Center, for instance, it is easier to surgically change the sex of a young male wrongly brought up as a female, than it is to change his cultural conditioning.

The first tragedy of this role-playing is personal. Men are made to feel they must earn their manhood by suppressing emotion, perpetuating their superiority over women (and, in racist societies, over non-white men as well), and imposing their will on others whether by violence or by economic means.

Women are made to feel they must earn their femininity by suppressing their intellect, accepting their second-class position, and restricting all normal ambitions to the domination of their children—so the cycle of conditioning can start all over again.

The second tragedy is political. That half of the population not brainwashed into aggressiveness is kept out of the political process, and expected to throw away socially valuable talents besides. The other half is left with the compulsion to prove manhood, and no more wilderness frontiers or natural enemies to prove it on.

There is no doubt that we pay a price in domestic policy. The National Commission on the Causes and Prevention of Violence noted that this country "is the clear leader among modern, stable, democratic nations in its rates of homicide, assault, rape and robbery, and at least among the highest in incidence of group violence and assassination."

Why? Well, the Commission adds that most of these violent crimes are committed by men between the ages of 15 and 24. "Proving masculinity" the report explains, "may require frequent rehearsal of toughness, the exploitation of women, and quick, aggressive responses."

For American leaders, however, domestic problems have traditionally been less of a proving ground for masculinity than have foreign relations. True, there is the constant Masculine Mystique pressure to be tough on law-breakers and youthful demonstrators, to "support your local police" and push for law and order. But domestic affairs are characterized by a short term political feedback which tends to restrain the transformation of psychological needs into policy.

Foreign affairs, on the other hand, are characterized by little feedback, and greatly increased opportunity to portray the adversary as different, and therefore evil; less than human.

Moreover, a leader afflicted by the Masculine Mystique need never confront the human cost to any of his victims—as he occasionally must if those victims are American minorities, or students, or unemployed.

Since World War II and the sanctifying of our overseas interventions, foreign policy has provided the ideal arena for politicians and intellectuals who feel the cultural need to play tough. Those few who buck the masculine ethic fare poorly.

Political reporter Richard Barnet provides this inside view of policy-making:

> One of the first lessons a National Security Manager learns after a day in the bureaucratic climate of the Pentagon, State Department, White House or CIA is that toughness is the most highly prized virtue. Some of the National Security Managers of the Kennedy-Johnson era . . . talk about the "hairy-chest syndrome." The man who is ready to recommend using violence against foreigners, even where he is overruled, does not damage his reputation for prudence, soundness, or imagination, but the man who recommends putting an issue to the UN, seeking negotiations, or—horror of horrors—"doing nothing" quickly becomes known as "soft." To be "soft"—that is, unbelligerent, compassionate, willing to settle for less—or simply to be repelled by homicide, is to be "irresponsible." It means walking out of the club.
>
> To demonstrate toughness, a National Security Manager must accept the use of violence as routine . . . Even the language of the bureaucracy—the diminutive "nucs" for instruments that kill and mutilate . . . "surgical strike" for chasing and mowing down peasants from the air—[are part of] the socialization process . . . designed to accustom bankers, lawyers and military technocrats . . . to the idea of killing in the national interest, much as at lower levels recruits are trained to grunt and shout "kill!" as they thrust their bayonets into sawdust bags.

Mr. Barnet's term for this behavior is "bureaucratic machismo." Even winning the Presidency doesn't seem to put an end to it.

Bill Moyers recalls being "deeply troubled by the problems of ego and pride" that afflicted the Johnson era. "It was as if there had been a transfer of personal interest and prestige to the war, and to our fortunes there," explains Mr. Moyers. "It was almost like a frontier test, as if he were saying, 'By God, I'm not going to let those little puny brown people push me around.' "

Aside from identifying one's notions of manhood with America's nationhood, there is the additional problem of comparing masculinity with other Presidents.

After a National Security Council meeting with McNamara and other ex-Kennedy men, Moyers recalls President Johnson's fear that they would think him "less of a man" than President Kennedy if Johnson did not carry through with Vietnam. He even mentioned his concern that the ex-Kennedy advisors would call up Joseph Alsop, tell Alsop that Johnson was "less of a man" than Kennedy and that Alsop would publicize that. Excesses of violence don't seem to worry our foreign policy makers nearly as much as peaceful and therefore unmanly behavior. It was Senator Charles Goodell whom Vice-President Agnew attacked for being a "Christine Jorgensen," not a Ku Klux Klan leader, or even a Vietcong chief.

President Nixon has accused those to the left of our Vietnam policy of being "appeasers," "compromisers," or "bums." Lt. Calley on the other hand, convicted of battlefield atrocities by a military court, was spared such reflections on his masculine character, and transferred from the stockade to the comfort of his own apartment by Presidential command.

Nixon's statements are full of concern that the United States may become a "pitiful, helpless giant," "a second rate power": that the country may be "defeated" or "humiliated."

He seems to identify strongly with wartime leaders, particularly Winston Churchill, and states often that he doesn't want to be the President "to see this nation accept the first defeat in its proud 190-year history." Two years ago in Saigon, he spoke of the Vietnam War as "one of America's finest hours."

After the Republican convention in 1968, Nixon was quoted as saying that he chose Agnew as Vice-President because, among other things, he had been a "tough guy" with Black leaders as Governor of Maryland. Nixon also admired his "forcefulness" and "strong-looking chin." At the same time, Agnew was not likely to be a "superstar," in Nixon's phrase, who would outshine him as a man.

In his book, *Six Crises,* Nixon describes his life experience in battlefield or sports terms, speaking often of "victory" or "defeat."

Unfortunately, foreign affairs rarely afford an opportunity for a clear victory or defeat, as required by the masculine ethic. Certainly, the war in Indochina does not.

So an obsession with winning becomes an even greater obsession with *not losing,* in appearances at least, an obsession with not losing face.

No single theme emerges more obviously from the Pentagon Papers than this conviction that any retreat would mean unbearable humiliation. It is the underlying premise of nearly every document.

John McNaughton, Assistant Secretary of Defense under McNamara, believes that this face-saving was the single most important goal of our policy in Vietnam—more than keeping territory from the Communists, and much more than permitting the South Vietnamese to enjoy a better, freer way of life.

Peace at any price is humiliation, but victory at any price—even genocide in Indochina and chaos at home—is quite all right. So goes the Masculine Mystique.

It's this kind of thinking that has caused us to consistently overestimate the domestic sacrifices Russia was willing to make for the arms race.

It's this kind of thinking that makes an SST crucial to our prestige, though it may be a disaster from every other point of view; that makes us add MIRVs to our existing capacity for overkill; that sees being Number One as an end in itself.

It's this kind of thinking that denies the courage in admitting mistakes, in forfeiting false positions, and so locks us into the unnecessary, inhuman gamesmanship of global showdowns in the O.K. Corral.

Increasingly, there are male leaders, not all of them young, with the courage to question the Masculine Mystique. Some of them work for the Government—though they are not faring very well, as we have seen. Some of them are even in Congress.

But women are the only large group not usually conditioned to believe their identity depends upon violence and aggression. Again, the difference is cultural, not biological. No one is preaching the superiority of women: in 50 years or so, after the sex roles have been humanized, it may turn out that men and women are aggressive in similar degrees.

But until then, it will be vital to have women in positions of power, particularly in the area of foreign policy. And not just one or two tokens, who may have to conform in order to survive. Enough of us so that we can challenge and change "bureaucratic machismo."

Challenge and change from women may be exactly what some men are afraid of, but that's their problem. (I do not believe, for instance, that women are spared military service because men want to protect us from being killed; if that were true, anti-abortion laws would be repealed so that American women would not be dying from butchered abortions at about the same rate American men are dying in Indochina. I believe men are afraid that women would not play the hierarchical game of the army, and would not be cruel enough. Which is, of course, exactly why we should be there.)

There are other men—Daniel Ellsberg, for instance—who are giving speeches about women's political power as a way of turning foreign policy around.

"Women don't respond to the issue of humiliation, prestige, and Number Oneism so important to Nixon's Imperial policy," Ellsberg explains. "Polls show that they are more against the war by any measure. I believe the sex differences in political opinion are much larger than we have been led to believe, and much more independent of social class and education."

One more point for those who still doubt the potential depth of this social revolution:

Geoffrey Gorer, an anthropologist who set out to study the few non-warring tribes, discovered that the less militaristic the society, the less polarized the sex roles—and vice versa, as we can see in the church-kitchen-children role of women in Hitler's Germany.

"What seems to me the most significant common traits in peaceful societies," concluded Gorer, "are that they manifest enormous gusto for concrete physical pleasures—eating, drinking, sex, laughter—and that they make very little distinction between the ideal character of men and women, particularly that they have no ideal of brave aggressive masculinity."

We may survive the Atomic Age, and get to humanism yet. But only if we are willing seriously to question the Masculine Mystique.

Physical Strength, Once of Significance

John H. Gagnon

DR. JOHN H. GAGNON, *whose research interests are in the fields of human sexual behavior, social change, and the family, is Professor of Sociology, State University of New York, Stony Brook.*

Once of high value in work and in war, physical strength was a standard by which were defined the roles, relationships and functions of males and females, of fathers and their families. These patterns of behaviour and of human relationships still persist, though strength is no longer of much importance. Thus, the man still provides courtesy services to the weaker woman and fills the dominant role in their social, sexual and professional relations. But today is a time of transition and we are approaching a "crisis of gender": the old definitions of manhood and womanhood based on differences in strength are decaying, while new ones have yet to be established.

Any traveller by car crossing the United States—or virtually any country—will be inevitably stopped one or more times by road building or repair projects. During these enforced waits he may see huge machines gouging the earth, filling chasms, carrying giant loads of earth and stone from one place to another. The thoughtful traveller may reflect on the amount of work that these machines can do and, if he has a historical bent, will think about the masses of human labour that it took to perform similar tasks in the past.

Such thoughts usually subside when the halt is over, but the traveller has experienced one of the central disjunctures of modern life: that physical strength, a basic evolutionary attribute of the body that increased the survival capacity of man when he lived in the world as nature made it, has lost much of its centrality to human existence.

In the recent historical past of most modernized societies, physical

From *Impact of Science on Society*, 1971, *21* (1) 31–42.

strength, as represented in the large musculature of the body, was a reasonably important parameter for social differentiation. It arranged men in crude hierarchies in both the world of work and the world of warfare. It differentiated men from women and was in some ultimate sense the basis for family authority.

As is characteristic in human affairs, what began as an instrumental attribute that distinguished between persons ultimately became a moral attribute as well. Stronger men came to be thought of as better men and men were (and are) elected to political office because they have a "strong" character (commonly recognized by an immobility of countenance). And temporary distinctions based on a transient capacity (for strength wanes) became hardened into what are thought to be just, true and beautiful social orders.

PHYSICAL STRENGTH IN WORK

It was with the movement from the land to the factory that characterized the Industrial Revolution that there occurred the major breaking point between a world where there was a relatively sure connexion between physical capacity and worldly rewards (though regulated by other status considerations) and a modern world where physical effort and consequent gain exist only in most abstract relation.

Many broad sectors of the early and later periods of the industrial world still had requirements for great physical strength, but the declining significance of strength can be seen in the large-scale employment of children and women in factories doing the same operations as men. While the utilization of child and female labour was also present in agriculture and cottage industry, there was a division of labour according to sex and age based on the levels of effort or skill required.

The application of the factory system and machinery to the extractive industries and to agriculture further eroded the role of physical strength in the world of work. The first impulse, as in the factories themselves, was to multiply output while retaining the requirement of gruelling work.

With the latter-day entry into the automation phase of the Industrial Revolution, however, the impulse has been toward totally labour-saving devices. The interposition of a complex series of automatic or semi-automatic mechanisms between the worker and his output has completed the near elimination of the general requirement of physical strength that was begun by the early factory system. Work is not raw effort, but is rather co-ordination and synchronization, the interfacing of man and machine—with the man operating as a more complex decision-making instrument linking together mechanical processes.

In my road-building example, the large-muscled earth-mover driver seen beside his huge machine, perhaps with a tattoo on his arm, is only a symbolic harking back to an older work style. The earth-mover cab is air-conditioned, his control pedals and levers are power-assisted and his work is co-ordinated with that of the steam shovel and the dump truck, with so many loads of earth to be moved a day. His muscles are irrelevant, as irrelevant as are those of the white-collar worker who runs the computer which makes out his pay-check or the industrial manager who handles the stock portfolios of the corporation. Their hierarchical status is not determined by strength, but by the abstraction of income differentials, which is convertible into variations in life styles.

PHYSICAL STRENGTH IN WAR

It is at the breakdown of peaceful cultural process that the erosion of physical strength as a major variable in human affairs is most obvious.

In the earliest days of warfare, strategy and tactics certainly played a significant role, but perhaps as significant—and very easily forgotten by bloodless historians of warfare—was the ability to bash or hack another man to death with club, axe or sword. The possession of great physical strength was given a further advantage through the employment of blunt or sharp instruments, and, while the arrow and spear are marginal equalizers, Davids rarely defeated Goliaths. Skill in combat, even when organized in the phalanx or the legion, still required a strong arm and vigorous body.

The armoured knight was, perhaps, the culmination of the union of physical strength and the social hierarchies of prestige in the West. But the knight and his castle were levelled by the gun, a weapon that made nearly all men equal. The armed infantryman of Cromwell's New Style Army marked the end of chivalry and opened the way to mass armies whose basic tools of war are fire-power and cannon fodder. The religious ideology that fathered the disciplined factory system in the West was the basis of its disciplined military system as well.

Modern weaponry, even in limited warfare, has taken on an industrial character to which a wide latitude of physical capacities can be conscripted. Automatic weapons in the hands of a determined local peasantry level differences between colonized and colonizer, and any man can press the button to fire an intercontinental ballistic missile. Indeed, in the film *Dr. Strangelove* a cripple is used to exemplify the cerebral quality of modern warfare.

The hand-gun, which is perhaps the most significant symbol of the levelling effects of modern technology on violence, is the central element in the mythic version of the American West presented in films. Its role in the democratizing of violence requires that its use be shrouded in rules that are as formal and restrictive as those of chivalry. Indeed, the obligatory fist fight in which the hero of the American western engages is a reaction against the equalizing influence of the portable gun: morality requires that older "man-to-man" codes of conduct be affirmed and older methods of creating hierarchy between men be retained.

PHYSICAL STRENGTH AND SOCIAL ROLES

It is apparent that societies which have heavily automated and cybernated their occupational and military sectors are in a stage where the necessity to differentiate the population on the basis of physical strength is nearly gone. Yet it is equally apparent that the distinctions between what different physical types of men do, what men and women do, and what adults and young people do, are still based on social patterns that were developed in days when physical strength was much more significant. Indeed, perhaps only the affluent sector of the current generation of young people growing up in the most advanced industrial countries has been largely free of this particular constraint on social and psychological life.

This is a transitional period, and there are still many alive who have experienced the need for physical strength and who have been allocated social and economic positions based on whether or not they possessed it. Further, the socialization procedures of even advanced societies—those procedures that condition children to fit into their society—still operate on the basis of the conventional historical distinctions between men and men, men and women, and adults and children which are founded on this attribute. Thus today, as during all periods of transition, we have the coexistence of differing styles of socialization and the continued existence of adults who operate according to a relatively inappropriate set of values and beliefs.

In our present style of socialization most parents still exhort their male children to be strong, to test themselves in sports, and to compete physically with other children. In the child's world, physical strength still retains some of its historical significance even though parents, especially of the middle class, seek to minimize the role of fighting and promote negotiations in settling disputes. Boys whose worlds are made up of both disorganized games and organized sport learn that physical strength is one of the measures of manhood. They see themselves as stronger or weaker than other boys, more skillful or less skillful in physical pursuits.

In an important sense, the possession of physical prowess is given too much weight and tends to acquire characterological implications. Physical strength and physical courage become identified with moral strength and moral courage, and the willingness to fight other boys for one's rights is an emblem of manliness. The physically weak boy may be bullied or left out of group play while the stronger boy will be selected for leadership positions and in most games becomes the chooser of sides or the captain of the team.

There are obviously substantial social class differences in the significance of physical strength in the creating of social hierarchies among boys, with the physically stronger being more important in working- and lower-class communities than in the middle class. One must be cautious not to see the child's world as the war of all-against-all and to recognize that a considerable body of social skills is required in all social classes for positions of leadership. However, the less complex the social environment, the less these skills tend to dominate the situation.

Though the environments of many children have become symbolically dense through television or mechanical toys, the primary resource that the young male has is still his own body. What he can and cannot do in comparison with others of his own age, those younger, and those older is one of the ways in which he gains and loses in social acceptance, and also conditions his acceptance of himself. In this sense the child's world is close to the pre-industrial world, and for most boys physical capability continues to be a powerful source of the sense of self and the sense of social position.

If strength serves to differentiate male children from each other, it at the same time serves to distinguish them from females. There is very little evidence that little boys are, in fact, stronger than little girls and given the wide variation in physical developmental rates there are substantial numbers of females who are larger and stronger than males of the same age. However, what is crucial is the socialization differences that determine the legitimacy for each sex of the expression of physical strength or the use of violence.

While overt aggressive behaviour is inhibited in both genders (once again, especially in the middle class) there is considerable covert approbation given to young men for engaging in aggressive physical activities. Superiority in physical strength, even if only presumed, or in the ability to use physical strength, is one of the primary signs to the young man that he is a man and not a woman.

As children grow older the training tracks for the two genders diverge, with a steady insistence that young men should be strong and young women weak. As they progress through secondary education the earlier hierarchies among young males based on strength tend to dissolve, and cognitive and socio-emotional skills begin to predominate. Nonetheless, those important previous experiences do not disappear from a young man's mind: if he was weak as a child, he may remember it with some shame or anger; if strong, those skills that brought him rewards in the past may be perseverated in long after they lose their utility.

The awareness of strength as a differentiator between men and women continues to be retained, however. Perhaps, it is even strengthened as the young male grows to full height, weight, and strength and is encouraged in his physical development by sports and recreations from which girls are excluded.

NONPHYSICAL COMPETITION IN WORK

At the end of the educational process and with the movement into an occupation the significance of physical strength among men tends to decline further, except for those who go into professional sports. Some few men enter those occupations where physical strength is still required (the police, furniture movers), and many others enter occupations which still have the fictional requirement of great strength. For most men, however, the world of work is not physically demanding, but rather involves the management of people and things in ways that are relatively remote from bicep size or the ability to lift weights. Except for exceptional circumstances, most men, most of the time, rarely find themselves in situations where great physical strength is required to deal either with other people or with objects.

For many men this decline of the necessity to engage in male-male competition of the physical kind is probably experienced with some relief. The broadening of the repertoire of assets used in competition with other men creates a wider range of opportunities to succeed. The tensions produced by rankings established on the basis of physical differences can now be avoided by that vast number of males whose physical capacities are unexceptional. Of course, while the movement into adulthood and the occupational world reduces drastically the importance of strength, it creates other tensions following out of the establishment of hierarchies of income, prestige and power, based on the possession of skills in the manipulation of symbols and people.

On the other hand, many men—including some of those who are relieved that adulthood frees them from the stresses of direct physical competition—sense the absence of the testing of strength that physical competition represents. They miss it as a ready affirmer of masculinity and they miss the simple, uncomplicated organizing of male relations done in their earlier years on the basis of strength and vigour. For these men there are two major domains of life in which the physical expression of malehood can still be acted out. The first of these is sports and the second is the sexual and non-sexual interactions with women.

SPORTS AS AN EXPRESSION OF MASCULINITY

Both spectator and participation sports activities have grown enormously over the last fifty years. It would be both foolish and false to attribute this growth entirely to a masculine need for some way to express male-male competitive physical behaviour, since it parallels the growth of other entertainment media that is a consequence of the increased amounts of time and income available to greater numbers of people. None the less, that the involvement with sports is a way of expressing masculinity needs is extremely plausible.

The male spectator in the stands (or before the television set) who is watching an athletic contest can feel himself as one with his "side," and "his team" can represent for him the expression of aggression and physical skill. Vicarious feelings of success and failure are acted out through skilled surrogates who win (or lose) for him. At the same time, the fan feels a sense of solidarity with other males who are on his side as fans as well as solidarity with the members of the team.

The existence of a large number of fans is important since then the spectator does not (as does the little boy who watches his more able peers play) feel alone in his lack of ability to play with the skill of those on the field. This is probably one of the reasons for the less ambivalent feelings about watching a professional sport as opposed to watching peers play the same sport in school. The skilled school athletes are competing with non-athletes (and with each other) for many of the same scarce resources (prestige, females) on the same campus, arousing mixed feelings about their success. On the other hand, the professional is a hireling whose success or failure does not reflect on the spectator, and athlete and fan are not competing against each other.

The increasing popularity of contact sports such as American football, as compared to the declining attendance, relative to population, at non-contact games such as baseball and cricket, suggests that there is an increased need among males for physical contact and at least the potentiality of violence. Indeed, the passionate identification with a team can sometimes lead to outbreaks of actual violence among the fans themselves. The outbreaks of "barracking" at European football (soccer) matches in England and the violence of fans at soccer matches in Latin American countries are indicators of the fact that these are collective occasions for acting out masculinity feelings.

During early adulthood many young men continue in sporting activities of one sort of another. Some of these are expressive of male-male competition, such as the informal neighbourhood (American) football games that used to be common in working-class communities as described by James T. Farrell in his novel *Studs Lonigan*. Baseball teams of out-of-school young men are still relatively numerous in some regions of the United States, but their importance seems to be declining. Such participation in team sports is more characteristic of the working class than the white-collar class, despite the fact that young American males who go on to institutions of higher education have available to them a continuing sports programme. However, with the advent of television-linked large-scale professional spectator sports, fewer and fewer young men of any class today participate in the tradition of informal sports.

There are supports for an older masculine style, at least symbolically, in many of the participation sports, though the situation is far more complex than in the case of spectator sports. Some of the sports, such as motorboating, are merely leisure-time activities in which competition between men is of the same form as competition in the purchase of expensive automobiles. It is conventional consumer behaviour, an evidence of masculine success in achievement that may be the final replacement of physical strength. Other sports such as tennis, squash and the like still have competitive elements of a traditional sort.

Those sports which parallel most closely the activities of primitive man, fishing and hunting, are presently so refined by technology that only through the most intricate symbolic transformations can the participant see himself in the traditional role of hunter or fisherman. Finally, there are sports like mountain climbing which demand such a high level of intellectual application and technical expertise, as well as highly sophisticated equipment, that they are nearly a cerebral exercise. Sports themselves appear to have taken on some of the technical and symbolic guises of the occupational culture.

STRENGTH IN MEN-WOMEN RELATIONS

Other than sports it is probably the relation between men and women that most sustains the continuing sense of the role of physical strength in the maintenance of masculinity. Rarely is the belief on the part of men that they are stronger than women ever tested, since the patterns of deference are so well learned that females rarely compete physically with men.

Men lift packages, move furniture, open jars for women—all of these are man's work. Each such act, and there may be a dozen of them a day, reaffirms to the man that he as a male is stronger than a woman. The act of applying increased physical tension and the resultant successful release before a female audience emphasizes the difference between them. Other tasks, such as carrying children or groceries, may be equally difficult physically, but for many men they are woman's work and as such demeaning for a man. Frequently, it is not the difficulty of the task, but its social definition which determines whether a male will do it willingly.

Though there are many non-sexual activities in which men are allowed to display physical superiority to women, it is probably in the domain of sex that a confirmation of the expected differences in physical strength is most important. Sexual activity in both its physical and social aspects is highly stylized, with a relatively firmly prescribed set of roles and meanings. Generally, it is expected that the man will initiate the sexual contact and both socially and physically guide their sexual activities.

While the female, over the course of a long-term relationship, may well develop a greater degree of initiative, the male still expresses mastery in the sexual relationship. Premonitory signs of this pattern can be seen in the playful behaviour of young adolescents as they wrestle together. The boy holds the girl against her will and in this interaction the linking of erotic responses with mildly aggressive behaviour is further developed.

In nearly all areas of the sexual relationship it would be severely traumatic if a woman demonstrated that she is in fact stronger than the male.

But even in the area of sex the increasingly abstract styles of modern life have begun to intrude. While the act of intercourse is thought to be explosive and powerful, it requires a sense of consideration and the sychronization of effort to create mutual satisfaction. And this emphasis on mutual satisfaction is central to a modern marriage based on companionship and romantic love. No longer is it sufficient for the man to take his pleasure and the woman to serve him. It has become recognized that the woman has the right to erotic satisfaction, too, and her satisfaction is derived more from socio-emotional skills than it is from gymnastic capacities. With the ubiquity of the marriage manual, fewer men today can take sexual pleasure without reciprocity, and in this reciprocity the gender-specific roles in initiation and response have begun to break down.

REACTIONS TO THE WANING IMPORTANCE OF STRENGTH

It is very apparent that there are going to be few refuges in the future for a sense of masculinity that has at its core differences in physical strength. The emphasis on the symbolic and socio-emotional that is characteristic of modern advanced societies enters all areas of social life.

Man's body as the primary tool in shaping the world is nearly obsolete and the distinctions between men that were created on the basis of it have lost their validity. One can see this process rapidly invading and reorganizing all aspects of life. From the work-place to the bedroom new symbolic forms and adaptations today exist which do not depend on strength.

For some men this shift will be felt as a catastrophe: something that had organized their lives is now missing. Yet for the larger collectivity this change can only be seen as the culmination of a long process that began with the Industrial Revolution.

The side-by-side existence of differently trained cohorts will be the source of considerable societal strain. There are still large numbers of males, even in Western industrialized countries, who have been trained to believe that differences in physical strength are the legitimate basis of social distinctions. Moreover, there are unskilled and skilled labourers who find the symbolic complexity of modern life, its pattern of delayed consummation of action, its attenuated relation between act and response, strange and uncomfortable. It is such tradition-minded men who will be the most discomfited as the cybernetic revolution progresses to its inevitable conclusion. They will not even have the pleasures of vicariously playing the heroic roles that were still available to men in the early twentieth century, when the explorer Robert Scott reached the South Pole and Charles A. Lindbergh flew solo across the Atlantic. The new heroes of today, those of the space age, are trained engineers, programmed elements of a huge technological operation, whose presence in the space vehicles is practically archaic: why send a man when an automatic system of sensors would do as well and weigh less?

For a long time to come societies and individuals in which strength remains an important organizing social attribute will continue to coexist with societies and individuals in which it has become insignificant. In a relatively advanced country like Australia there is a very powerful all-male culture in which sport, drink, and other forms of male-male competition are the central organizing theme of social life. In the United States there still remains a large population of young men in the working class and lower economic classes for whom physical combativeness is a major source of an ongoing sense of manhood.

IN SUMMARY

Let me summarize our observations.

The change in the meaning of physical strength has had a major impact on two male worlds, those of work and of warfare. These worlds, historically dominated by men, are primarily arenas for male-male competition, resulting in the organization of men into hierarchies. The only involvement of women in these competitions is to suffer the consequences of their successful or unsuccessful conclusions.

The erosion of the importance of strength in these worlds has been going in the West at a steadily increasing rate for at least 300 years, with cybernation and automation being the culmination of this process. The rapid pace of change means that there co-exist today large populations with different investments in physical strength as a standard for social differentiation, with conflicts in views and consequent social tensions.

However, I would argue that while there will continue to be some minor problems, the crisis is probably past as far as the acceptance of the change in the value of strength is concerned. Male-male competition today is rarely physical; it takes the form, instead, of competition for status, income and occupational position. Thus, between viewpoints on physical strength as a social determiner the struggle is nearly over, though we still observe a few final outcroppings of the traditional definitions of manhood.

The changing role of strength in distinguishing between men and women is part of vast changes taking place in what is accepted as the appropriate package of behaviours for the two genders. The rate of change in the past has been relatively slow and it is only at the present time that serious shifts might occur.

One reason for the historical stability of the traditional role of strength in male-female relations is that it provided compensations to men for the rewards that they had lost with the decline in the value of physical strength in other areas. There will probably continue to be greater resistance to change in this area primarily because unlike the situation in the world of work, where money (for example) can serve to differentiate status and power between males, there is hardly any available substitute for strength as a differentiator between the genders.

Strength, like noble birth, has become (or is becoming) one of those attributes that has lost its saliance in the organization of human societies. We are past the crisis of work and are at the beginning of the crisis of gender—and I suspect that the latter will be more painful than the former. And I am sure that what we mean now by men and women will not be what those who live after the crisis will mean.

7

MEN'S LIBERATION

Many men have seen the shortcomings of working at getting ahead and staying cool. But what are the alternatives? Our training as males makes it hard for us to see that there are any. Our restless striving for achievement hampers our knowing the inner satisfaction work can provide. Our demand for emotional self-control impedes our experiencing the pleasure of emotional awareness and growth.

Yet this recognition of the shortcomings of the masculine role is a crucial first step toward change. From this can follow a search for the alternatives the role has obscured, and for ways to realize them in our lives. In this search, we men have started talking more openly with other men about how we feel. Some of us are doing this in men's consciousness-raising groups—the main vehicle so far of male liberation.

Many men, like Stan Levine, who tells here of his own experience, came to such a group initially seeking help in understanding and relating to changes women are making. Men in these groups are more or less aware of how traditional sex roles encourage men to oppress women. We struggle against playing this role. But working not to oppress women is not enough to free men. We need to learn what it is in our own role that oppresses us and take action ourselves to change this. Helping men identify and overcome the limitations of the masculine role is the main function of men's groups.

A men's group might typically include six to eight men meeting an evening a week at someone's home. As Barbara Katz's article reports, these groups include older and younger men, single and married, in big and small towns. The key feature of men's groups is the attempt to talk openly about our own feelings and experiences. If we talk about sports, it is not about a spectacular play we watched last Sunday, but about how we have felt about our own athletic participation. Michael Weiss relates some actual discussion from a men's group he belonged to.

Often, talking openly with other men is difficult. Our experience has not led us to fully trust one another to show understanding and sympathy. But we try, and trust builds up gradually, as "A Men's Group Experience" relates. We admit our doubts to other men—and find that they, too, have doubts. The pressure to appear always certain, composed, confident—regardless of our true feelings—is reduced.

What occurs in men's groups varies widely—both between groups, and in a single group at one time and another. Topics may be specified for each meeting or discussion left open. Members may relate to each other in ways that are more confrontive and challenging or more supportive. Discussion may focus more on members' lives outside the group or more upon interpersonal experiences within the group. Activities may include not only discussion, but also dinners, camping, dance, sports, or massage—all done with some consicousness of how we are relating to one another.

Most men's groups start when one or more men ask friends if they would like to come to an exploratory meeting with other men, to see what such a group might be like, and whether they would like to be in one. Some groups have started from workshops at conferences or meetings called by existing groups. Some ongoing groups have taken responsibility for collecting the names of men who are interested in being in groups and organizing a first meeting whenever enough new men are available.

The personal experience and life change of the men involved is the main outcome of men's efforts to liberate themselves. However, some individuals and groups have set out definitions of the liberation of men as they see it. Two such statements are included here, one by Jack Sawyer in 1970, and a more recent one by the Berkeley Men's Center. There is now a growing literature on the masculine role, including psychological and sociological studies as well as personal accounts of men changing themselves. The final section, "References on Men and Masculinity," lists a large number of these articles.

A Quiet March for Liberation Begins

Barbara J. Katz

The word "brother" is taking on a new meaning.—*Men Against Cool,* a Chicago group.

BARBARA J. KATZ *is a staff writer for* The National Observer, *the national weekly newspaper published by Dow Jones & Company. Before joining the* Observer, *Ms. Katz wrote for United Press International, CBS Radio, and U.S. Senator Birch Bayh. A native Clevelander, she holds degrees from the University of Chicago and Columbia University. Her major avocation is the feminist cause, which she believes involves men's as well as women's liberation.*

The men are on the march. But it's a quiet, decidedly uncoordinated march, so hidden from view that one must listen very carefully to hear its stirrings. It's the first, faltering footsteps of a men's liberation movement.

Men's liberation? That's right. In cities, suburbs, and small towns as diverse as Fresno, Calif., Lawrence, Kan., and Fort Lee, N.J., an estimated 300 men's groups now meet regularly to explore the ways in which sex-role stereotypes limit and inhibit them. In heart-of-the-country places like Oberlin, Ohio; Lansing, Mich.; and Iowa City, Iowa, conferences on such topics as "the new masculine consciousness" attract hundreds of participants. And once in a while, in sophisticated urban centers like New York City and Chicago, small groups of men demonstrate against the "crippling sex-role training" found in children's books and the "exploitation of the insecurities of men" practiced by Playboy king Hugh Hefner.

Some men put their new views into print in publications like Brother: A Forum for Men against Sexism, published in Berkeley, Calif. Some are writing books: At least five books on men's liberation

---

Barbara J. Katz, "Women's Lib Auxiliaries?," *The National Observer,* December 29, 1973, p. 8. Reprinted by permission.

are now in the works. Others form organizations, like Boston's Fathers for Equal Justice, to try to dispel what they regard as a widespread view of men—particularly divorced men—as bystanders unconcerned with the rearing of their children. Others act as individuals, like the teacher from New York City who has successfully challenged a school policy denying men the right to take child-care leaves.

Generally, though, the men taking part in this new movement—mostly white, middle-class, and in their mid-20s to mid-50s—are more introspective than political. Most have become involved in response to the women's movement: At first defensive under female questioning of accepted sex roles, they soon came to question these roles themselves.

Unlike the members of the women's movement, however, they have not yet formulated a widely accepted set of social and political goals, nor produced a highly visible structure to fight for these goals. Some would even deny they are members of a "movement." Eschewing rhetoric, they explore their concerns about the traditional male sex role on an intensely personal level, usually within groups of from 6 to 10 members.

In a brightly lit, comfortable living room in North Arlington, Va., four men, one of them with his 3-month-old son on his knee, are "rapping." Jean, a 37-year-old sandy-haired, craggy-faced lawyer, is talking:

I was brought up in a family where traditionally the males keep everything to themselves. You grin and bear it and never recognize that there are any problems. Or if there is a problem, you just take a deep breath, throw back your shoulders, and say, "I'm a big guy and I'm just gonna live through it and override it."

Competitive pressures are something else I've always felt strongly—"Get in there and compete and work your 10-hour days and work every week end." I've always done a lot of that, sort of following the road map that others have laid out, neglecting my family and my personal desires in the process. I'm trying to get out of both these binds now, but it's not that easy to change the rules after playing the game the old way for so long.

" 'Getting ahead' and 'staying cool'—these have been the two main prescriptions of the male role in our society," says Joseph Pleck, a psychology instructor at the University of Michigan and a frequent speaker at men's conferences. "But it's becoming clear to many of us that many of our most important inner needs cannot be met by acting in the ways we have been expected to act as men."

Dr. Robert Gould, a psychiatrist at New York's Metropolitan General Hospital and speaker at a recent men's conference at Oberlin College, agrees: "It's more difficult to appreciate men's distress, since they have the dominant role in society, but their role is just as rigidly defined and stereotyped."

The idealized male sex-role, Gould explains, is to be tough, competitive, unfeeling, emotionally inexpressive, and masterful—"to come as close as possible to satisfying the John Wayne image." But trying to play that role exacts its price. Says Gould: "By striving to fulfill the role society sets forth for them, men repress many of their most basic human traits. They thus cut off about half their potential for living."

Men's consciousness-raising, or "rap," groups are one tool for increasing that potential. In these groups, men simply try to talk honestly about their lives to other men—a new experience for many—and to raise the questions that have begun to bother them.

Why, the men ask, aren't men supposed to express emotions? Why must men never reveal weakness? Why can't men be more than "buddies" with one another, sharing their feelings, not just their views on sports, women, and work? Why can't men touch one another, the way women do, without being thought homosexual?

Why must men be the sole or major breadwinner? Why must they always assume the dominant role with women? Why must they prove their "manliness" by "putting down" or "beating out" the next guy? Why must men always strive to "get ahead" instead of just enjoying their work? Why aren't men supposed to have too much to do with children, even their own?

Warren Farrell, who teaches "sexual politics" at American University and heads the National Organization for Women's task force on the "male mystique," believes that men's groups are "the basic instrument of the men's liberation movement." Farrell, whose book, *The Liberated Man,* will be published in the autumn, travels around the country lecturing on men's liberation and after each talk invites members of the audience to become the nucleus of a new group. "So far we've formed at least 50 groups this way," he says. So great is the demand for men's groups, he says, that he and other concerned men are now planning a national conference to train group "facilitators."

Why this sudden concern for men's liberation? Most men in the movement today credit the growing strength of the women's liberation movement. For every woman rethinking *her* role, they say, there's probably a man somewhere rethinking *his.*

In a small, pleasant living room in Berwyn, Ill., a Chicago suburb, eight men, one with a 7-month-old daughter, and four cats of mixed descent sit in the overstuffed furniture and sprawl on the floor. Bowls of turkey soup—made by one of the men—and jugs of wine and apple juice are passed around. George, a tall, gangly, 47-year-old Unitarian minister, is talking:

When my wife got involved in the women's movement several years ago, her thinking and questioning about her role started having an effect on both our lives. I saw I had to start dealing with some of the issues she was raising.

When I first joined a group, about four years ago, we did some "guilt-tripping" at first—flagellating ourselves for the ways we were oppressing women—but we soon moved on to sharing other problems. We soon came to see that it wasn't just the women in our lives who were having problems and whom we were having problems relating to, but we also had problems within ourselves, and problems relating to each other. We discovered that in some way we had been dehumanized, and we came to want to find out what it means to be a male human being.

But is the move toward greater awareness only a process of raising questions? No, reply the men who've stayed with it. There are answers and gains.

For some men, it's meant their first close male friendships. For others, it's meant a lessening of competitive pressure and a greater recognition of the importance of personal and family desires.

For Jean, the Virginia lawyer trying to emerge from his double bind, it's meant "being able to show more emotion with our little daughter" and a willingness to take "an enormous amount of time off of work"—even at the risk of cutting his salary—to help his wife through a difficult pregnancy.

For George, the Chicago minister, it's meant a "net energy gain" from the support provided by "people I really dig." It's meant being able to share the most personal of concerns with peers who understand and share his concerns—even his emotional struggle over the "finality" of the vasectomy he's considering.

For Mark, a 40-year-old burglar-alarm specialist in Chicago, it's meant being able to view his wife "more as an equal partner, a whole person, a friend. Before I saw her primarily as a mother and housekeeper, and I was always playing the big protector, the big man around the house. That's really a pretty crummy role, and besides, you can't have a really open relationship with a servant. It's been a lot nicer lately."

And for Jeff, a 26-year-old advertising executive in Deale, Md., it's meant the discovery that "vulnerability isn't necessarily a bad thing," and that "crying is a tremendous release." It's also enabled him to face the fact that, although successful at his job, he doesn't like what he's doing. "It's so easy to get caught up in simply doing what you're trained to do, what you're expected to do, even if you know it's not what you really want," he says. Jeff is planning to switch to an entirely different field—ecological architecture.

Liberation, these men say, does not mean that men will be "liberated" from the need to work or to share family responsibilities. It does mean becoming aware of what they see as the subtle ways they are forced into doing things because they must satisfy society's expectations of "what it takes to be a man."

Those who have given some thought to men's liberation say there are two major obstacles to overcome if one is to "unlearn" those expectations: The first is recognizing and unlearning the underlying contempt they say most men feel for women; the second is questioning the male "hierarchy of values."

"Men learn from the time they're boys that the worst possible thing is to be considered feminine—a 'sissy,'" says Warren Farrell. "The male's fear that he might be thought of as a female—with all the negative implications that carries—has been the central basis of his need to prove himself 'masculine.' A more positive image of women frees a man to come in contact with the so-called feminine parts of his personality and allows him to start displaying human emotions without fear of being called feminine."

The male "hierarchy of values," with its emphasis on competition and "success," is so ingrained in our society that "it takes a revolution in one's thinking to see what it's about," says psychiatrist Robert Gould. "In American society, success has nothing to do with how you live your life," he says, "but with whether you satisfy American values of what success is—wealth, power, and status. One learns very early that if you're bigger and stronger and louder, you'll win all the marbles. One seldom questions whether what is given up in the process of winning the marbles—meaningful relationships with people, enjoyment of work for its own sake—is worth it."

The men taking part in the men's movement *are* doing that questioning. But their movement is small and, while growing, not yet at the pace of the women's movement. Some, like Jim, a 33-year-old reporter in Washington, D.C., believe "the real guts of this is in the children we bring up.

"Surely our impact, for good or ill, is going to have an impact on them," he says. "We're not going to find exact answers to all our questions immediately, but certainly we're setting a different example from what we had."

One Man's Experience

Stan Levine

STAN LEVINE *is a jazz musician, a free-lance writer and the creative director (advertising) for a major record company. He's also the proud daddy of three children who are growing up with what he hopes are better ideas about sex roles.*

Stan Levine, "One Man's Experience," *Ms.*, February 1973, p. 14. Reprinted by permission.

Who needed a men's group? Who needed more competition? At 47½ years of age, hadn't I already won enough and lost enough competitions on ball fields and battlefields? in classrooms and conference rooms? Was I honest enough for a men's group? *Man* enough? Who needed yet another commitment? Another organization?

Questions or not, I finally joined in self-defense. Joan was into a women's group. She was clearly growing, and growth is her natural state. She loves me and I love her, and we both want our marriage and our family to keep on being together. However, I didn't love Joan's group so much. I had no quarrel with the general idea. I mean, who could argue with discussion, self-expression, equality, truth, and so forth? I offered surface support while I masked my resentment with "humor."

In fact, I was scared. From her group, Joan would find out (for the first time, of course) that men are not gods. Or that some men are more godlike than I. And better lovers. That marriage is perhaps obsolete. That I'm a shit. That she wouldn't need me. That she doesn't love me.

All but one of my fears have been realized. Joan knows now (and always did) that men are *not* gods. That other men *are* more godlike than I. There *are* better lovers. Marriage *is* perhaps obsolete. I *am* a shit. She does *not* need me. But, and this is the important one, she *does* love me.

She loves me even more because I got myself into a men's group. I didn't want to get left behind—not only by Joan, but by other people who seemed to be so much alive, including our own three children. I was in serious danger of becoming near-extinct as I settled down with my chauvinism, my role playing, my fantasies, and my fears. I still have these things, but no longer settle.

If there were reasons for my joining a men's group, there were even more reasons for *not* joining. It has been years since I was able to get it on with other men. I guess the end of my getting-it-on days was the end of my high school football career. I thought I was a hero and I thought everyone else thought so, too. The Marine Corps (the place for heroes) finished that fantasy. After World War II, I returned home, to college and to varsity football. The heroism and camaraderie were gone. Forever.

In the world of men, I was alone, jealous, angry, untrusting, and uptight. Only with women could I let it hang out. Of course, with the advantages of hindsight, a few affairs, a bad first marriage, and the men's group, I know now that my ease with any woman was based on her ability to worship me. I was a *man*. She was merely a woman.

What we (eight of us, all white, mostly college educated, and more or less professional) have been doing beween 8 P.M. and midnight every Monday has run a gamut. When we were new to each other we spoke about our jobs, our families (especially about our fathers), our women (or men). Then we talked about the roles we play. What it meant to each of us to be a son, a boy, a teen-ager, an athlete, a soldier, a scholar, a wage earner, a lover, a husband, a father. A *man.* A *super man.* And what it meant *not* to be some of these things.

And we talked "topics." Violence. How we sought it. How we feared it. How we actually dealt with it. We talked about the meaning of *macho.* We talked about "scoring." Winning. Losing. Crying. Fucking. Fidelity. Loneliness. Sometimes we got off on eight personal trips. Sometimes there was understanding. Sometimes, none.

There's been much inquiry into why each of us remains in the group. Without plan or schedule, it seems that every week one member or another takes a turn at serving notice to the others that he has alternatives for his Monday nights. The inquiry is framed with questions like: "Am I getting mine from the group?" "Shouldn't the group be part of something bigger?" "Is this just another therapy group?" "Why can't we be more like a therapy group?" "Why should I expose myself when others don't?" Why should I be on time when others aren't?" There is much inquiry but little defection.

Each of us has felt big disappointments with the group. I've had two. Once I emptied our beach house of wife and family and volunteered it to the group for a weekend. It was our only non-Monday night gathering of the entire group and for me it was a disaster. The greedy food-getting and sloppy housekeeping were not what I was used to in those cherished surroundings and I was pissed. But as host and general good guy and originator of the Weekend Idea, how could I complain? So I didn't. I withdrew. They sensed my anger but couldn't identify it. And wouldn't identify it if I wouldn't. We dealt with this at our next regular meeting in the city. The group was more together than before. My next "second thoughts" about the group were almost my last ones. I learned I had cancer. I got the news on a Monday and told the group that night. There was much deep concern and warm, honest support.

But during the next days of hospital and extensive major surgery and doctors and excruciating anxiety, there was not a word from anyone in the group except Al. I knew the others all cared, but they didn't know how to handle it. This time I knew it was the group's problem, not mine. I was in bed but they were crippled. I felt disgust and sadness along with my anger. Through Al, I told the "men's group" it was no men's group. They worked it out at their next meeting. A meeting of cross-accusations and confessions. One by one, they were able to visit the hospital. There was much love. And there still is.

I've been freed from cancer, but the experience forced a new look at things. And things look all the way from different to better to beautiful. Things with myself, with me and my wife, with my children, my friends, the people I work with. All these people haven't changed, but I am changing. Along with the Monday night men's group.

A Men's Group Experience

Our men's group has been in existence for about a year now. During this time we've gone through a lot of experiences that we feel good about sharing with other men. The group has gone through a lot of changes in members, having as many as nine and as few as four during the year. So this article is actually speaking for the present group, although we feel that others who have been in the group share many of our ideas about it.

One of the main reasons we joined a men's group was a feeling of dissatisfaction with ourselves, our jobs, our relationships with men and women, and what we saw as our alienating futures. The group gives us a way to share our feelings and experiences with others in an intimate and honest way. We also feel the need to understand our alienation from each other and our selves; to see how our roles, problems, sexual fears, and personal frustrations are shared by nearly everyone in the society. Being an all men's group gives us a common base of male experience to share and open up with one another.

As we began to share our problems and feelings with one another we began to see that the solutions to our alienation have to come about collectively. Individual approaches lead only to more frustration and loneliness, while spilling out troubles to a group gives strength, a feeling that there's nothing to be defensive about, being more accepting of ourselves, and being more at ease with others. We continue to meet as a group because we see the need to keep struggling with the old patterns of relating, the old fears, and the old roles which we have found unsatisfactory. We see the need to begin carrying out the ideas of the group in our private lives and to use the group as a sounding board to test our experiences and rethink our actions.

When we began meeting we spent a lot of time talking about our pasts—growing up as men, learning to compete and be masculine, to

---

"A Men's Group Experience," from *Brother: A Forum for Men Against Sexism* (P. O. Box 4387, Berkeley, Calif. 94704), Summer 1972, #5, p. 12. Reprinted by permission. This article by itself should not be considered representative of the politics of the staff of *Brother*. Each issue was meant to be seen as a whole.

think and not to feel, to "succeed" and feel bad if we "failed," to treat women as inferior sexual objects, and the host of male roles we've been taught to play. We talked about how we were often out of touch with our feelings or how we simply refused to admit to ourselves that we felt incompetent with women, unable to live up to the images expected of us by parents and society, unable to communicate with other people, lonely and isolated. It was and is extremely hard to admit that we feel left out when we see "happy" couples together and we are not relating to a woman, or that we feel our own relationship is inadequate and that what we really need is a "better woman." We also talked about subjects that still cause us guilt and confusion such as masturbation; we continue to have difficulty talking about homosexuality and our fears about becoming intimate with men.

As we continued to meet once a week, we changed the form of our meetings. We closed each meeting with a group criticism, both positive and negative, of individuals, the general meeting, and other aspects of the men's group. This gave us a chance to work to improve the meetings and search for new ways to relate. It also opened the whole area of criticism and how it should be handled; we have tried to learn to offer our ideas with love and with the intention of improving our lives and not to trash other people. Only with growing trust and openness were we able to accept or give criticism openly; this continues to be a critical aspect of the group meetings.

We also learned that it was important to begin and close meetings in a fairly consistent and dependable way. The initial tendency for meetings to drag on late at night proved a considerable burden to the working men in the group. Also missing meetings or coming late tended to destroy trust and commitment among group members. We found it critical to set aside one consistent time for the meetings and hold it as the highest priority of our weekly schedules. We also learned the importance of paying close attention to what another man is saying to try to glean the truth from often confusing explanations.

As trust built up we began to talk more about our current lives and the problems we face day to day. We opened our meeting with a brief discussion of subject matter for the meeting; when a focus was agreed to, we tried to stick to that subject for the evening or until it was exhausted. We spent considerable time exploring our personal relations with women, and some time on our living groups, school, jobs projects and other day to day crises. We found this approach to be very helpful in some cases; other times it seemed that headway was made only slowly. Since most of us were not living or working together, it was often difficult to grasp the full details of another man's dilemma; it was necessary to ask careful questions and fully empathize with one another to succeed in helping each other.

We have questioned whether it is possible to achieve collective unity for our group even though we do not live and work together. We have dealt with this to some extent by getting together outside the group during the week. Also we feel that the group's attitude is the most basic feature of collectivity, and that unity does grow with time and commitment.

Most recently the group has begun to focus internally on our relations with one another. We have spent one night on each person in the group talking about how we feel about him. These meetings have been among the most satisfying we have had. It has required both a willingness to be vulnerable and a trust in the group. It has allowed us to deal with our feelings in a very first hand manner, in the here and now. The feelings expressed have been positive and negative; a possible tendency has been to overstress positive characteristics, which may not be very helpful to the person. Only a full-sided appraisal is helpful; providing one has been an effort requiring preparation and forethought. Also fairly recently we have experimented with sensory awareness and group trust exercises involving physical contact.

During the life of our group, numerous men have come and gone. We have tried to understand why people tend to be turned off by the group or attracted with only partial commitments. Some men seemed unable to concentrate or give their full attention to the discussion; others left to travel or attend school elsewhere; some seemed to feel that "men's liberation" was a rhetorical trip or that it was stressing too much of the negative and not leading in positive directions. In some ways the group is threatening to our images and could be viewed as an admission of weakness in traditional ways of thinking. In any event, the high turnover has been symptomatic of the difficulty we have in remaining committed to each other over a long period of time and the difficulty men have in getting close. Of the six men who have left the group only one is still involved in men's groups.

So we are still faced with the question of the direction of our group. We feel strongly that as men we need to see our problems as products of the larger society, and that ultimately our solutions can only come with a collective unity of men, women, minorities, gays, and working people. The men's group has been one form of dealing with the oppression we feel by being forced to conform to the narrow and lonely roles of men in this society. We are continuing to examine that oppression, attempting to alter our daily lives and environments, and creating new forms for people to relate in cooperative loving ways. Our men's group teaches us that there is a new way to do things that isn't tied up in competitiveness and feeling better than others. We want to spread this feeling to more and more of our personal relationships, and encourage more men to form men's groups.

Unlearning

Michael Weiss

MICHAEL WEISS *is 31 years old, and the father of two children. He works as a freelance writer and a sometime teacher. He is the author of* Living Together: A Year in the Life of a City Commune.

At the first meeting of my men's group we arranged ourselves in a circle on the floor and talked about ourselves for four or five hours. It was an incredible high because none of the seven of us had ever before met alone with other men to talk about our feelings as men.

We continued to meet every Thursday night. Sometimes we would touch and hug; most of the touching, though, came in huddle-like masses. When, at one meeting, somebody suggested that we all sit together on the bed and communicate without talking we avoided it. None of us seemed to know how a men's consciousness raising group should proceed, so we just talked about what was on our minds. Sometimes that was an immediate problem at home or at work, sometimes our parents or childhood. It was months before we really began to talk about whether we trusted one another, and except for political discussions we never talked about the competitiveness with other men we all acknowledged feeling.

It was apparent from the beginning that our feelings for one another were intense and insecure. We were full of jealousy and coyness as well as simplicity and honesty. We fell into a certain shy affection in greeting that reminded me in its tenderness of puppy love. We were learning not to be afraid of one another. We hugged when we met, whether on the street or in our houses, and I was soon beginning to feel the bodies of the men I was touching, not merely giving and receiving a blunt embrace and a quick squeeze before retreating.

Only one of the men in the group has had a post-adolescent sexual experience with another man. He said the most remarkable aspect of the love-making was that he had no model in his mind of what was

---

expected, no criteria for good and bad performance against which to measure himself and his experience. He felt free to explore.

But although we talked about gay liberation and our ambiguous feelings about our own potential for homosexual relationships, the men in the group are all living with or dating women, and it is about ourselves in relation to women that we most often talked. There are some things about what it does and does not mean to be a man that most of us agreed about. Six of us, for instance, live in communes where there are no distinctions between women's work and men's work—all tasks are shared equally. Competing to be a provider for my family, assuming a pose of strength or wisdom whether or not I possess either at the moment, maintaining an air of worldly wiseness—in short, being somebody else's conception of a man—does not satisfy my actual needs. There are many other things, however, about which I am more uncertain and troubled.

The men in the group joined for many reasons. All of us are between 25 and 30, white and college-educated. Like most men in similar groups, we are all living with or close to women who are trying to change what have been their traditional sex roles. Two of us have children, although one father is divorced and does not live with his kids most of the year. Besides me, only one other man is married. Two of the men do not live with women. The rest of us do.

In my own case, my wife had become involved in the women's liberation movement. Some of her concerns I was able to respond to in ways that made us happy at the ease of our re-adjustment. It made sense to me, for instance, when she questioned the notion that housecleaning or cooking was her job, with which I sometimes helped out (we were not living communally at the time). It was, after all, my house and my meals too. But more crucial issues left me feeling isolated: she was questioning some basic patterns, and even when I agreed with her intellectually I wondered if I would be less of a man if I gave up some of the rights and privileges that represented my dominance. Why were most of our friends my friends? Why did where we lived always seem to be determined by what I was doing? Why did I win most of our arguments? Why was it so difficult for her to get really angry with me and show me how angry she was? Why did I seem to be able to give or withhold approval of what she was about, and why was she so responsive to that? Answers to these questions, and many others, were peculiar to our relationship. But it also appeared to us that the same kinds of questions could be asked about most relationships between men and women, that the questions seemed to be political as well as personal.

Often, feeling endangered by her growing independence, I argued with her vehemently. But there were times I knew (but could not say) that I was arguing to protect myself from identifying things I had always kept hidden from her, and often from myself.

I was able to see much more about myself than just what she was indicating. I was thinking more about what it meant to me to be a man, how I thought of other men and women. And I needed help in finding answers. I also needed to be able to talk to people other than my wife, because too much was at stake between us to make it possible for us to work these things out alone together. I watched her sharing experiences and understandings with other women in her consciousness raising group. I was threatened by these new relationships she was developing exclusive of me, but I also saw that the same path was open to me.

We tape-recorded the fifth session of my men's group so that I could incorporate some of it into this article. We met often since then, until the group broke up about a year after forming. Many times we talked more intimately. But the things that concerned us in this meeting are part of every man's life: looking at women's bodies and arguing with other men.

My experiences in the group taught me that I am not alone in being trapped by sensations, thoughts, and actions which do not feel comfortable but which have been hard to call into question because they have been so deeply learned. To some degree, I think we helped one another unlearn those self-images which bring us to hurt and limit ourselves and others.

This evening we met in my living room. An argument developed about staring at women's bodies. It seems surprising to me now that feelings ran so high. Surely there was more at stake than any of us understood. Perhaps we were approaching our feelings about our own sexuality. At any rate, we were discussing what we considered a political issue and we did it by being righteous, by yelling, and by working out all kinds of feelings about how the world has treated us.

David, a forceful, outspoken man with a bushy black beard, initiated the discussion. "What do you think about," he wanted to know, "when you're walking down the street and an attractive woman is coming toward you with no bra on? Do you look at her, and if you do, does that make you a pig? Or are you exercising a kind of erotic thing you need?"

"Well," said Alan, "that kind of depends on whether she's looking too, you know? I can't say I feel there's anything wrong with looking."

"But have you ever heard women talk of how they feel disgusted when they walk down the street and every man's eyeballs go up and down?" David asked.

"Well," said Alan, a thin, precise, 26-year-old writer, "I really feel that some women who still feel that way and want to liberate themselves sexually have got to start learning that that's not true. Every man looking at them isn't ogling them. And there's nothing wrong with your body being looked at."

Alan's voice was rising and he was sounding defensive, I think, because he knew there were men in the group who would object to what he had said.

Brian responded angrily. He grew up in Atlantic City where, he told us, he was part of a scene which put a premium on laying as many of the tourist girls as possible. He has reacted strongly against that experience. He's now a medical student living in a commune with a number of women who work full time in the women's movement, and probably more in touch with the evolving ideology of women's liberation than anybody else in the group.

"Alan," Brian said, "maybe you could write up what you just said and hand it around to a few women's groups and tell them how if they really want to be sexually liberated they can do that, and how they have to learn that being looked at by men isn't being ogled."

"Listen," Alan said, "I didn't say that men don't ogle women. I said that looking and ogling aren't the same thing. I walk down the street and I see a woman and she's really beautiful and I look at her and say to myself, 'Wow, she's beautiful.' I don't think there's anything wrong with that."

Alan once said he might feel more at home in a group with six women than with six Brians. He grew up believing that sex could not be disconnected from love and in high school refused to sleep with a girl who felt more strongly about him than he did about her. He seems to behave as though his growth results from a gradual process beginning at a basic, deeply rooted posture. Brian, on the other hand, appears to feel a need for deep, wrenching, and sudden change in his life.

Ralph intervened in the argument at this point. "I think what's really bothering women is that we're isolating something that I don't think can be isolated. What women are objecting to is that they have been thought of as sexual objects. They haven't been dealt with as complete human beings."

"But there's another problem," said Steve, a short, quiet social worker. "If a woman dresses to look sexy and beautiful, then it's really hard to expect me not to react to her sexually. I mean if she walks around with no bra, in a tight-fitting top, and then doesn't want me to stare at her, that really puts me in a double bind."

"I just know," David said, "that when I look at a woman I draw conclusions about her as a person that I never would about a man. Like I'll think, 'I'd like to know her better' because I think she's physically attractive. About a man I'm more apt to think, 'Well, he seems interesting but I'll have to know him better before I decide whether or not I like him.' "

"The men I work with at the hospital," Brian said, "if you ask them what they think of such and such a girl, they all say 'Well, she's really pretty,' or 'She's too fat.' And right down the line they're judging them on the way they look, and by the standards of the white American beauty."

"But what I was saying," Steve explained, "is that if a woman is going to get angry at me for looking at her then I think she has to take part of that responsibility."

"But the question is not whether she's trying to promote it, it's what I do for myself," said David. "Looking at women's bodies is not something I want to eliminate. But I do feel as though I'm relating to them as physical objects and I don't know what to do about it."

"How else can you relate to someone when you're just walking down the street?" asked Jerry.

"There's also a question of cultural values," said Brian. "Women were brought up to look at a potential mate in terms of status, the kind of life he's going to give them, money. And we were brought up to believe that the most important thing about a woman is her beauty."

"There's also the whole question of passivity," said Alan. "It seems to me that one of the reasons men ogle women is that they're supposed to make the advance, whether it's a rape or a proposal."

"Like women don't really stare at men," added Jerry, "because they know that if they do it's likely to lead to an approach, whether they want it or not. If women shared the responsibility for taking the initiative it would give them a lot more freedom."

"I don't know," said David. "If women came to have the same aggressiveness that men are socialized into we'd just be twice as bad off."

"Well, I don't know if it would happen that way," said Alan. "I think the reason men can be so uptight and awful in their aggressiveness is because this big burden has been placed on us that we're responsible for the initiation, the approach. And your manhood rests on it. If that isn't a critical thing for me to do, then both roles are going to adjust in a better way."

One of the difficulties I think we had in our men's group, and one which I suspect other groups are also encountering, is making the transition from the motivating energy of our reactions to the women's movement to the sustaining energy of building a growing understanding of men's liberation. A lot of us got into the group because we were guilty and confused and eventually reached a point where our reasons for remaining had more to do with getting closer to other men and more in touch with our own changing feelings about manliness than spilling our guilty guts.

In my own case, I sympathized with the women's movement and began to respond to it largely out of guilt and fear. I was guilty because reading women's literature I had begun to see the ways in which I controlled my wife and other women by maneuvering out of a learned sense of natural dominance to keep them dependent on me. I had always known, somewhere in the back of my mind, what I was doing. And now I began to feel like a heel—and worse, a heel about to be caught out. I blamed myself for everything that made us unhappy about our marriage.

One of the things I've gotten out of my men's group is an understanding of the pointlessness of that blame. As I listened to the other men talk about the women in their lives I began to see that we have been encouraged to subjugate, depersonalize, maim, and manipulate women. Such a god-awful social process has had its effects on us. The same social structures generate pressures that force most men to be dominant, callous, devoid of gentleness, unable to express feelings, and desperately afraid of losing control. It would be as senseless to blame myself for having acted out so much of what I was taught it means to be "masculine" as it would be to blame my wife for having been so "feminine"—passive, scared, dependent. We were and are victims of the same insanity. To change it we have to begin by changing the kinds of relations that exist between us and among the people our lives touch.

My wife began to alter the balance in our relationship by trying to be more assertive when she wanted to be, or less easily cowed, or more able to state what she wanted and to be angry. I wanted the relationship to endure and to continue to make us both happy, so I was going to have to become part of that process of readjustment. But I was still running scared.

It took me quite a while to accept that all I can do is *try* to free myself from what makes it necessary to hurt, oppress, and isolate myself from other people. I think the only way I can do that effectively is together with other people who share that goal. I need their collective strength and wisdom if I am going to change in a society which rewards me at every turn for continuing to behave in the same old ways. A men's group seemed one way to start that process. I live most of my life in contact with women. A great deal of my competitive behavior seems to grow out of how I want women to view me. Getting together alone with men has been a respite from a pressure I've accepted in my own life. It created room for different kinds of honesty.

Some six months after the discussion we had about looking at women's bodies, it still seems good to have shared the contradictory things that seemed to be going on in each of us. But as Ralph said at the time, whether or not we stare at women's bodies is not really the issue. How I treat women (and men) is. And how I treat women depends on how I feel about myself and how they want to be treated.

Later that same evening we began to talk about how we act toward one another in the group, and toward other men in general. It was a preliminary attempt to get at the issue of competition. Why do I feel that I have to outdo other men? What is it about me that makes me feel superior/inferior to other people, and not merely in relation to them? Why can men's bodies frighten me? Why is it harder to look at a naked man than a naked woman? In conversations we so often seem to be using our minds and our voices to build up the size of our cocks. That's what somebody in the group calls macho arguing. Why is it so much harder for me to be gentle or open with another man than to be witty, or garrulous, or cool and foreboding?

We had been arguing for a while when Ralph intervened. Ralph, whose training is as a clinical psychologist, now is a part-time teacher and auto mechanic. He is short, blond, sometimes stubborn, and especially effective, I think, in summing up what seems to be common sentiment or in seeing group dynamics.

"I'm just getting some bad feelings," he said. "It seems like there's a really competitive thing going on. People are being put down and we're yelling at one another. Is anyone else feeling that?"

"If we're going to sit around here and talk about feelings then we're going to get excited," David said heatedly. "And I don't see what's wrong with attacking someone if it's done in a feeling of friendship."

"It seems to me," I said, "that the one kind of emotion our society encourages men to express is a kind of argumentative anger with other men. And that's the kind of thing that's most often been expressed tonight. But not the other things we might have been feeling."

"I don't really agree," said David. "Alan said women will have to learn there's nothing wrong with men looking at their bodies. Brian and I disagreed. And we reacted to it."

Don, who had remained silent most of the evening, spoke up. Don joined the men's group just a short while after he began to live with a woman whose devotion to the women's movement occupied most of her time. He is frequently confronted by her in the overtly political context with some of the kinds of problems the group is trying to puzzle out.

"It hits home so hard the way you guys were coming across in an authoritarian way," he said. "I wasn't bothered by your getting emotional. It was the way David was coming across and the way Brian attacked Alan for what he said about ogling women. When I come on that way with Joyce, she walks out on me."

"It was Brian's sarcasm that bothered me, too," Ralph agreed. "It seemed like a way of putting Alan down."

"It's also a way of softening your anger," Brian said.

"We argue by banging on each other," Don said. "And we can take it because that's what we've been doing to each other for all our lives."

"I don't know how well we can take it," said Steve. "I just pulled out of the whole thing. Don wasn't saying much and Brian and Jerry were just laying flat on their backs."

"There are a lot of ways to get out your feelings without attacking other people," said Jerry, sitting up.

"But when you do feel really strongly about something what do you think is the appropriate way to express it in this group?" asked David.

"Well," answered Don, "I don't think it's appropriate to use the volume of your voice as an aggressive tactic. That's a male kind of thing. I do it a lot."

"Okay," said Brian. "So it's a male kind of thing and we all do it. Where do we go from there? Does that make it bad?"

"What fucked up my marriage," Ralph said, "was my trying to control my wife. I got out a lot of emotion but it wasn't what I was really feeling. Instead of saying I feel jealous, I would try to direct her. I'd say, 'I don't want you to see that person,' and I'd make up a rationalization why she shouldn't. And then I'd say it over and over again and louder and louder. I think it's valid if I'm jealous or upset to scream or yell, but I can't force someone else to do what I want."

"David," said Steve, "it seems to me that if you say something that really makes me angry I could come back to you in two ways. One is that I could tear your argument to shreds and put you down and show you how wrong you are. I could do that angry or I could do that calm. It makes no difference, that's one way. The other way would be to say that what you said makes me angry because it contradicts my experiences and beliefs, and explain what they are."

"Well," said David, "nobody's explained to my satisfaction yet the difference between expressing anger in a legitimate way and using it in a manipulative or controlling way. We just sit here and analyze every fucking word and we take any spontaneity out of it. If we analyze every word, how do we keep from suppressing emotion?"

For a moment we were all quiet. Then Alan turned to Brian.

"I felt in other weeks that we started with the assumption that we were a group that was going to build trust, and a group that has a common understanding and experience because we're all men. But we never really asked if that was there. And I feel very awkward about it. I know there's been an antagonism between you and me, Brian, since the first week, and we've never talked about it."

"I really liked you a lot when I came over here to visit and we were just sitting in the back yard playing guitar," Brian answered. "And it carried over to when I walked in tonight and maybe that's what brought out my anger, feeling disappointed."

"There's one thing I want to say before we go on," said Ralph. "Maybe what we're experiencing is that we're accustomed to relating to one another on an aggressive, macho, verbal basis. Like, David, you're saying that you find it really weird that we're agreeing and being supportive and trying to understand each other instead of getting into disagreements. And what that says to me is that we come from a background that says disagree, disagree. That's normal for me. And suddenly we're not disagreeing all the time and you're having trouble with that."

Earlier this year the group disbanded. Jerry and Steve had quit previously; Alan had left town. We had added a few new men. Some individual antagonisms finally made it impossible to continue in a productive way. We had lost our momentum and were bogged down in discussing whether to emphasize political considerations or intergroup relationships.

At this point I am not interested in joining another men's group. I think they have a limited, but significant, usefulness. All of the men in the group thought they were made more aware than they had been of the kinds of roles women are made to play. But we were also put deeply in touch with the kinds of poses we men are bullied into adopting.

In ways I had never before known I came close to the men in my group. It is hard to say exactly what we shared. Perhaps for the first time I was able to say to other men: I am tired and I am scared. It is surprisingly easy to shoulder a bit of responsibility for one another once we realize we are burdened by the same beasts.

On Male Liberation

Jack Sawyer

Male liberation calls for men to free themselves of the sex-role stereotypes that limit their ability to be human. Sex-role stereotypes say that men should be dominant; achieving and enacting a dominant role in relations with others is often taken as an indicator of success. "Success," for a man, often involves influence over the lives of other persons. But success in achieving positions of dominance and influence is necessarily not open to every man, since dominance is relative and hence scarce by definition. Most men in fact fail to achieve the positions of dominance that sex-role stereotypes ideally call for. Stereotypes tend

---

Jack Sawyer, "On Male Liberation," *Liberation*, Aug–Sept–Oct 1970, *15*(6–8), 32–33. Reprinted by permission.

to identify such men as greater or lesser failures, and in extreme cases, men who fail to be dominant are the object of jokes, scorn, and sympathy from wives, peers, and society generally.

One avenue of dominance is potentially open to any man, however —dominance over a woman. As society generally teaches men they should dominate, it teaches women they should be submissive, and so men have the opportunity to dominate women. More and more, however, women are reacting against the ill effects of being dominated. But the battle of women to be free need not be a battle against men as oppressors. The choice about whether men are the enemy is up to men themselves.

Male liberation seeks to aid in destroying the sex-role stereotypes that regard "being a man" and "being a woman" as statuses that must be achieved through proper behavior. People need not take on restrictive roles to establish their sexual identity.

A major male sex-role restriction occurs through the acceptance of a stereotypic view of men's sexual relation to women. Whether or not men consciously admire the Playboy image, they are still influenced by the implicit sex-role demands to be thoroughly competent and self-assured—in short, to be "manly." But since self-assurance is part of the stereotype, men who believe they fall short don't admit it, and each can think he is the only one. Stereotypes limit men's perception of women as well as of themselves. Men learn to be highly aware of a woman's body, face, clothes—and this interferes with their ability to relate to her as a whole person. Advertising and consumer orientations are among the societal forces that both reflect and encourage these sex stereotypes. Women spend to make themselves more "feminine," and men are exhorted to buy cigarettes, clothes, and cars to show their manliness.

The popular image of a successful man combines dominance both over women, in social relations, and over other men, in the occupational world. But being a master has its burdens. It is not really possible for two persons to have a free relationship when one holds the balance of power over the other. The more powerful person can never be sure of full candor from the other, though he may receive the kind of respect that comes from dependence. Moreover, people who have been dependent are coming to recognize more clearly the potentialities of freedom, and it is becoming harder for those who have enjoyed dominance to maintain this position. Persons bent on maintaining dominance are inhibited from developing themselves. Part of the price most men pay for being dominant in one situation is subscribing to a system in which they themselves are subordinated in another situation. The alternative is a system in which men share, among themselves and with women, rather than strive for a dominant role.

In addition to the dehumanization of being (or trying to be) a master, there is another severe, if less noticed, restriction from conventional male sex roles in the area of affect, play, and expressivity. Essentially, men are forbidden to play and show emotion. This restriction is often not even recognized as a limitation, because emotional behavior is so far outside the usual range of male activity.

Men are breadwinners, and are defined first and foremost by their performance in this area. This is a serious business and results in an end product—bringing home the bacon. The process area of life—activities that are enjoyed for the immediate satisfaction they bring—are not part of the central definition of men's role. Yet the failure of men to be aware of this potential part of their lives leads them to be alienated from themselves and from others. Because men are not permitted to play freely, or show affect, they are prevented from really coming in touch with their own emotions.

If men cannot play freely, neither can they freely cry, be gentle, nor show weakness—because these are "feminine," not "masculine." But a fuller concept of humanity recognizes that all men and women are potentially both strong and weak, both active and passive, and that these and other human characteristics are not the province of one sex.

The acceptance of sex-role stereotypes not only limits the individual but also has bad effects on society generally. The apparent attractions of a male sex role are strong, and many males are necessarily caught up with this image. Education from early years calls upon boys to be brave, not to cry, and to fight for what is theirs. The day when these were virtues, if it ever existed, is long past. The main effect now is to help sustain a system in which private "virtues" become public vices. Competitiveness helps promote exploitation of people all over the world, as men strive to achieve "success." If success requires competitive achievement, then an unlimited drive to acquire money, possessions, power, and prestige is only seeking to be successful.

The affairs of the world have always been run nearly exclusively by men, at all levels. It is not accidental that the ways that elements of society have related to each other has been disastrously competitive, to the point of oppressing large segments of the world's population. Most societies operate on authoritarian bases—in government, industry, education, religion, the family, and other institutions. It has been generally assumed that these are the only bases on which to operate, because those who have run the world have been reared to know no other. But women, being deprived of power, have also been more free of the role of dominator and oppressor; women have been denied the opportunity to become as competitive and ruthless as men.

In the increasing recognition of the right of women to participate equally in the affairs of the world, then, there is both a danger and a promise. The danger is that women might end up simply with an equal share of the action in the competitive, dehumanizing, exploitative system that men have created. The promise is that women and men might work together to create a system that provides equality to all and dominates no one. The women's liberation movement has stressed that women are looking for a better model for human behavior than has so far been created. Women are trying to become human, and men can do the same. Neither men nor women need be limited by sex-role stereotypes that define "appropriate" behavior. The present models for men and women fail to furnish adequate opportunities for human development. That one-half of the human race should be dominant and the other half submissive is incompatible with a notion of freedom. Freedom requires that there not be dominance and submission, but that all individuals be free to determine their own lives as equals.

Berkeley Men's Center Manifesto

The Berkeley Men's Center is a collective of men struggling to free themselves from sex-role stereotypes and to define themselves in positive, nonchauvinistic ways. It has been active since 1970 and includes men of all sexual orientations. It distributes material on men's struggles and gayness and helps in the formation of men's consciousness-raising groups in the Bay Area. Projects include antisexist actions, television and radio programs, bake sales, and men's work-playshops every few months, with child care.

We, as men, want to take back our full humanity. We no longer want to strain and compete to live up to an impossible oppressive masculine image—strong, silent, cool, handsome, unemotional, successful, master of women, leader of men, wealthy, brilliant, athletic, and "heavy." We no longer want to feel the need to perform sexually, socially, or in any way to live up to an imposed male role, from a traditional American society or a "counterculture."

We want to love ourselves. We want to feel good about and experience our sensuality, emotions, intellect, and daily lives in an integrated way. We want to express our feelings completely and not bottle them up or repress them in order to be "controlled" or "respected." We believe it requires strength to let go and be "weak." We want to enjoy masturbating without feeling guilty or that masturbation is a poor substitute for interpersonal sex. We want to make love with those

Prepared in February, 1973, and used by permission of the Berkeley Men's Center.

who share our love, male or female, and feel it should not be a revolutionary demand to be either gay, heterosexual, or bisexual. We want to relate to our own personal changes, motivated not by a guilt reaction to women, but by our growth as men.

We want to relate to both women and men in more human ways—with warmth, sensitivity, emotion, and honesty. We want to share our feelings with one another to break down the walls and grow closer. We want to be equal with women and end destructive competitive relationships between men. We don't want to engage in ego battles with anyone.

We are oppressed by conditioning which makes us only half-human. This conditioning serves to create a mutual dependence of male (abstract, aggressive, strong, unemotional) and female (nurturing, passive, weak, emotional) roles. We are oppressed by this dependence on women for support, nurturing, love, and warm feelings. We want to love, nurture, and support ourselves and other men, as well as women. We want to affirm our strengths as men and at the same time encourage the creation of new space for men in areas such as childcare, cooking, sewing, and other "feminine" aspects of life.

We believe that this half-humanization will only change when our competitive, male-dominated, individualistic society becomes cooperative, based on sharing of resources and skills. We are oppressed by working in alienating jobs, as "breadwinners." We want to use our creative energy to serve our common needs and not to make profits for our employers.

We believe that Human Liberation does not stem from individual *or* social needs alone, but that these needs are part of the same process. We feel that all liberation movements are equally important; there is no hierarchy of oppression. Every group must speak its own language, assume its own form, take its own action; and when each of these groups learns to express itself in harmony with the rest, this will create the basis for an all embracing social change.

As we put our ideas into practice, we will work to form a more concrete analysis of our oppression as men, and clarify what needs to be done in a socially and personally political way to free ourselves. We want men to share their lives and experiences with each other in order to understand who we are, how we got this way, and what we must do to be free.

References on Men and Masculinity

1. GENERAL

Adolph, J., "The South American macho: mythos and mystique," *Impact of Science on Society,* Jan–March 1971, 21(1), 83–92.

Benson, Leonard, *Fatherhood: A Sociological Perspective.* Random House, 1967.

Brenton, Myron, *The American Male.* Fawcett Premier, 1966.

Brugger, W., "The male (and female) in Chinese society," *Impact of Science on Society,* Jan–March 1971, 21(1), 5–20.

Calderone, Mary, "It's really the men who need liberating," *Life,* Sept 4, 1970, 24–25. Reprinted in Gwen Carr, ed., *Marriage and Family in a Decade of Change,* Addison-Wesley, 1972, 139–141.

Chenoweth, Gene, "The cultural bind on the American male," *National Association of College Admissions Counselors Journal,* Sept 1969, 14(2), 6–9.

"Dress and male liberation: symbols of sex roles," in Jan L. and Cornelia B. Flora, *Readings in Introductory Sociology: The Self and Social Structure,* Xerox College Publishing, 1973, 3–19.

Farrell, Warren, *The Liberated Man: Freeing Men and Their Relationships with Women.* Random House, 1974.

* Indicates that the work is included in the present volume.

Note: The Humanities Library of the Massachusetts Institute of Technology maintains an extensive archival "men's studies" collection, including both published and unpublished materials—articles, reports, papers, leaflets, etc.

Fasteau, Marc, *The Male Machine.* McGraw-Hill, 1974.
Hacker, Helen, "The new burdens of masculinity," *Marriage and Family Living,* 1957, 3, 227–233.
Hearn, Thomas, "Jesus was a sissy after all," *Christian Century,* Oct 7, 1970, 1191–2.
Kirchenbaum, D., "Masculinity and racism: breaking out of the illusion," *Christian Century,* Jan 10, 1973, 43–46.
Levinson, Daniel, "The male mid-life decade," in David Ricks, ed., *Life History Research in Psychopathology,* Vol. 3. Univ. of Minnesota Press, 1974.
"Men," *Win,* April 11, 1974, 10(13), entire issue.
Men and Masculinity. Transcript of a course at Univ. of Wisconsin (Madison) Extension (Fall, 1971). $1, from Center for Women's and Family Living Education, 610 Langdon St., Madison, Wisc. 53706.
Miller, Jean Baker, "Sexual inequality: men's dilemma," *American Journal of Psychoanalysis,* 1972, 32(2), 147–155.
Olstad, Keith, "Brave new men: a basis for discussion," *Oberlin Alumni Magazine,* Sept–Oct 1973, 5–11.
Pleck, Joseph, "Psychological frontiers for men," *Rough Times,* June–July 1973, 3(6).
———, "Psychosocial change in men," in *Encyclopedia of the American Woman,* 1974, forthcoming.
Rudy, Arthur & Peller, Robert, "Men's liberation," *Medical Aspects of Human Sexuality,* Sept 1972, 84–96.
Ruitenbeek, Hendrik, *The Male Myth.* Dell, 1967.
Shostak, Arthur, "Middle-aged working class Americans at home: changing definitions of manhood," *Occupational Mental Health,* 1972, 2(3), 2–7.
Steinman, Anne, "Male and female perceptions of Male sex roles," in *Proceedings, 76th Annual Convention, American Psychological Association,* 1968, 421–422.
"The Embattled Human Male," *Impact of Science on Society,* 1971, 21(1). Entire issue.
Turner, Ralph, "Strains of masculinity," in Turner, *Family Interaction,* Wiley, 1970, 294–303.
"What's Next for Manhood?" *London Sunday Times Magazine,* April 23, 1972, entire issue.
Yachnes, Eleanor et al., "The myth of masculinity," *American Journal of Psychoanalysis,* 1973, 33(1), 56–67.

2. PHYSIOLOGY AND PHYSIQUE

Dalton, Katherina, "No evidence of male cycles," in Dalton, *The Menstrual Cycle,* Warner Paperback Library, 1972, 148–152.

Gilkinson, H., "Masculine temperament and secondary sex characteristics," *Genetic Psychology Monographs,* 1937, 19, 105–154.
Kurtz, R., "Body image—male and female," *Transaction,* Dec 1968, 6, 25–27.
Levine, Seymour, "On becoming male," in I. Ramsey & R. Porter, eds., *Personality and Science,* Churchill & Livingston CIBA Foundation Blueprint, London, 1971.
Owen, David, "The 47, XYY male: a review," *Psychological Bulletin,* 1972, 78, 209–233.
Ramey, Estelle, "Men's cycles," *Ms.,* Spring 1972, 8ff.
Rasmuson, M., "Men, the weaker sex?" *Impact of Science on Society,* Jan–March 1971, 21(1), 43–54.
Seltzer, C., "The relationship between the masculine component and personality," in C. Kluckhohn & H. A. Murray, eds., *Personality in Nature, Society, and Culture,* Knopf, 1948, 84–96.

3. SOCIALIZATION AND DEVELOPMENT

*Allen, Brian, "Liberating the manchild," *Transactional Analysis Journal,* 1972, 2(2), 68–71.
Biller, H. & Borstelmann, L., "Masculine development: an integrative review," *Merrill-Palmer Quarterly,* 1967, 13, 253–294.
Harford, T. et al., "Personality correlates of masculinity-femininity," *Psychological Reports,* 1967, 21, 881–884.
*Hartley, Ruth, "Sex role pressures in the socialization of the male child," *Psychological Reports,* 1959, 5, 457–468.
Knox, W. & Kupferer, H., "A discontinuity in the socialization of males in the United States," *Merrill-Palmer Quarterly,* 17, July 1971, 251–261.
Mead, Margaret, "Sex and achievement," in Mead, *Male and Female,* 1949, chap. 15.
Mussen, P. H., "Long-term consequents of masculinity of interests in adolescence," *Journal of Consulting Psychology,* 1962, 26, 435–440.
Sullivan, H. S., "Male adolescence," in Sullivan, *Personal Psychopathology,* Norton, 1973.

4. AFFILIATION AND EMOTIONAL EXPRESSIVENESS

Balswick, J. & Peek, C., "The inexpressive male: a tragedy of American society," *Family Coordinator,* 1971, 20, 363–368.

Booth, Alan, "Sex and social participation," *American Sociological Review,* 1972, 37, 183–192.

*Clark, Don, "Homosexual encounter in all-male groups," in L. Solomon & B. Berzon, eds., *New Perspectives on Encounter Groups,* Jossey-Bass, 1972.

Clark, Lige & Nichols, Jack, *Roommates Can't Always Be Lovers—An Intimate Look at Male/Male Relationships.* St. Martin's, 1974.

Elias, N. & Dunning, E., "Dynamics of group sports with special reference to football," *British Journal of Sociology,* 1966, 17, 388–401.

*Jourard, Sidney, "Some lethal aspects of the male role," in Jourard, *The Transparent Self,* Van Nostrand, 1964.

Pleck, Joseph, "Is brotherhood possible?" in N. Glazer, Malbin, ed., *Old Family/New Family: Interpersonal Relationships,* Van Nostrand Reinhold, 1974.

Useem, R. et al., "Functions of neighboring for the middle-class male," *Human Organization,* 1960, 19, 68–76.

Wayne, June, "The male artist as a stereotypical female," *Art Journal,* Summer 1973, 32, 414–416.

5. SEXUALITY[1]

Balswick, J., "Attitudes of lower class males toward taking a male birth control pill," *Family Coordinator,* 1972, 21, 195–201.

Cole, S. & Bryon, D., "A review of information relevant to vasectomy counselors," *Family Coordinator,* 1973, 22, 215–221.

Finger, F., "Sex beliefs and practices among male college students," *J. Abnormal Psychology,* 1947, 42, 57–67.

Ginsberg, G. et al., "The new impotence," *Archives of General Psychiatry,* 1972, 26, 218–220.

Glassberg, B., "The quandary of a virginal male," *Family Coordinator,* 1970, 19, 82–87.

Kanin, E., "Male aggression in dating-courtship relations," *American Journal of Sociology,* 1957, 63, 197–204.

———, "An examination of sexual aggression as a response to frustration," *Journal of Marriage and the Family,* 1967, 29, 428–433.

Kinsey, A. C. et al., *Sexual Behavior in the Human Male.* W. B. Saunders, 1948.

Kirkendall, L., "Toward a clarification of the concept of male sex drive," *Marriage and Family Living,* 1958, 20, 367–372.

[1] These references deal only with heterosexuality. For a bibliography on gay liberation, send a stamped, self-addressed long envelope to Task Force on Gay Liberation, P.O. Box 2383, Philadelphia, PA 19103.

Kirkpatrick, C. & Kanin, E., "Male sex aggression on a university campus," *American Sociological Review,* 1957, 22, 52–58.

*London, Irving, "Frigidity, sensitivity, and sexual roles," in Anne Kent Rush, *Getting Clear: Body Work for Women,* Random House/Bookworks, 1973, 228–230.

"Sex and marginality in American men," *Transaction,* March–April 1971, 21–51.

Steiner, Roberta, "The sacred bull: a bibliography on male birth control," *Synergy* (San Francisco Public Library Bulletin), Spring 1973, (40), 18–23.

6. RELATIONSHIPS WITH WOMEN

Bass, Bernard et al., "Male managers' attitudes toward working women," *American Behavioral Scientist,* 1971, 15, 221–236.

Dentler, R. & Pineo, P., "Sexual adjustment, marital adjustment and personal growth of husbands: a panel analysis," *Marriage and Family Living,* 1960, 22, 45–48.

Garland, T. N., "The better half? The male in the dual profession family," in C. Safilios-Rothschild, ed., *Toward a Sociology of Women,* 1972, 199–215.

Holmstrom, L., *The Two-Career Family.* Schenkman, 1972, 133–144.

Janeway, Elizabeth, "The weak are the second sex," *Atlantic,* Dec 1973, 91–104.

Komarovsky, Mirra, "Cultural contradictions and sex roles: the masculine case," *American Journal of Sociology,* 1974, 78, 873–884.

Martinson, F., "Ego deficiency as a factor in marriage—a male sample," *Marriage and Family Living,* 1959, 21, 48–52.

Pleck, Joseph, "Male threat from female competence: an experimental study in college dating couples," Ph.D. dissertation, Dept of Social Relations, Harvard, 1973. Xerox University Microfilms 74-11,721.

Rapoport, Rhona and Robert, *Dual-Career Families.* Penguin, 1971, 23–30, 282–301.

———, "Family enabling functions I: The facilitative husband in the dual-career family," in R. Gosling, ed., *Support, Innovation, and Autonomy,* Tavistock, 1973.

7. RELATIONSHIPS WITH CHILDREN

Aberle, D. & Naegele, K., "Middle-class fathers' occupational role and attitudes toward children," *American Journal of Orthopsychiatry,* 1952, 22, 366–378.

Benson, Leonard. *Fatherhood: A Sociological Perspective.* Random House, 1967.

Bigner, Jerry, "Fathering: research and practice implications," *Family Coordinator,* 1970, 19, 357–362.

Caughlan, Jeanne, "Psychic hazards of unwed paternity," *Social Work,* 1960, 5, 29–35.

Klein, Carole, "The single parent—male," in Klein, *The Single Parent Experience,* Walker & Co., 1973, 43–59.

Kotelchuck, Milton, "The nature of the child's tie to his father," Ph.D. dissertation, Dept of Social Relations, Harvard Univ., 1972.

Lacoursiere, Roy, "Fatherhood and mental illness: a review and new material," *Psychiatric Quarterly,* 1972, 46, 109–124.

Lee, P. & Wolinsky, A., "Male teachers of young children: a preliminary empirical study," *Young Children,* August 1973, 342–353.

Nash, John, "The father in contemporary culture and current psychological literature," *Child Development,* 1965, 36, 261–297.

Polatnick, M., "Why men don't rear children: a power analysis," *Berkeley Journal of Sociology,* 1973–74, 18, 45–86.

*Seifert, K., "Some problems of men in child care center work," *Child Welfare,* 1973, 102, 167–171.

8. WORK

Aldous, Joan, "Occupational characteristics and the male's role performance in the family," *Journal of Marriage and the Family,* 1969, 31, 707–712.

*Bartolomé, Fernando, "Executives as human beings," *Harvard Business Review,* Nov–Dec 1972, 62–68.

Clopton, Will, "Personality and career change," *Industrial Gerontology,* Spring 1973, 9–17.

Gronseth, Erik, "The husband-provider role: a critical appraisal," in A. Michel, ed., *Family Issues of Employed Women,* E. J. Brill, Leiden, 1971, 11–31.

———, "The breadwinner trap," in L. Howe, ed., *The Future of the Family,* Simon & Schuster, 1972, 175–191.

Haavio-Manilla, E., "Satisfaction with family, work, leisure, and life among men and women," *Human Relations,* 1972, 24, 585–601.

Kelleher, Carol, "Second careers—a growing trend," *Industrial Gerontology,* Spring 1973, 1–8.

Tausky, C., "Meanings of work among blue collar men," *Pacific Sociological Review,* 1969, 12, 49–55.

Turner, Ralph, "The male occupational role," in Turner, *Family Interaction,* Wiley, 1970, 255–266.

Useem, J. & Useem, R., "Social stresses and resources among middle

management men," in E. Jaco, ed., *Patients, Physicians, and Illness,* Free Press, 1958, 74–91.
Wilmott, P., "Family, work and leisure conflicts among male employees," *Human Relations,* 1972, 24, 575–584.

9. POWER AND VIOLENCE

Elkin, S., "Aggressive and erotic tendencies in Army life," *American Journal of Sociology,* 1946, 51, 408–413.
Fannin, L. & Clinard, M., "Differences in the conception of self as a male among lower and middle class delinquents," *Social Problems,* 1966, 13, 205–214.
Fast, Julius, "The predator with a brain: how men see themselves," in Fast, *The Incompatibility of Men and Women,* Avon, 1972, 95–115.
*Gagnon, John, "Physical strength: once of significance," *Impact of Science on Society,* Jan–March 1971, 21(1), 31–42.
Komisar, Lucy, "Violence and the masculine mystique," *Washington Monthly,* July 1970, 39–48.
Schuman, S. et al., "Young male drivers: impulse expression, accidents, and violations," *Journal of the American Medical Association,* 1967, 200, 1026–1030.
*Steinem, Gloria, "The myth of masculine mystique," *International Education,* 1972, 1, 30–35.
*Stone, I. F., "Machismo in Washington," *New York Review of Books,* May 18, 1972, 14–16.
Stouffer, Samuel, "Masculinity and the role of the combat soldier," in Stouffer et al., *The American Soldier,* vol. 2, 131–135.
Toby, J., "Violence and the masculine idea: some qualitative data," *Annals of the American Academy of Political and Social Science,* March 1966, 36, 19–27.

10. BLACK MALE SEX-ROLE

Bond, J. & Peery, P., "Has the black man been castrated?" in R. Staples, ed., *The Black Family,* Brooks-Cole, 1971, 140–144.
Hannerz, Ulf, "Growing up male," in Hannerz, *Soulside,* Columbia Univ. Press, 1971.
Hare, N., "The frustrated masculinity of the Negro male," in R. Staples, ed., *The Black Family,* Brooks-Cole, 1971, 131–134.
Staples, R., "The myth of the important black male," *Black Scholar,* June 1971, 2(10), 2–9.

"The Black Male," *Black Scholar,* June 1971, 2(10), entire issue.
"The Black Male," *Ebony,* Aug 1972, entire issue.

11. HISTORICAL

Barker-Benfield, B., "The spermatic economy: a nineteenth century view of sexuality," *Feminist Studies,* Summer 1972, 1(1), 48–72.
Kingsdale, J., "The 'poor man's club': social functions of the urban working-class saloon," *American Quarterly,* 1973, 25, 472–489.
McGovern, J., "David Graham Phillips and the virility impulse of the Progressives," *New England Quarterly,* 1966, 39, 344–355.
Rosenberg, C., "Sexuality, class and role in nineteenth century America," *American Quarterly,* 1973, 25, 131–153.

12. LITERARY

Fiedler, Leslie, "Good good girls and good bad boys," in Fiedler, *Love and Death in the American Novel,* Stein & Day, 1966.
———, "The male novel," *Partisan Review,* 1970, 37(1), 74–89.
Heilbrun, C., "The masculine wilderness of the American novel," *Saturday Review,* Jan 29, 1972, 41–44.
Martin, T., "*One Flew over the Cuckoo's Nest* and the high cost of living," *Modern Fiction Studies,* 1973, 19, 43–55.

13. PERSONAL ACCOUNTS

Farber, Jerry, "Growing up male in North America," in Farber, *The University of Tomorrowland,* Pocket Books, 1972, 93–113.
Glenn, Michael & Kunnes, Richard, *Repression or Revolution? Therapy in the United States Today.* Harper and Row, 1973, 74–80.
*Keith, Jeff, "My own men's liberation," *Win,* Sept 1, 1971, 7(14), 22–26.
Lyon, Dale, "On woman-man awareness: a conversation that still has me spinning," *Newsletter of the Association for Humanistic Psychology,* Nov 1972, 1–3.
"Men," a regular feature in *Ms.* magazine.
*Miller, S. M., "The making of a confused middle-aged husband," *Social Policy,* July–Aug 1971, 2(2), 33–39.
Pleck, Joseph H., "My male sex role—and ours," *Win,* April 11, 1974, 10(13), 8–12.
*Silverstein, Michael, "Power and sex roles in academia," *Journal of Applied Behavioral Science,* 1972, 8, 536–563.

Unbecoming Men: A Men's Consciousness-Raising Group Writes on Oppression and Themselves. Times Change Press, 1971.

14. MEN'S LIBERATION

Brother: A Forum for Men Against Sexism. P.O. Box 4387, Berkeley, CA 94704. Subscription $3. Issue No. 9 (1974) contains a contact list of men and men's groups.

Brothers: A Men's Liberation Newsletter. c/o Rising Free, 197 King's Cross Rd., London WC1.

DeGolia, Rick, "Thoughts on men's oppression," *Issues in Radical Therapy,* 1(3), Summer 1973, 14–18.

Farrell, Warren, "Guidelines for consciousness-raising," *Ms.,* Feb 1973, 12ff.

———, "Women's and men's liberation groups: political power within the system and outside the system," in J. Jacquette, ed., *Women in Politics,* Wiley, 1974.

———, "Male consciousness and the anti-power culture," *Sociological Focus,* Winter 1971.

———, "Is there a need for men's liberation?" *Medical Aspects of Human Sexuality,* Sept 1973.

Plank, David & Weiss, Randy, "The men's liberation movement: a manifesto," *Oberlin Review,* April 13, 1973.

*Sawyer, Jack, "On male liberation," *Liberation,* Aug–Sept–Oct 1970, 15(6–8), 32–33.

———, "On the politics of male liberation," *Win,* Sept 1, 1971.

Steiner, Claude, "Letter to a brother: reflections on male liberation," *Issues in Radical Therapy,* Jan 1973, 1(1), 15–19.

*Weiss, Michael, "It's never too late to unlearn," *Village Voice,* Aug 24, 1972.

*———, "Getting in touch with our manliness," *Village Voice,* Aug 31, 1972.

15. FILMS

A Day Off Two men take a day off together, embark on a series of male adventures which end badly, and part without ever really making contact. (Awareness Films, 815 Murray Ct., Ann Arbor, Mich., 1973, 25 mins.)

A Male Condition (Antioch Documentary Films, Yellow Springs, Ohio 54387, 1974, 60 mins.)

Masculinity A four-part filmstrip series. (Schloat Productions, 150 White Plains Rd., Tarrytown, NY, 1974.)

Pillar of Wisdom Fifty young freshmen, smeared with grease, try to get a cap on top of a 20-foot pole. Produced by National Film Board of Canada. (Carousel, 1970, 9 mins.)

Sticky My Fingers, Fleet My Feet Deflates one of the classic American myths: the middle-aged male who clings to a youthful standard of physical prowess and virility. (Time-Life, 1970, 23 mins.)

The Game High school student, provoked by friends to prove his claimed ability as a seducer, seeks to demonstrate his masculinity by winning over a young woman in his class. Produced by National Film Board of Canada. (McGraw-Hill, 1967, 28 mins.)